R.D. VILLAM

Civilization: What If...?

Copyright © 2024 by R.D. Villam

All rights reserved. No part of this publication may be reproduced, stored or transmitted in any form or by any means, electronic, mechanical, photocopying, recording, scanning, or otherwise without written permission from the publisher. It is illegal to copy this book, post it to a website, or distribute it by any other means without permission.

First edition

*This book was professionally typeset on Reedsy.
Find out more at reedsy.com*

Contents

Preface	v
What If Alexander the Great Had Lived to Old Age?	1
What If Hannibal Had Decisively Conquered Rome After the...	6
What If the Persian Empire Had Successfully Conquered...	12
What If the Library of Alexandria Had Never Been Destroyed?	18
What If Julius Caesar Had Not Been Assassinated?	25
What If Cleopatra and Mark Antony Had Won the Battle of...	32
What If the Trojan War Had Never Happened?	39
What If the Hebrews Had Never Left Egypt?	46
What If the Assyrian Empire Had Survived Longer?	53
What If the Indus Valley Civilization Had Not Collapsed?	60
What If Sparta Had Won the Peloponnesian War?	67
What If the Etruscans Had Maintained Control Over Rome?	74
What If the Celtic Tribes Had Successfully Unified Against...	81
What If Buddhism Had Spread Widely in the West Instead of...	88
What If the Silk Road Had Never Been Established?	95
What If Sargon of Akkad's Empire Had Lasted Longer?	102
What If the Mycenaean Civilization Had Not Collapsed?	109
What If the Roman Empire Had Never Adopted Christianity?	116
What If Socrates Had Never Been Executed?	123
What If the Phoenicians Had Established a Dominant...	131
What If the Minoans Had Not Been Destroyed by the Volcanic...	138
What If the Chinese Han Dynasty Had Not Fallen?	145
What If the Macedonian Phalanx Had Been Defeated by the...	152
What If the Carthaginian Explorer Hanno Had Discovered the...	159
What If the Ancient Egyptian Pharaoh Akhenaten's Religious...	167

What If the Qin Dynasty's Legalism Had Spread Throughout...	175
What If the Roman Empire Had Successfully Conquered...	182
What If the Greek City-States Had Unified Before the Persian...	190
What If the Ancient Israelites Had Established a...	198
What If the Maurya Empire Had Not Declined After Ashoka?	206
What If the Hittites Had Successfully Expanded into Egypt?	214
What If the Ancient Athenian Democracy Had Never Been...	222
What If the Etruscans Had Developed a Writing System That...	230
What If the Sumerians Had Discovered the Use of Iron...	238
What If the Wars of the Diadochi Were Taken to the Next...	246
What If the Romans Had Never Conquered Britain?	254
What If the Early Christian Church Had Not Split from...	261
What If the Visigoths Had Failed to Sack Rome in 410 CE?	269
What If the Ancient Olmecs Had Developed a More Advanced...	276
What If Pharaoh Ramses II Had Died Young?	284
What If the Ancient Chinese Had Invented the Printing Press...	291
What If the Parthian Empire Had Defeated the Romans...	298
What If the Ancient Scythians Had Established a Lasting...	306
What If the Ancient Greeks Had Colonized More of North...	314
What If the Ancient Celtic Tribes Had Built Cities and...	321
What If the Byzantine Empire Had Reconquered the Entire...	328
What If the Ancient Mayans Had Established a Vast Empire?	335
What If the Roman Empire Had Fully Integrated Christianity...	343
What If the Huns Had Settled and Established a Kingdom in...	351
What If the Ancient Polynesians Had Discovered the Americas...	358

Preface

History is often seen as a grand, unchangeable narrative, a chain of events so inevitable that they seem almost predestined. But what if history were less a straight line and more a vast tapestry, woven from the threads of countless "what ifs"? What if Alexander the Great, that unstoppable force of ambition, had lived to old age, reshaping the world in his image? What if Hannibal had done the unthinkable and decisively conquered Rome, forever altering the course of Western civilization? What if the Persians had successfully conquered Greece, and the philosophical foundations of Western thought had been crushed under the sandals of Xerxes' soldiers?

"Civilization: What If…?" invites you to journey down the roads not taken, where history veers off its familiar path and plunges us into the realms of alternate realities. These are the histories that might have been, each one a tantalizing glimpse into a world where the great Library of Alexandria still stands, its scrolls intact, its knowledge vast; where Julius Caesar, unstabbed and undeterred, reshapes the Roman Republic; where Cleopatra and Mark Antony, victorious at Actium, craft an Egyptian empire that dominates the Mediterranean.

In these pages, the Trojan War never erupts, and the stories that shaped Greek identity remain untold. The Hebrews, never leaving Egypt, transform the religious landscape of the ancient world. The Assyrian Empire, surviving the test of time, continues to exert its brutal yet sophisticated influence over the Near East. And across the seas, the Indus Valley Civilization thrives, its urban sophistication pushing the boundaries of what was possible in ancient South Asia.

But the journey doesn't stop there. What if Sparta's iron grip had crushed Athenian democracy, snuffing out the flicker of philosophy and arts that would define Western culture? What if the Etruscans had held onto Rome, or if the Celtic tribes had unified against the Roman juggernaut? How different might our world be if Buddhism, rather than Christianity, had spread widely in the West? What if the Silk Road had never been woven, leaving East and West isolated in their respective cultural bubbles?

This book explores these and many more scenarios, not with the intent to rewrite history, but to revel in the possibilities that history could have offered. Imagine Sargon of Akkad's empire enduring the ages, or the Mycenaean civilization surviving the tumult of time. Picture a world where the Roman Empire never embraced Christianity, or where Socrates' voice continued to challenge the youth of Athens.

The scope of these alternate histories is vast, stretching from the ancient shores of the Mediterranean to the highlands of the Andes, from the courts of Pharaohs to the steppes of the Scythians. What if the ancient Greeks had colonized more of North Africa, blending cultures in ways unimaginable? What if the ancient Polynesians had discovered the Americas before Columbus, their canoes making landfall on shores unknown to Europe for centuries?

Each chapter in this book is a doorway into a different world, a world shaped by the question "What if?" Through clever, humorous, and sometimes downright sarcastic narratives, we delve into the ripple effects of these alternate events, tracing how a single change might have altered the course of civilizations, sparked new empires, or prevented others from ever rising.

"Civilization: What If...?" is not just a collection of stories; it is an invitation to reimagine history, to play with the infinite possibilities that lie just beyond the horizon of what was. So, take a step into the unknown, where history meets imagination, and where the past is anything but certain. What if? Well, let's find out.

R.D.V.

What If Alexander the Great Had Lived to Old Age?

The Background

Let's set the scene: It's 323 BCE, and Alexander the Great, fresh off conquering half the known world, is doing what he does best—conquering the other half. But instead of catching a nasty fever and dying at the tender age of 32 in Babylon, let's say he takes a detour to a more health-conscious lifestyle. Maybe he cuts back on the wine, switches to a Mediterranean diet, and discovers yoga. The point is, instead of dying young, he lives well into his 80s, with a six-pack, a flowing beard, and the unquenchable thirst for conquest.

One day, instead of feverishly planning his next war from his deathbed, Alexander decides he's had enough of early demise. So, he downs a miraculous potion—let's call it "The Elixir of Eternal Conquest" (sponsored by an ancient version of Gatorade)—and instantly feels rejuvenated. Now, he's got the energy of ten men and the lifespan to match. Rather than bowing out early, Alexander sets his sights on uniting Europe, Asia, and Africa under one massive, glittering empire.

The 10 Possible Things That Would Happen

1. The Unification of the World (Well, Most of It)

Alexander, with his new lease on life, marches his armies westward and southward. He doesn't stop until his empire stretches from the British Isles to the southern tip of Africa and as far east as China. The world, now under a single banner, enjoys an unprecedented period of peace. Well, if by "peace," you mean everyone's too terrified to revolt, lest they face Alexander's wrath. The world's cultures start blending in strange ways. Picture this: Egyptians adopting Greek philosophy, Greeks mastering Chinese martial arts, and Romans trying (and failing) to rock the Indian sari. History's first attempt at global fusion cuisine is born, with dishes like "Spartan Tandoori" and "Athenian Sushi."

2. A New Capital of the World: Alexandropolis

Forget Babylon or Rome. Alexander builds a shiny new capital, Alexandropolis (because what else would he call it?), at the crossroads of his empire—right smack dab in modern-day Turkey. This city becomes the heartbeat of a multicultural, multiethnic empire. It's a metropolis of unimaginable grandeur where philosophers, scientists, and artists from every corner of the empire gather to create, argue, and get drunk together. Alexandropolis becomes the Silicon Valley of the ancient world, where the latest tech includes steam-powered gadgets, early versions of eyeglasses, and a prototype for the "iScroll," a device that's essentially a really fast scribe with a chisel.

3. The Great Olympic Games: Now Featuring Elephants

Alexander, always one for spectacle, decides the Olympic Games need an upgrade. So, he introduces new events like Elephant Polo, Full-Contact Philosophizing, and the Marathon Chariot Race. The games, held in Alexandropolis, become the ultimate entertainment spectacle, drawing competitors and fans from across the empire. The sports culture becomes so embedded in society that ancient gyms start popping up everywhere. Instead of today's CrossFit, people brag about their achievements in the "Alexander's Bootcamp," which includes training regimens like "Siege Warfare 101" and "How to Wrestle a Persian."

4. The Universal Language: Alexandrian

Alexander, tired of having to use translators every time he conquers a new region, decrees that the entire empire will speak one language: Alexandrian, a mix of Greek, Persian, Sanskrit, and whatever the Macedonians were mumbling in the back. It's a linguistic mashup that's as confusing as it is unifying. The world's first attempts at international diplomacy occur, though they're hindered by the fact that nobody can quite figure out how to pronounce certain words without offending someone. The phrase "Oops, I invaded your country" becomes a common diplomatic apology.

5. Conquest of the Americas: The Alexander Way

After uniting the Old World, Alexander, ever the overachiever, sets his sights on the mysterious lands across the Atlantic. With a fleet of specially designed ships, he discovers the Americas centuries before Columbus. Naturally, he claims them in the name of Alexandropolis. The indigenous peoples of the Americas, seeing this strange guy with a helmet and cape, decide to trade knowledge. The result? The ancient world gets its hands on corn, potatoes, and chocolate, leading to the creation of "Choco-Gyro," a culinary disaster that's popular for about five minutes.

6. Philosophy Wars: The Epic Debates

In his later years, Alexander grows bored with fighting actual wars and instead sponsors massive debates between the greatest philosophers of his empire. Think Plato vs. Confucius in a verbal smackdown. These debates are held in grand arenas, with the audience deciding the winner by applause—

or by throwing ripe fruit. The debates spark a new tradition of intellectual duels, where philosophers and scientists compete not just in logic, but in insults. The phrase "Your ideas are as empty as a Spartan's dinner plate" becomes a classic burn.

7. The Eternal Senate: A Political Experiment

Always interested in new ideas, Alexander creates the Eternal Senate, a political body where representatives from every part of his empire can debate laws. It's an experiment in ancient democracy, though it quickly devolves into chaos as senators from vastly different cultures try to out-shout each other. Political satire is born, with plays and puppet shows mocking the Eternal Senate's never-ending debates. A popular character is "Senator Druncus," a perpetually tipsy senator who accidentally declares war on a neighboring empire because he misread his notes.

8. The Alexandrian Calendar: The Year of Conquest

Dissatisfied with existing calendars, Alexander invents his own. The year now begins on the anniversary of his birth, and each month is named after one of his greatest battles. It's a confusing system, but everyone uses it because, well, Alexander said so. The confusion over dates leads to a thriving business in "historical recalibration," where scribes are paid to figure out when things actually happened. Entire industries are built around deciphering what day it is.

9. The Alexander Academy: The Birth of Universal Education

In an unprecedented move, Alexander founds the Alexander Academy, where children from all over the empire are sent to learn warfare, philosophy, and how to properly admire a statue of Alexander. It's the world's first attempt at universal education. The academy churns out a generation of highly educated, overly confident youth, who then spread throughout the empire, annoying their elders by insisting on debating everything from the merits of different sword techniques to whether the earth is round or, as they call it, "Alexander-shaped."

10. The Great Revolt: When the World Says 'Enough'

As Alexander ages, his empire becomes so vast and so unwieldy that even he can't keep it together. Discontent simmers across the empire, with regional leaders, tired of being ruled by a guy who insists on naming everything after himself, rising in revolt. The world's first synchronized, global rebellion occurs. The empire fractures into dozens of smaller states, each claiming to be the true successor of Alexander's glory. The result is centuries of bickering, wars, and alliances, with historians looking back and saying, "Honestly, this was bound to happen."

Conclusion

Alexander the Great living to old age would have been a world-altering event, leading to a unified, yet chaotic, ancient world where cultures blended, philosophies clashed, and everything from calendars to cuisine bore his unmistakable mark. The ripple effects would be felt for millennia, with future generations either cursing or praising the man who could never resist adding a little more to his empire—or his name to everything.

What If Hannibal Had Decisively Conquered Rome After the Battle of Cannae?

The Background

It's 216 BCE, and Rome is having a very bad day. Hannibal, the Carthaginian general with a flair for dramatic entrances (remember those elephants crossing the Alps?), has just handed them one of the worst defeats in their history at the Battle of Cannae. Rome, bruised and battered, is teetering on the brink. Historically, the Romans, being the stubborn lot they were, dug in their heels, restructured, and eventually turned the tide. But what if, instead of regrouping, Rome crumbled under the weight of its losses?

Picture this: Instead of regrouping after Cannae, the Romans are paralyzed by fear, indecision, and a severe lack of pasta (morale, as it turns out, is heavily influenced by carbs). The Senate bickers endlessly, the legions are in disarray, and the citizens start Googling—err, discussing—what life might be like under Carthaginian rule. Sensing an opportunity, Hannibal doesn't just sit on his victory; he marches on Rome itself, laying siege to the Eternal City. After a few tense months, Rome, unable to muster a defense, opens its gates, effectively ending the Republic and ushering in a new era: The Age of Carthage.

The 10 Possible Things That Would Happen

1. Carthage Becomes the New Rome

With Rome conquered, Carthage becomes the undisputed master of the Mediterranean. The city, once content to focus on trade and occasionally roasting Roman legions, now embraces its role as the dominant imperial power. The Mediterranean Sea becomes a Carthaginian lake, complete with tolls and heavily armed "lifeguards." The Roman roads that once connected the vast empire now serve as Carthaginian trade routes. The Carthaginians, being more mercantile than military, turn the old Roman provinces into bustling trade hubs, where you can buy anything from Numidian spices to freshly squeezed Gaulish wine. Pax Romana is replaced by Pax Carthagina, a time of peace where the only wars are fought over shipping tariffs.

2. Latin Becomes a Dead Language (Much Earlier)

With the fall of Rome, Latin goes the way of the dodo—extinct. The new language of power is Punic, and all those future scholars who would have spent their days conjugating Latin verbs now scratch their heads over Punic grammar, which is as elusive as it is confusing. Western literature as we know it takes a bizarre turn. Instead of Cicero, Virgil, and Ovid, future generations study the works of Carthaginian poets and orators. Shakespeare's "Julius Caesar" becomes "Hannibal the Great," and the line "Et tu, Brute?" is replaced with "You too, Barca?"

3. The Roman Senate: Carthaginian Edition

Hannibal, ever the strategist, decides to keep the Roman Senate intact— sort of. He fills it with Carthaginian sympathizers, ex-slaves, and a few bewildered Romans who now have to pretend they know how to run a Phoenician empire. The Senate's new job? Approving Hannibal's latest conquests and debating which Mediterranean port has the best seafood. The

Senate becomes a shadow of its former self, rubber-stamping whatever Hannibal desires. Satirical plays mocking the Senate become popular in Carthage, with characters like "Senator Patheticus" and "Lord of the Leek and Carrot" becoming household names. The Roman tradition of dignified oratory is replaced by speeches that involve more hand gestures and loud arguments about olive oil prices.

4. The Rebranding of Carthage

With Rome under his control, Hannibal decides Carthage could use a bit of a makeover. The city undergoes a massive rebuilding project, complete with new temples, a colossal harbor, and a grand coliseum where gladiators fight...well, more gladiators, but with more style and fewer rules. Carthage becomes the cultural capital of the ancient world, attracting artists, poets, and philosophers. Greek and Egyptian influences blend with Punic traditions, creating a unique culture. Carthaginian fashion becomes the trendsetter, with everyone from Spain to Syria wearing the latest in Punic couture—flowing robes with just the right amount of sandal bling.

5. The Carthaginian Calendar

Hannibal, ever the innovator, introduces a new calendar. The year now starts with the anniversary of the Battle of Cannae, and the months are named after his greatest victories. The Romans, grudgingly, adapt to this new system, though they never quite forgive Hannibal for renaming "April" to "Barcalis." Future historians have a field day trying to reconcile the old Roman calendar with the new Carthaginian one. Dates become a jumbled mess, with scholars debating whether Julius Caesar was assassinated in the year of the "Second Punic" or "Barcalis the Eleventh." The confusion leads to the invention of the world's first historical footnote, which simply reads: "Honestly, we have no idea."

6. The Rise of Carthage's Navy

With Rome's navy sunk or captured, Carthage becomes the supreme naval power. The Mediterranean is patrolled by sleek, fast Carthaginian triremes, making piracy a thing of the past and trade a much safer—and profitable—venture. Hannibal's fleet even explores beyond the Pillars of Hercules, discovering new lands and trade routes. The Carthaginian discovery of the British Isles leads to the establishment of a colony, "Nova Carthago," where the locals learn the joys of olive oil, wine, and endless taxation. The Punic influence spreads north, bringing with it Mediterranean architecture, which clashes hilariously with the local weather, leading to the invention of the world's first waterproof toga.

7. The Great Carthaginian Library

Not to be outdone by the Greeks, Hannibal orders the construction of the Great Carthaginian Library, a repository of knowledge that dwarfs even Alexandria. The library collects scrolls, tablets, and manuscripts from every corner of the empire, making it the center of learning for centuries. The library's vast collection includes works on philosophy, science, and history that would have been lost to time. Scholars flock to Carthage, creating a golden age of knowledge. Unfortunately, the library's bureaucratic system is so complex that it takes weeks to check out a single scroll, leading to the creation of the world's first interlibrary loan service.

8. Hannibal's Heirs: The Barcid Dynasty

With Rome subdued, Hannibal establishes the Barcid dynasty, ensuring his descendants rule for generations. The Barcids are a colorful bunch, known for their military prowess, love of luxury, and tendency to name everything after Hannibal. They rule with a mix of cunning and charisma, keeping the empire in check through a combination of charm and intimidation. The Barcid dynasty lasts for centuries, with each successive ruler trying to outdo the previous one in terms of conquests and extravagant palaces. The empire's stability leads to the development of early banking systems, as wealthy Carthaginians look for safe places to stash their gold. The concept of "Barcid Banking" is born, complete with vaults, interest rates, and the occasional Hannibal-themed savings bond.

9. The Punic Pax: A New World Order

Under Carthaginian rule, the Mediterranean enjoys a long period of peace and prosperity, known as the Punic Pax. Trade flourishes, cities expand, and cultures intermingle. Carthage becomes the world's first true melting pot, where people of all backgrounds live, work, and argue about the best way to make garum (fish sauce). The Punic Pax leads to an explosion of cultural exchange, with everything from Egyptian hieroglyphs to Greek theater being adapted and transformed by Carthaginian artists. The empire's peace also allows for the development of new technologies, including early forms of the compass, steam-powered devices, and a primitive version of the catapult-powered selfie stick.

10. The Carthaginian Renaissance

With the empire secure and the Pax in full swing, Carthage experiences a renaissance of art, science, and philosophy. Thinkers from all over the known world gather in the city, debating everything from the nature of the gods to the best method for brewing beer. This golden age of creativity leads to advancements that will shape the future of the world. The Carthaginian Renaissance spreads throughout the empire, influencing everything from architecture to literature. The Barcid rulers commission grand works of art and philosophy, many of which survive into the modern era. The Renaissance also leads to the creation of the world's first university, where students can major in subjects like "Advanced Hannibal Studies" and "Elephant Herding for Conquest."

Conclusion

If Hannibal had decisively conquered Rome after the Battle of Cannae, the world would have been a very different place. Carthage, once a trading city on the edge of the Mediterranean, would have become the heart of a vast, multicultural empire. The legacy of the Barcid dynasty would have shaped the course of Western civilization, with Carthaginian culture, language, and philosophy dominating the ancient world. The Mediterranean would have been a peaceful, prosperous region, where trade and cultural exchange flourished under the watchful eye of Hannibal's descendants. And somewhere, in a small corner of history, a Roman poet would still be trying to rhyme something with "Barcalis."

What If the Persian Empire Had Successfully Conquered Greece?

The Background

It's the early 5th century BCE, and the Persian Empire, the biggest, baddest superpower of the ancient world, is looking at Greece with the same expression a cat gives a particularly slow mouse. The Persian kings, Darius and later Xerxes, have a simple plan: absorb those pesky little Greek city-states into their ever-expanding empire. Historically, the Greeks, fueled by their love for freedom, democracy, and not wanting to be Persian subjects, managed to fend off the invaders. But what if things had gone differently? What if, instead of that famous "Greek Miracle," we got the "Persian Marvel"?

During the Battle of Salamis, instead of the Greek fleet pulling off their sneaky victory, a storm—let's call it "Zeus Took a Nap"—wreaks havoc on the Greek ships. Meanwhile, the Persian navy, suspiciously dry and intact, sweeps in and crushes the remaining Greek forces. The Battle of Salamis is a catastrophic loss for Greece. Without their navy, the Greeks can't stop the Persian juggernaut from rolling through their city-states. Athens burns, Sparta is humbled, and the once-unthinkable becomes reality: Greece is now a province of the Persian Empire.

The 10 Possible Things That Would Happen

1. Persian Culture Becomes the Standard

With Greece firmly under Persian control, Persian culture starts to seep into every aspect of Greek life. Instead of Greek columns, you start seeing Persian palaces in Athens, complete with those awesome bull-headed capitals. Greek citizens find themselves wearing Persian robes and debating the merits of Zoroastrianism over wine—well, diluted wine, as the Persians find undiluted Greek wine barbaric. Greek gods start to blend with Persian deities in a bizarre pantheon mashup. Zeus becomes Ahura-Zeus, the thunderbolt-wielding embodiment of light and truth, while Athena develops a fondness for Persian fashion and starts appearing in statues wearing a chador. Meanwhile, the Olympics are rebranded as the "Royal Persian Games," featuring new events like chariot archery and "Who Can Bow the Lowest."

2. The Death of Democracy (Literally)

The Persian Empire, being a fan of centralized power, looks at this "democracy" thing the Greeks have and decides it's a bad idea. The Athenian Assembly is dissolved, and in its place, a satrap—a Persian governor—runs the show. The concept of democracy is relegated to the philosophical musings of disgruntled Athenians, who gather in underground taverns to discuss what could have been. Political philosophy takes a dark turn. Instead of celebrating the virtues of democracy, Greek philosophers start writing about the benefits of absolute monarchy and the "benevolent satrap." Plato's "Republic" becomes "The Satrapy," where he waxes lyrical about the ideal Persian ruler who, like all rulers, is infallible and deserves tribute (preferably in gold or sheep).

3. Persian-Greek Fusion Cuisine

The Greeks may have lost their autonomy, but they retain their love of food. Persian-Greek fusion cuisine becomes all the rage, with dishes like "Moussaka à la Cyrus" and "Spanakopita with a Saffron Twist" dominating the tables. Greek symposiums, now under Persian supervision, serve kebabs alongside the traditional olives and cheese. Greek wine culture takes a hit as the Persians introduce their refined drinking customs. Drinking parties become more sophisticated, with guests reclining on couches discussing philosophy, but now they have to do so while nibbling on pistachios and sipping watered-down wine mixed with rosewater. The phrase "Eat, drink, and be merry" is replaced with "Eat, drink, and try not to offend the satrap."

4. The Persianification of Greek Art

Greek sculptors and painters, now under Persian patronage, start incorporating Persian themes into their work. Statues of gods and athletes sport Persian hairstyles and clothes, and scenes of Persian kings in grand processions become common motifs in Greek art. The famous Greek ideal of the "nude hero" is quickly replaced with the "modestly dressed and heavily adorned hero." The Parthenon is rebuilt—this time with Persian funds and under Persian architectural influence. It's grander, with intricate reliefs showing the glorious battles of Xerxes, and it's topped with a massive golden statue of Ahura-Zeus. Art historians centuries later scratch their heads, trying to figure out why Athena looks like she's about to start a fire ritual.

5. Philosophy Takes a Persian Turn

With Persian scholars and magi arriving in Greece, Greek philosophy undergoes a major shift. The Greeks, who once debated the nature of the universe and man's place within it, now find themselves incorporating Zoroastrian concepts like dualism and the cosmic struggle between good and evil. Socrates might still be asking questions, but now he's asking, "What would Ahura Mazda do?" The Stoics take their philosophy of self-control and merge it with Persian asceticism, leading to a new movement known as "Mazdaism," where true wisdom is found in denying oneself worldly pleasures, except when it comes to Persian dates—they're still allowed to eat those. Epicureans, meanwhile, are labeled heretics and forced to justify their love of pleasure as part of the grand cosmic plan.

6. Greek Mythology Gets a Rewrite

As Persian influence grows, the old Greek myths start to change. The Iliad is rewritten, with the gods playing a much more hands-off role (after all, Ahura Mazda doesn't micromanage), and Achilles is portrayed not as a tragic hero but as an enlightened warrior fighting for the greater good. The Odyssey becomes a tale of Odysseus's spiritual journey to find the true path of righteousness—guided, of course, by Persian sages. The Greek pantheon's more chaotic deities, like Dionysus and Ares, are sidelined in favor of more orderly and wise gods. Temples dedicated to these wild deities fall into disrepair, and the cult of Dionysus becomes an underground movement, with secret parties held in olive groves where people still drink wine undiluted and dance like maniacs, thumbing their noses at the satrap.

7. The Persian School of Athens

Athens, once the cradle of Greek philosophy, becomes a center of Persian learning. The Persian king establishes the "Royal Academy of Athens," where the brightest minds study everything from astronomy to medicine, all under the watchful eyes of Persian scholars. The Academy is also a propaganda machine, teaching the virtues of Persian governance and the divine right of the king. Plato's Academy and Aristotle's Lyceum are absorbed into the Royal Academy, where students now study Persian philosophy alongside Greek. The famous "Allegory of the Cave" is updated to include the wise satrap who leads the prisoners out of the cave and into the light of Persian truth. Meanwhile, Aristotle's "Golden Mean" becomes "The Satrap's Mean," where the ideal is to be moderate in all things, except when it comes to paying taxes.

8. The Persian Peace: An Era of Stability

With Greece under control, the Persian Empire enjoys an extended period of peace and prosperity. The Greeks, known for their constant bickering and wars, are forced to play nice under Persian rule. Trade flourishes, roads are built, and the Greek economy booms—though much of the profit ends up in Persian coffers. The economic prosperity leads to a building boom, with new cities springing up all over Greece, each one more Persian than the last. The agora, once the heart of Greek city life, is transformed into a bustling bazaar where Greek merchants hock Persian rugs, spices, and luxury goods. The phrase "All roads lead to Rome" is replaced with "All roads lead to Persepolis," though the Greeks still grumble about the tolls.

9. The Spread of Zoroastrianism

With the Persians in charge, Zoroastrianism begins to spread throughout Greece. Temples to Ahura Mazda are built alongside the ruins of old Greek temples, and Zoroastrian fire rituals become a common sight. While the Greeks are initially resistant, many eventually adopt Zoroastrian practices, blending them with their own traditions. Zoroastrianism's focus on the cosmic struggle between good and evil influences Greek thought and religion. New mystery cults emerge, blending Greek and Persian beliefs, and the Eleusinian Mysteries are updated to include a final test where initiates must choose between the paths of light and darkness. Greek dramas also take a darker turn, with playwrights exploring themes of fate, cosmic justice, and the battle between good and evil—usually ending in everyone's tragic demise, just for good measure.

10. The Persian Empire's Western Capital: New Persepolis

To better govern the newly conquered Greece, the Persian king establishes a second capital in Athens, renaming it New Persepolis. The city becomes a symbol of Persian power in the West, complete with grand palaces, sprawling gardens, and a royal road that connects it directly to the original Persepolis in Iran. New Persepolis becomes the cultural and administrative hub of the western Persian Empire. Greek architects, now under Persian patronage, develop a new style that blends Greek and Persian elements, leading to the birth of "Persegreek" architecture. The city attracts scholars, artists, and merchants from across the empire, creating a cosmopolitan center that rivals the old Persepolis in grandeur. Meanwhile, the original Acropolis is converted into a giant administrative complex, complete with a satrap's palace, where the old Parthenon is used as a glorified filing cabinet.

Conclusion

If the Persian Empire had successfully conquered Greece, the history of Western civilization would have taken a dramatic turn. Persian culture, philosophy, and governance would have overshadowed Greek achievements, leading to a unique blend of traditions that defined the ancient world. Democracy and the Greek pantheon would have been relegated to the annals of history, while Persian influence spread across Europe, shaping the development of Western thought, art, and politics. The Greek spirit, once defined by independence and innovation, would have been reshaped by Persian ideals, creating a new, blended civilization where the legacy of both cultures lived on—albeit in a way that would leave future historians both fascinated and utterly confused.

What If the Library of Alexandria Had Never Been Destroyed?

The Background

Imagine the scene: The Library of Alexandria, the greatest repository of knowledge in the ancient world, stands tall and proud on the shores of the Mediterranean. Founded by Ptolemy I in the 3rd century BCE, it's a beacon of learning where scholars from all over the world gather to study, debate, and write on everything from philosophy to mathematics to what exactly makes a good wine. Historically, this wonder of the ancient world suffered several tragedies—a few accidental fires, the occasional political upheaval, and a general lack of proper fire insurance—leading to its eventual destruction. But what if the library had survived the millennia, unscathed and continuously expanding, preserving every scrap of knowledge from the ancient world?

Let's say, instead of burning to the ground during one of history's infamous "Oops, we accidentally set the most valuable library on fire" moments, the Library of Alexandria becomes the ultimate fortified citadel of learning. Ptolemy III, sensing the vulnerability of this intellectual treasure, orders the construction of fireproof walls, earthquake-resistant columns, and a staff of librarians who are trained not only in cataloging scrolls but also in fire-fighting, diplomacy, and anti-vandalism tactics. Thus, the library survives every potential disaster, from Julius Caesar's accidental torching to the later invasions by overzealous conquerors who would rather see the world burn than read.

The 10 Possible Things That Would Happen

1. An Unbroken Chain of Knowledge

With the Library of Alexandria intact, the accumulated knowledge of the ancient world—from Greek philosophy to Egyptian medicine to Persian astronomy—remains preserved, meticulously copied, and updated by generations of scholars. Instead of losing priceless scrolls, we get a continuous, unbroken intellectual tradition that connects the ancients directly to the Renaissance and beyond. The Dark Ages never really darken. With the library's resources, Europe bypasses the intellectual stagnation and instead experiences an early Renaissance around 500 CE, roughly a thousand years ahead of schedule. Monks in monasteries find themselves studying Euclid instead of just copying manuscripts, and the church debates scientific theories alongside theology. The term "medieval" becomes synonymous with "surprisingly advanced."

2. The Scientific Revolution Begins Early

The library, housing the works of Archimedes, Eratosthenes, and countless others, becomes the hub of early scientific inquiry. Scholars from across the known world flock to Alexandria to conduct experiments, share ideas, and argue over whose theory of the cosmos is less likely to get them laughed out of the forum. The Scientific Revolution kicks off in Alexandria in the 2nd century CE, with inventions like the steam engine, primitive computers, and even early prototypes of eyeglasses emerging far earlier than they did historically. By the time Leonardo da Vinci is born, the world has already seen flying machines (though they're more like giant kites), and his notebooks are filled not with groundbreaking ideas but with doodles of things that have already been built. The term "Renaissance man" loses its meaning since everyone is one.

3. The Alexandrian Empire of Knowledge

Alexandria becomes the intellectual and cultural capital of the world, overshadowing Rome and later Byzantium. Its influence spreads across the Mediterranean, with scholars from India, China, and even distant Britannia sending emissaries to study at the feet of the world's greatest minds. The city itself evolves into a melting pot of ideas, where Greek, Egyptian, and Eastern philosophies blend into a unique Alexandrian worldview. The world map changes as other cities try to emulate Alexandria's success. "Mini Alexandrias" spring up in places like Antioch, Athens, and Carthage, each vying to be the next intellectual powerhouse. The competition between these cities leads to rapid advancements in urban planning, public education, and the development of the world's first "university league tables," sparking debates among scholars over which city has the best philosophy department.

4. Technology Takes Off

With an unbroken tradition of engineering and scientific experimentation, the world sees technological advancements centuries ahead of their time. The ancient world, armed with knowledge preserved and expanded in Alexandria, begins to experiment with everything from windmills to water clocks to complex machinery that would have made Heron of Alexandria proud. The Industrial Revolution happens about a thousand years early. By the time Rome falls (if it ever does), factories powered by water and wind dot the Mediterranean landscape. Roman aqueducts are retrofitted to drive massive grain mills, and the term "Roman roads" comes to refer to well-paved highways lined with early steam-powered carts. The Roman Empire's fall is delayed as the empire leverages its advanced technology to fend off barbarian invasions with steam-powered legions.

5. Philosophy Meets Science: The Birth of the Alexandrian Method

The ongoing debates at the Library of Alexandria lead to the development of a new method of inquiry, blending Greek philosophical reasoning with empirical observation. This "Alexandrian Method" becomes the standard for scientific research, influencing everything from medicine to physics to alchemy (which, thanks to the library's resources, starts evolving into early chemistry). The separation between philosophy and science never fully develops. Future generations see no distinction between pondering the nature of reality and conducting experiments to test those ideas. "Philosopher-scientists" like Hypatia become the norm, and universities worldwide adopt the Alexandrian curriculum, where students must study both Aristotle and Archimedes before they can graduate. The debate over whether philosophy or science is more important is resolved with the saying, "Why not both?"

6. Religious and Cultural Syncretism

The library, a melting pot of ideas, becomes a center for religious and cultural syncretism. Greek gods merge with Egyptian deities, and Zoroastrianism, Hinduism, and Buddhism all influence each other in unexpected ways. The scholars of Alexandria, curious about everything, begin writing treatises on the commonalities between all religions, sparking a movement toward a more unified, philosophical spirituality. Religious conflicts are significantly reduced as the world's major religions develop a common philosophical foundation. Alexandria's influence leads to the formation of a global council of religious leaders, who gather every decade to debate, philosophize, and occasionally argue about whose turn it is to bring the wine. The concept of religious wars becomes almost unthinkable, and the Crusades never happen. Instead, there's a series of friendly, if heated, debates over whether fasting or feasting brings you closer to enlightenment.

7. The Global Trade of Ideas

With the library as the epicenter, a global trade network for knowledge develops, with scholars exchanging letters, scrolls, and even visiting each other's academies. Alexandria's harbor is filled not only with grain and spices but also with the latest manuscripts on mathematics from India, medicine from China, and astronomy from Persia. The spread of ideas leads to an early form of globalization, where cultures begin to share and adopt each other's best practices. Roman architects start incorporating Chinese feng shui principles into their building designs, while Indian mathematicians introduce the concept of zero to Greek scholars. The result is a world that's more interconnected and cooperative, with less focus on conquest and more on collaboration—though the occasional intellectual rivalry still leads to some spirited debates (and the first-ever "academic burn" in history).

8. Medicine Makes a Quantum Leap

The medical knowledge preserved and expanded in Alexandria leads to unprecedented advancements in health and medicine. Greek, Egyptian, and Indian medical practices are combined, leading to early forms of surgery, herbal medicine, and even a rudimentary understanding of germs. Lifespans increase significantly, with people regularly living into their 70s and 80s. Ancient leaders, no longer plagued by short life expectancies, have time to think more long-term, leading to more stable governments and fewer wars of succession. Hospitals become standard in every major city, and the phrase "Take two herbs and call me in the morning" becomes the ancient world's version of a doctor's prescription.

9. The Great Alexandrian Codex

As the library's collections grow, the librarians develop an early form of the codex, a bound book that replaces cumbersome scrolls. These codices, filled with everything from Plato's dialogues to cutting-edge astronomical theories, become the preferred method of knowledge transmission. The library even starts producing "bestsellers," with the works of Homer, Sophocles, and even an early cookbook by a mysterious "Apicius" topping the ancient charts. The invention of the codex accelerates the spread of literacy across the ancient world. Public reading rooms (the ancient equivalent of libraries) pop up in every major city, where citizens can check out the latest "scroll-busters" and engage in heated discussions about whether Socrates or Aristophanes was the better writer. The codex format also leads to the development of early encyclopedias, with the Great Alexandrian Codex being the go-to reference for everything from how to build a catapult to the best way to prepare a roast lamb.

10. A Legacy That Lasts

The Library of Alexandria's survival ensures that its influence extends far beyond the ancient world. As the centuries pass, the library becomes a symbol of intellectual achievement, inspiring future generations to value knowledge above all else. The Renaissance, when it eventually comes, is not so much a rebirth as it is a continuation of the Alexandrian tradition. The Enlightenment happens in the 10th century instead of the 18th, leading to an earlier spread of democratic ideas, human rights, and scientific inquiry. By the time the 20th century rolls around, humanity has already colonized the moon, cured most diseases, and developed a global network of knowledge-sharing that's essentially the Internet, but with scrolls. The phrase "Standing on the shoulders of giants" is replaced with "Reading from the shelves of Alexandria," and every major city has its own version of the library, ensuring that knowledge is preserved and expanded for all time.

Conclusion

If the Library of Alexandria had never been destroyed, the course of human history would have been radically different. The preservation and continuous expansion of ancient knowledge would have accelerated scientific and technological advancements by centuries, leading to a world where the Dark Ages never happened, the Renaissance came early, and humanity reached heights of intellectual and cultural achievement far beyond what we know today. The Library of Alexandria would have stood as the eternal heart of human progress, ensuring that the flames of knowledge never dimmed, but instead, illuminated the path to a brighter future. And who knows? Maybe by now, we'd all be flying around in steam-powered chariots while debating the finer points of Zeno's paradoxes over a nice cup of Egyptian coffee.

What If Julius Caesar Had Not Been Assassinated?

The Background

It's the Ides of March, 44 BCE, and Julius Caesar, fresh off a string of victories, both military and political, is heading to the Senate. Historically, we all know what happens next—a group of disgruntled senators, fed up with Caesar's growing power and his apparent disdain for the old ways of the Republic, stab him 23 times, ending not just his life but, eventually, the Roman Republic itself. But what if, instead of meeting his untimely demise on the Senate floor, Caesar had managed to avoid the conspiracy—perhaps by deciding to take a sick day, or maybe just having a better security detail? What if Caesar had lived on, reshaping Rome in his image without the need for an emperor's crown?

So, let's say on that fateful day, Caesar gets a bad feeling—maybe he actually listens to the soothsayer for once, or perhaps Calpurnia's nightmare is enough to convince him to skip the Senate meeting. Either way, Caesar avoids the assassination attempt, and the conspirators, caught with their daggers out and no one to stab, awkwardly pretend they were just planning a surprise... birthday party? Embarrassed and exposed, they scatter, leaving Caesar to continue his rule.

The 10 Possible Things That Would Happen

1. Caesar's Reforms Continue (But with a Twist)

Caesar, now aware of just how precarious his position is, doubles down on his reforms but with a newfound caution. He starts reshaping the Republic with a more inclusive Senate, packed with loyalists and a few well-paid former conspirators who suddenly discover they really like the idea of one-man rule, as long as it's not called "dictatorship." The Senate becomes less of a debating chamber and more of a rubber-stamp club, with senators enthusiastically agreeing to whatever Caesar suggests—be it land reforms, calendar changes, or the introduction of Caesar-brand togas. The Republic, technically still intact, becomes a de facto monarchy in all but name, but with lots of paperwork to make it look official.

2. The Roman Republic 2.0

With Caesar at the helm, the Roman Republic undergoes a facelift. It's no longer the chaotic mess of competing aristocrats and endless squabbles; instead, it's streamlined, efficient, and—surprise!—run by Caesar. He introduces a series of reforms aimed at strengthening the Republic while ensuring that he remains the "First Citizen," not an emperor, but definitely more important than everyone else. The reforms lead to a more centralized and stable government. The title of "Dictator for Life" is replaced with "First Citizen for an Indefinite but Definitely Not Life-Long Period," which sounds much friendlier. Future historians scratch their heads trying to classify this new system, eventually settling on "Caesarian Republic," though a few rebellious types insist on calling it what it is: "Empire Lite."

3. Brutus and the Boys Get a Second Chance

Having dodged the knives, Caesar surprises everyone by not having Brutus, Cassius, and the other would-be assassins executed. Instead, he pardons them in a grand gesture of magnanimity—or as a clever ploy to keep them close and under surveillance. Brutus, now forced to live with the shame of his failed conspiracy, spends the rest of his days writing very gloomy philosophical treatises on how not to overthrow a dictator. Brutus becomes the ancient equivalent of a disillusioned political pundit, warning about the dangers of unchecked power while sipping wine at fancy parties paid for by Caesar. His works, though filled with biting critiques, are largely ignored by a populace that's more interested in Caesar's latest gladiatorial games. Eventually, Brutus fades into obscurity, remembered more as the guy who almost killed Caesar but instead ended up on the wrong side of history.

4. The Eternal Senate (Now with More Caesar!)

To appease the old Republican guard while still maintaining control, Caesar introduces a series of constitutional amendments that grant the Senate more "responsibilities"—mostly in name only. The Senate, now stuffed with Caesar's supporters, becomes a lively place where senators debate things like the best way to honor Caesar's victories or whether to rename Rome to "Caesaria." The Senate turns into a grand theater, with endless discussions about trivial matters while real power remains firmly in Caesar's hands. This faux-republicanism satisfies the masses who still cling to the idea of the Republic, even as Caesar's influence grows unchecked. Future Roman leaders adopt the same strategy, maintaining the façade of republicanism long after its substance has been hollowed out.

5. The Conquest of Parthia (At Last!)

Caesar, still the ambitious military genius, turns his attention eastward after dealing with his domestic troubles. He finally gets around to his planned invasion of Parthia, determined to avenge Crassus's humiliating defeat and expand Rome's borders even further. The campaign is a resounding success, with Caesar adding "Conqueror of the East" to his already impressive list of titles. The successful conquest of Parthia leads to an unprecedented expansion of the Roman Empire, stretching its borders deep into the East. The influx of wealth and exotic goods from the newly conquered territories sparks a cultural revolution in Rome, with Parthian fashions, foods, and even philosophies becoming the latest trends. The Senate, of course, debates the best way to incorporate Parthian culture into Roman society—before unanimously agreeing to Caesar's proposal to rename the Parthian capital "Caesarabad."

6. The Caesarian Calendar: Now with Extra Days!

Having already reformed the calendar once, Caesar decides that it could use a bit more tweaking. He introduces a few extra months here and there, all named after his victories or favorite pastimes. The Julian Calendar becomes the Caesarian Calendar, and everyone celebrates the new holiday "Caesarday," where citizens are encouraged to reflect on the greatness of Caesar—and buy more togas. The calendar changes lead to some confusion across the Empire, especially among the provinces that still haven't quite adjusted to the last set of reforms. Future historians have a field day trying to figure out what year things actually happened, leading to the creation of the first historical timeline charts, which, of course, start with "Year One: Caesar's Victory Over Common Sense."

7. Caesar the Patron of the Arts

With his power secure and no immediate threats to his rule, Caesar turns his attention to the arts. He commissions poets, playwrights, and sculptors to create works that glorify Rome—and, naturally, Caesar himself. Rome enters a golden age of culture, with artists vying for Caesar's favor by producing increasingly elaborate and flattering portrayals of the "First Citizen." The Roman arts scene explodes with creativity, albeit with a slightly one-sided focus on Caesar. Theaters across the Empire stage epic dramas about Caesar's life, while sculptors work overtime crafting marble statues of him in every conceivable heroic pose. The phrase "to Caesarize" enters the Roman lexicon, meaning to excessively flatter someone in the hopes of getting ahead, a practice that becomes so common it eventually spawns the first anti-flattery movement in history.

8. The Caesar Doctrine

As his rule solidifies, Caesar introduces the "Caesar Doctrine," a foreign policy strategy that emphasizes peace through overwhelming military might. Neighboring kingdoms and tribes are "encouraged" to join the Roman fold, not through outright conquest, but through treaties that just happen to favor Rome. Caesar becomes the ultimate diplomat, expanding Rome's influence without necessarily marching legions into every corner of the known world. Rome's borders expand in a more subtle manner, with new client states popping up across Europe and the Near East. These states, nominally independent, follow the "Caesar Doctrine," adopting Roman laws, culture, and coinage, all while paying hefty tributes to Rome. Caesar's strategy of diplomacy backed by military threat becomes the blueprint for future Roman leaders, who use it to maintain Rome's dominance for centuries. The term "Romanization" is replaced with "Caesarization," though both essentially mean "Do it our way or else."

9. The Caesar Succession Plan

Realizing that his rule won't last forever (despite his best efforts), Caesar begins planning for a smooth succession. He grooms a series of potential heirs, emphasizing loyalty to the Republic (and by Republic, he means himself). His preferred successor, a young and ambitious military commander (let's call him Octavian), is carefully positioned to take over when Caesar eventually decides to "retire." Caesar's well-planned succession avoids the chaotic power struggles that plagued Rome after his assassination in our timeline. Octavian takes over as "First Citizen" without much fuss, ensuring a smooth transition of power. The tradition of grooming a successor becomes a hallmark of the "Caesarian Republic," preventing the kind of bloody civil wars that historically tore Rome apart. However, this also leads to a new problem: future leaders are judged not on their merit but on how well they can imitate Caesar's style, leading to a series of increasingly absurd "Caesar impersonation" contests.

10. The Myth of Caesar

As time passes, the man and the myth of Caesar begin to blur. Historians, poets, and orators alike contribute to the growing legend of Caesar, casting him as the ultimate Roman hero, philosopher-king, and military genius. He becomes a larger-than-life figure, a symbol of Rome's greatness, even as his successors continue to build on his legacy. The mythologization of Caesar leads to the creation of the first Roman "superhero" stories, with bards telling tales of Caesar's exploits that grow more fantastical with each retelling. Future generations are taught the "Three Cs" in school: Courage, Conquest, and Caesar. The Roman pantheon, once filled with a host of deities, finds itself overshadowed by the cult of Caesar, with statues of him popping up in temples alongside those of Jupiter and Mars. The line between history and myth becomes so blurred that by the time the Empire falls, future civilizations aren't sure if Caesar was a man, a god, or just a really successful toga salesman.

Conclusion

If Julius Caesar had not been assassinated, the Roman Republic might have evolved into something entirely different—a strange hybrid of republican ideals and monarchical rule, where Caesar's influence loomed large over every aspect of Roman life. The rise of emperors could have been delayed or even avoided, with the Republic continuing in name, but with the reality of power firmly in the hands of Caesar and his successors. The preservation of the Republic, however, would come at the cost of true democracy, as Rome drifted further into the realm of autocracy, wrapped in the comforting illusion of republicanism. And in the end, the name of Caesar would echo through history not as the man who destroyed the Republic, but as the one who transformed it into something entirely new—something neither fully a republic nor an empire, but something uniquely... Caesar.

What If Cleopatra and Mark Antony Had Won the Battle of Actium?

The Background

It's 31 BCE, and the stakes couldn't be higher. The forces of Mark Antony and Cleopatra, the power couple of the ancient world, are squaring off against Octavian (the future Augustus) in the waters off the coast of Actium. Historically, Octavian's forces won the day, leading to Antony and Cleopatra's tragic end, and the rise of the Roman Empire under Augustus. But let's rewind and give our star-crossed lovers a break. What if, against all odds, Antony and Cleopatra emerged victorious from the Battle of Actium? What if instead of Octavian's Rome, the Mediterranean world was shaped by the influence of the last pharaoh of Egypt and her Roman lover?

So, let's say a clever tactical maneuver—perhaps Cleopatra's legendary charm paired with Antony's military prowess—turns the tide at Actium. Octavian's fleet, caught in a cunning trap, is decimated. His forces, demoralized and leaderless, crumble. Octavian himself either flees or is captured, depending on which historian you ask in this alternate universe. With Rome's golden boy out of the picture, Antony and Cleopatra seize control of the Roman world, or at least a large portion of it. The Ptolemaic Kingdom of Egypt, instead of being absorbed into Rome, becomes the dominant power in the Mediterranean, reshaping the future of Western civilization.

The 10 Possible Things That Would Happen

1. The Ptolemaic-Roman Empire

With their victory at Actium, Antony and Cleopatra establish a new power structure—an empire that's part Roman, part Egyptian. Cleopatra, ever the astute ruler, plays up her divine status as the reincarnation of Isis, while Antony, the Roman general, maintains the loyalty of the legions. Together, they create a hybrid empire that stretches from the Nile to the Tiber. The new Ptolemaic-Roman Empire becomes a unique cultural fusion. The Senate in Rome still exists, but it now answers to Cleopatra, who rules from Alexandria, where she's more interested in building libraries and temples than listening to old senators drone on about the Republic. The empire's official language is a mix of Latin and Greek, with Egyptian hieroglyphs making a stylish comeback in official documents.

2. Cleopatra: The New Augustus

Cleopatra, ever the pragmatist, uses her victory to position herself as the rightful ruler of Rome. She presents herself not just as the Queen of Egypt, but as the Empress of Rome, effectively taking on the role that Augustus would have played. Temples are built in her honor across the empire, and she's worshipped as a goddess in both Egypt and Rome. Cleopatra's image becomes synonymous with power, femininity, and divine right. Roman women, once relegated to the shadows, begin to see her as a role model, leading to an early feminist movement in Rome. The phrase "What would Cleopatra do?" becomes the ancient world's version of modern motivational posters, complete with stylized portraits of the queen wearing a laurel wreath and holding a scroll.

3. Antony's New Rome

Antony, basking in the afterglow of victory, decides to reshape Rome in his image. He moves the capital from the city of Rome to Alexandria, arguing that it's more strategically located (and, let's face it, it's closer to Cleopatra). Alexandria becomes the new center of the empire, a city where Roman legions march past Egyptian obelisks and philosophers debate in the shadow of the Great Library. Rome, now a secondary city, becomes a bit of a backwater compared to the glittering, cosmopolitan Alexandria. The traditional Roman values of austerity and simplicity give way to Egyptian opulence, with Romans adopting Egyptian fashion, art, and religion. The Colosseum, instead of being built in Rome, is constructed in Alexandria, where gladiators fight under the watchful eyes of sphinxes.

4. Octavian's Exile

Octavian, the defeated would-be emperor, is forced into exile. Rather than being executed, he's sent to the farthest reaches of the empire, perhaps a desolate outpost in Gaul or Hispania, where he spends the rest of his days plotting a comeback that never materializes. He writes bitter memoirs, detailing how he was wronged, but no one in Alexandria bothers to read them. Without Octavian to stabilize Rome, the old aristocracy struggles to maintain control. The Senate, now largely ceremonial, becomes a playground for wealthy elites who pretend to govern while Cleopatra and Antony pull the real strings from Alexandria. Political satire becomes a popular genre, with plays mocking the old senators' inability to adapt to the new world order. Octavian, meanwhile, becomes a tragic figure in history, remembered more for his whining than his statesmanship.

5. Cleopatra's Heirs

Cleopatra and Antony's children, including Caesarion (the son of Julius Caesar), are groomed to inherit this new empire. Caesarion is declared co-ruler, his status as the son of Caesar giving him a claim to both the Roman and Egyptian thrones. The dynasty that follows blends Roman military tradition with Egyptian divine kingship, creating a ruling family that's both feared and revered. The Ptolemaic dynasty, now with Roman blood, becomes even more entrenched in power. The concept of divine kingship, long a staple in Egypt, spreads to Rome, where the emperors are seen as living gods. Future rulers are expected to embody both the Roman virtue of "gravitas" and the Egyptian ideal of "maat" (justice and harmony). The empire's official portraits show rulers in both Roman togas and Egyptian robes, holding the symbols of both civilizations—a fasces in one hand and an ankh in the other.

6. The Cult of Isis Goes Global

Cleopatra's identification with the goddess Isis becomes a powerful tool for unifying the empire. The cult of Isis, already popular in Egypt, spreads throughout the Roman world, with temples dedicated to the goddess popping up in every major city. The worship of Isis, with its promise of eternal life and its elaborate rituals, becomes the dominant religion in the empire. The spread of the Isis cult leads to the gradual decline of the traditional Roman pantheon. Jupiter, Mars, and Venus take a backseat to Isis, Osiris, and Horus, as the Roman gods are slowly assimilated into the Egyptian pantheon. The concept of a single, all-powerful goddess appeals to many in the empire, leading to the early rise of monotheistic tendencies. Christianity, when it eventually emerges, faces stiff competition from the established and state-sponsored cult of Isis.

7. Rome's New Allies: Egypt's Old Enemies

With Cleopatra in charge, Rome's foreign policy takes a decidedly Egyptian turn. Old enemies of Egypt, such as the Nubians and Parthians, become Rome's new targets. Antony leads campaigns into these territories, expanding the empire further south and east, securing Egypt's borders, and bringing even more wealth into the empire. The Roman legions, now seasoned veterans of desert warfare, become experts in both conventional and guerrilla tactics. The empire's expansion into Africa and the Near East brings a wealth of new resources and trade routes, making Alexandria the richest city in the world. Meanwhile, the Roman Senate is left grumbling about how they miss the good old days of fighting Gauls and Germans, while trying to figure out what to do with all these new exotic animals Cleopatra keeps sending them.

8. The Alexandrian Renaissance

Alexandria, already a center of learning, becomes the cultural and intellectual heart of the empire. The Great Library, spared from destruction, continues to expand, becoming the repository of knowledge from across the known world. Scholars from every corner of the empire flock to Alexandria to study, debate, and innovate under the patronage of Cleopatra and Antony. The Alexandrian Renaissance leads to significant advancements in science, medicine, and philosophy. The knowledge preserved in the library fuels early developments in everything from steam power to early forms of chemistry. The concept of the university is born, with Alexandria hosting the world's first true institution of higher learning. Future generations refer to this period as the "Golden Age of Cleopatra," with her name synonymous with wisdom, power, and cultural flourishing. Rome, once the heart of Western civilization, is now seen as a quaint, historical footnote.

9. The Fusion of Roman and Egyptian Art

The victory at Actium leads to an unprecedented blending of Roman and Egyptian art and architecture. Temples, statues, and public buildings throughout the empire incorporate both Roman realism and Egyptian symbolism. The result is a unique style that comes to define the art and architecture of the Ptolemaic-Roman Empire. The new art style spreads throughout the empire, with Roman cities adorned with sphinxes, obelisks, and colossal statues of the gods. The Roman Colosseum, if it is ever built, is decorated with hieroglyphics, and gladiators fight under the watchful eyes of statues of Horus and Mars. The artistic fusion also extends to literature, with Roman poets composing epic verses about the gods of Egypt and Egyptian scribes chronicling the deeds of Roman heroes. The result is a cultural legacy that blends the best of both worlds, admired by future civilizations as the pinnacle of ancient artistry.

10. The End of the Roman Republic

With Cleopatra and Antony in control, the Roman Republic, already weakened by decades of civil war, is effectively dead. The Senate, once the center of Roman political life, becomes little more than a ceremonial body, rubber-stamping the decisions made in Alexandria. The idea of republican governance fades into obscurity, replaced by the concept of divine monarchy as embodied by Cleopatra and her heirs. The death of the Republic leads to the complete reorganization of the Roman government. Local governors are appointed directly by Alexandria, with the Senate serving as a glorified advisory council. The concept of citizen participation in government becomes a relic of the past, remembered only in the dusty annals of history. As the centuries pass, Rome is absorbed fully into the Egyptian-centric empire, with future generations knowing it more as a province of Cleopatra's realm than the mighty Republic it once was.

Conclusion

If Cleopatra and Mark Antony had won the Battle of Actium, the course of Western civilization would have taken a drastically different path. The Ptolemaic Kingdom of Egypt, instead of fading into history, would have become the dominant power in the Mediterranean, reshaping Rome in its image and blending Egyptian and Roman culture into a unique hybrid civilization. The Roman Republic, already on life support, would have been fully eclipsed by the rise of a new, Egyptian-centric empire that valued divine monarchy over republicanism, and cultural fusion over traditionalism. Cleopatra's legacy, rather than ending in tragedy, would have been one of unparalleled influence, creating a world where the Nile and the Tiber flowed together, shaping the future of both East and West. And who knows? Maybe, in this alternate history, Cleopatra's famous asp would have been just another exotic pet in the royal menagerie, rather than the symbol of her tragic end.

What If the Trojan War Had Never Happened?

The Background

The Trojan War, that legendary conflict sparked by a beauty contest gone terribly wrong, has been the subject of countless tales, poems, and debates. According to legend, it all started when Paris, a Trojan prince, awarded the golden apple to Aphrodite, who in turn promised him the most beautiful woman in the world—Helen of Sparta. Unfortunately, Helen was already married to King Menelaus, which led to a full-scale Greek invasion of Troy. The war, lasting ten long years, became the backdrop for Homer's *Iliad* and *Odyssey*, epic poems that shaped Greek culture and Western literature for millennia. But what if that fateful beauty contest had gone differently, or if Paris had simply stayed home? What if the Trojan War had never happened?

So, let's imagine that Paris, instead of causing a scandal that would launch a thousand ships, decides that the whole "golden apple" thing isn't worth the trouble. Maybe he chooses wisdom over beauty and hands the apple to Athena (who promptly makes Troy a center of learning instead of war), or maybe he's just too busy with other matters to bother with goddesses and their petty disputes. Either way, Helen stays in Sparta, Menelaus remains unbothered, and the Greek coalition never sets sail for Troy. The war that would have defined an era simply… doesn't happen.

The 10 Possible Things That Would Happen

1. *Homer's Career Crisis*

Without the Trojan War, Homer (assuming he was a real historical figure) finds himself in a bit of a bind. With no epic war to chronicle, he has to turn his attention to other subjects. Instead of *The Iliad*, Homer ends up writing about the agricultural practices of the Peloponnesian Peninsula or a really detailed account of Mycenaean tax collection—riveting stuff, really. Without the *Iliad* and *Odyssey*, Greek literature takes a very different turn. The oral tradition shifts away from epic tales of heroism and instead focuses on the mundane realities of daily life. Future students groan not over the adventures of Achilles and Odysseus, but over lengthy verses describing crop rotations and sheep herding techniques. The phrase "Homeric hero" is replaced with "Homeric farmer," and the world's first agricultural manuals are born.

2. *No Achilles, No Problem*

Achilles, the nearly invincible Greek hero, never gets his chance to shine—or die gloriously in battle. Instead, he becomes a local legend for his athletic prowess, perhaps winning a few Olympic medals before retiring to a quiet life of farming. His anger issues, without an outlet in battle, manifest in some very aggressive plowing techniques. With no Achilles to serve as the archetype of the tragic hero, Greek mythology shifts focus. Heroes are less about tragic flaws and more about practical virtues like endurance, hard work, and the ability to wrestle an ox into submission. Greek sculpture, instead of depicting muscular warriors, favors statues of robust farmers, and the great Greek hero myths are replaced with tales of agricultural triumphs. The Olympics feature a new event: the Achilles Plow Race.

3. A Peaceful Mycenae

The Mycenaeans, instead of launching a massive expedition across the Aegean, focus on domestic development. Mycenaean Greece becomes a land of bustling trade, rich culture, and, most importantly, no long-term sieges that would drain the treasury and the populace. King Agamemnon, instead of being remembered as a warlord, is known as a master builder who erects grand palaces and expands the Mycenaean trade network. Without the war, the Mycenaean civilization doesn't collapse as quickly. The Greek Dark Ages are delayed, or perhaps even avoided, as the Mycenaeans maintain their grip on power longer. This extended period of stability leads to earlier advancements in art, architecture, and government. The famous Lion Gate at Mycenae is still built, but now it's just the entrance to a massive shopping district, complete with ancient versions of luxury boutiques and a thriving market for olive oil and pottery.

4. The Rise of Troy: A Cultural Powerhouse

Without a Greek invasion to worry about, Troy continues to thrive as a wealthy and influential city-state. Under King Priam, Troy becomes the cultural and intellectual center of the ancient world, rivaling even Athens in its later years. The city's strategic location on the Hellespont ensures that it controls trade between the Aegean and Black Seas, filling its coffers with riches from far and wide. The city of Troy becomes the Florence of the ancient world, attracting artists, philosophers, and scholars. The "Trojan School" of thought emerges, blending Eastern and Western philosophies in a unique way that influences generations of thinkers. The legendary wooden horse, instead of being a symbol of Greek cunning, becomes the mascot of Troy's elite university, where students study rhetoric, engineering, and diplomacy. The term "Trojan Horse" is only ever used to describe a particularly clever debating tactic.

5. Helen of Sparta: A Political Force

Without the whole "abduction by Paris" episode, Helen remains in Sparta, where she becomes more than just a pretty face. She uses her status as the most beautiful woman in the world to influence politics, broker alliances, and secure peace across Greece. Menelaus, grateful to avoid a war, supports her endeavors, and the two become the ultimate power couple of the ancient world. Helen's influence leads to a more stable and unified Greece, where city-states cooperate rather than compete. The idea of a pan-Hellenic league, under Spartan leadership, gains traction much earlier, paving the way for a more unified Greece that can better resist external threats. Helen becomes the poster child for early feminism, with later writers extolling her virtues not just for her beauty, but for her political acumen and diplomatic skills. Statues of Helen depict her with a scroll in one hand and a scepter in the other, a symbol of both wisdom and power.

6. The Odyssey: A Fishing Trip

With no Trojan War, Odysseus doesn't have to spend ten years trying to get home. Instead, he enjoys a peaceful reign on Ithaca, known more for his shrewdness in governance than his epic adventures. *The Odyssey* becomes a much shorter tale, recounting a particularly eventful fishing trip where Odysseus almost caught a really big fish, but it got away. Without Odysseus's epic journey, the concept of the "hero's journey" in literature evolves differently. Future epics focus less on physical quests and more on intellectual or spiritual journeys. The phrase "an Odyssean adventure" comes to mean "a mildly interesting day at the office," and Homeric heroes are praised for their wit and wisdom rather than their ability to stab things. The Mediterranean's fishing industry, however, experiences a brief boom thanks to the popularity of Odysseus's fishing techniques.

7. Greek Drama: A Shift in Focus

Without the tragic backdrop of the Trojan War, Greek playwrights turn their attention to other themes. Instead of the doomed house of Atreus, dramatists focus on everyday life, politics, and the occasional romantic comedy. Aeschylus writes a hit play about a merchant's struggle to open a new market stall, while Sophocles pens a hilarious farce about a love triangle involving a shepherd, a nymph, and a particularly talkative goat. Greek theater takes on a lighter tone, with comedies far outnumbering tragedies. The tradition of Greek drama becomes more focused on social commentary and satire, with Aristophanes emerging as the most influential playwright of the era. The gods, rather than being depicted as vengeful and capricious, become figures of fun, with Zeus portrayed as a bumbling bureaucrat and Hera as the long-suffering wife who's had enough of his antics. The concept of catharsis is still there, but now it's achieved through laughter, not tears.

8. Athens and Sparta: Best Frenemies

With no Trojan War to set the stage for future conflicts, Athens and Sparta maintain a more cooperative, if still competitive, relationship. Instead of the Peloponnesian War, the two city-states engage in a series of highly competitive athletic and artistic festivals, where they try to outdo each other in everything from wrestling to pottery-making. The rivalry between Athens and Sparta becomes more about cultural achievements than military might. The Olympic Games, rather than being an occasional event, become an annual festival where city-states showcase their best athletes, artists, and philosophers. The rivalry pushes both cities to greater heights, leading to a golden age of Greek culture that lasts even longer than in our timeline. The phrase "Spartan discipline" takes on a new meaning, referring to their rigorous artistic training, while "Athenian democracy" is synonymous with intellectual openness and innovation.

9. The Gods Go Global

With no Trojan War to occupy their attention, the Greek gods start to get restless. Instead of meddling in mortal affairs, they turn their divine attention outward, influencing other cultures across the Mediterranean and beyond. Zeus makes a guest appearance in Egyptian mythology as a storm god, while Apollo decides to take a trip to the Indus Valley, where he's worshipped as a sun deity with a penchant for poetry. The Greek pantheon becomes a global phenomenon, with Greek deities being incorporated into various cultures. Temples to Zeus, Athena, and Apollo pop up in Carthage, Egypt, and even distant Persia. The spread of Greek religion leads to an early form of cultural exchange, where myths and religious practices blend together in fascinating ways. The result is a more interconnected ancient world, where gods and heroes cross borders as easily as traders and merchants.

10. The Absence of Epic Heroes: A New Ethos

Without the Trojan War, the Greek concept of heroism undergoes a major shift. Instead of glorifying warriors who achieve greatness through violence, Greek culture begins to celebrate those who excel in peace. The ideal hero is now the philosopher-king, the wise ruler, or the clever diplomat who wins wars without bloodshed. The absence of epic warrior-heroes changes the trajectory of Western thought. The focus on intellect over brawn leads to earlier developments in philosophy, science, and governance. Plato's Republic is written much earlier, and Aristotle's works on ethics and politics become the foundation of Greek education. Future generations look back on this era as the time when Greece chose the pen over the sword, laying the groundwork for a society that values knowledge and wisdom above all else. The phrase "Achilles heel" never enters the lexicon—instead, people speak of having a "Socratic wit" or "Pericles' diplomacy."

Conclusion

If the Trojan War had never happened, the entire course of Greek history and culture would have been fundamentally altered. Without the epic tales of Homer to shape Greek identity, the concept of heroism would have evolved in a different direction, focusing more on intellectual achievements than martial prowess. Greek literature, art, and philosophy would have developed along different lines, leading to a world where the ideals of wisdom, diplomacy, and cultural exchange took precedence over the glorification of war. The legacy of Greece, instead of being defined by tales of gods and heroes clashing on the battlefield, would be remembered for its contributions to peace, knowledge, and the arts—a legacy that, while different, would be no less profound. And somewhere in a quiet corner of the world, an old poet named Homer might still be spinning yarns—this time, about the greatest cheese maker in all of Mycenae.

What If the Hebrews Had Never Left Egypt?

The Background

The story of the Hebrews' exodus from Egypt, led by Moses, is one of the most defining narratives in the Bible. It's a tale of liberation, divine intervention, and the birth of a nation that would carry profound religious significance for millennia. The Exodus not only shaped Jewish identity but also laid the foundation for Christianity and Islam. But what if that dramatic flight from Pharaoh's oppression never happened? What if the Hebrews, instead of crossing the Red Sea and wandering the desert, had simply stayed in Egypt, blending into the fabric of one of the world's most powerful ancient civilizations?

Let's imagine that Moses, instead of confronting Pharaoh with plagues and miracles, takes a different approach—maybe he decides that a full-scale exodus isn't the best idea after all. Perhaps negotiations with the Egyptian rulers lead to a settlement where the Hebrews are granted more freedom and better living conditions without leaving the land. The Hebrews stay, not as slaves, but as a distinct community within the Egyptian Empire, gradually integrating while retaining their unique cultural and religious identity.

The 10 Possible Things That Would Happen

1. The Great Hebrew-Egyptian Synthesis

With the Hebrews remaining in Egypt, a cultural and religious synthesis begins to form. Over generations, Hebrew and Egyptian traditions blend, creating a unique hybrid culture. Hebrew monotheism coexists with Egyptian polytheism in a strange but functional religious system where Yahweh is worshipped alongside Ra, Osiris, and Isis. Passover might involve a nice Seder plate with some hieroglyphic inscriptions. The fusion leads to some interesting theological developments. Egyptian priests, intrigued by the concept of monotheism, begin incorporating elements of Hebrew faith into their own practices. The result is a new, state-sponsored religion that combines the moral codes of the Torah with the rituals of Egyptian worship. Temples are built where statues of Moses and Thoth stand side by side, and sacred texts are written in both Hebrew and hieroglyphics. Future historians are baffled by scrolls that include both "Thou shalt not kill" and detailed instructions on mummification.

2. The Pharaohs of Israel

As the Hebrew community prospers in Egypt, they begin to climb the social ladder. By the time Ramses XII takes the throne, Hebrews hold prominent positions in government, trade, and the military. Eventually, a charismatic Hebrew leader—let's call him "Moshe the Great"—rises to power and becomes the first Hebrew Pharaoh. This marks the beginning of a new dynasty, the "Pharaonic Kings of Israel," where the Egyptian crown is worn with a Star of David emblem. The new Hebrew dynasty leads to a period of unprecedented prosperity for Egypt. The Pharaonic Kings of Israel bring a unique blend of Egyptian statecraft and Hebrew legalism, resulting in a more just and efficient government. The Pyramids of Giza get a few new neighbors: towering ziggurats dedicated to Yahweh, where both Egyptians and Hebrews come to worship. The history books record this period as the

"Golden Age of Egypt," though scholars debate whether to classify it as Egyptian or Israelite history.

3. No Ten Commandments (But Some Pretty Solid Guidelines)

Without the Exodus, there's no dramatic revelation on Mount Sinai, no tablets of stone with the Ten Commandments. Instead, Moses—or perhaps a later Hebrew sage—pens a more pragmatic set of guidelines for living within Egyptian society. These "Twenty Suggestions" become the cornerstone of Hebrew-Egyptian law, blending moral teachings with practical advice on how to navigate life in the bustling, bureaucratic Egyptian state. The absence of the Ten Commandments means that the ethical foundation of Judaism, Christianity, and Islam is significantly different. The "Twenty Suggestions" are more like helpful life hacks than divine edicts: "Thou shalt not covet thy neighbor's pyramid" and "Honor thy Pharaoh and thy elders." As a result, the concept of sin is less rigid, and the moral landscape of Western religion becomes more nuanced, with fewer hard and fast rules. Religious debates revolve around whether it's okay to bend the suggestions in certain circumstances—leading to the first religious think tanks.

4. Egyptian Christianity: The Birth of Coptic Judaism

As centuries pass, the Hebrew-Egyptian community continues to evolve. When the teachings of a certain radical preacher named Jesus of Nazareth begin to spread, they don't encounter a distinct Jewish identity, but rather a hybrid culture steeped in both Hebrew and Egyptian traditions. Christianity takes root, but instead of branching out from Judaism, it emerges as a sect within the broader Hebrew-Egyptian religious framework, leading to a faith known as Coptic Judaism. The spread of Coptic Judaism across the Roman Empire changes the course of Western religion. The New Testament is written in both Greek and Egyptian demotic script, with gospel stories that include Egyptian parables and Hebrew prophecies. The Coptic Church, with its unique rituals and iconography, becomes the dominant Christian tradition in the Eastern Mediterranean. Rome adopts Christianity much later, and when it does, it's Coptic Christianity that shapes the early church. Michelangelo's "Last Supper" features a distinctly Egyptian backdrop, complete with a Nile view and a few strategically placed obelisks.

5. Islam Without the Exodus

The absence of the Exodus narrative has profound implications for the development of Islam. Without the story of Moses leading his people to freedom, the Quran's emphasis on liberation and the struggle against oppression takes on a different tone. Islam still emerges in the Arabian Peninsula, but it is less focused on the themes of deliverance from slavery and more on communal harmony and coexistence, influenced by centuries of Hebrew-Egyptian synthesis. The Five Pillars of Islam might include a pilgrimage not just to Mecca, but also to a great temple in Alexandria, where Hebrew-Egyptian traditions are honored. Islamic law, shaped by the "Twenty Suggestions," becomes more flexible, with scholars debating the nuances of morality in a multicultural context. The Dome of the Rock, when it's built, features a distinctive blend of Hebrew, Egyptian, and Arabic architectural styles, complete with hieroglyphic inscriptions praising Allah, Yahweh, and the Pharaohs.

6. A More Unified Mediterranean World

With the Hebrews fully integrated into Egyptian society, the region becomes a more cohesive cultural and economic unit. The Eastern Mediterranean thrives as a hub of trade, knowledge, and diplomacy. The influence of the Hebrew-Egyptian synthesis spreads throughout the ancient world, leading to a more unified Mediterranean civilization where Greek, Egyptian, and Semitic cultures blend seamlessly. The unity of the Mediterranean world leads to an earlier and more sustained period of peace and prosperity. The great empires of antiquity—Greece, Rome, Persia—interact more as equals than rivals, with cultural exchanges becoming the norm. Greek philosophers study in Egyptian temples, Roman engineers learn from Hebrew architects, and Persian poets compose verses in praise of both Apollo and Yahweh. The famous Library of Alexandria, enriched by Hebrew texts, becomes the intellectual capital of the ancient world, where scholars from across the empire debate everything from philosophy to the best methods of pyramid construction.

7. The Torah Becomes the Papyrus

Without the Exodus, the Torah—or what would become the Torah—takes on a different form. Instead of a strict set of laws given by God, it becomes a collection of wisdom literature, parables, and practical advice for living a righteous life in Egyptian society. Known as the "Papyrus," this text is a best-seller in both Hebrew and Egyptian communities, with sections on everything from crop rotation to the proper way to honor one's ancestors. The Papyrus becomes the foundation for not just one, but multiple religious traditions in the Mediterranean. Future prophets and teachers draw upon its wisdom to craft their own teachings, leading to a more diverse religious landscape. The Papyrus is eventually translated into Greek and Latin, becoming one of the most influential texts in the ancient world. When the Roman Empire converts to Coptic Christianity, the Papyrus is adopted as part of the new canon, influencing the development of Western moral philosophy and law. The concept of "Mosaic Law" is replaced with "Papyrus Ethics," taught in schools from Alexandria to Athens.

8. Pharaohs as Patrons of Monotheism

The Egyptian rulers, impressed by the stability and unity of the Hebrew-Egyptian community, begin to take an interest in monotheism. Pharaohs start to experiment with worshiping a single god—initially as a way to consolidate power, but eventually out of genuine spiritual curiosity. This leads to the establishment of a state-sponsored monotheism that coexists with traditional polytheistic practices. The Pharaohs' patronage of monotheism leads to an era of religious innovation in Egypt. Temples dedicated to Yahweh, Ra, and Osiris are built side by side, and a new priestly class emerges that specializes in monotheistic worship. Over time, the idea of a single, all-powerful god gains traction across the empire, influencing religious thought far beyond Egypt's borders. The monotheistic experiment eventually spreads to the broader Mediterranean, laying the groundwork for the later adoption of Christianity and Islam in a more unified religious landscape.

9. The Hebrew-Egyptian Calendar

With the Hebrews remaining in Egypt, the development of a unique calendar is inevitable. The Hebrew lunar calendar and the Egyptian solar calendar are combined to create a new, hybrid system that balances the cycles of the moon and the sun. This "Hebrew-Egyptian Calendar" becomes the standard throughout the region, used for everything from agriculture to religious festivals. The new calendar leads to a more organized and efficient society, where time is meticulously tracked and festivals are celebrated with greater regularity. The Hebrew-Egyptian calendar eventually spreads to other cultures, influencing the development of timekeeping in Greece, Rome, and beyond. The combination of lunar and solar cycles becomes the foundation for later advancements in astronomy and mathematics. By the time the Gregorian calendar is introduced, it's seen as a minor update to the already sophisticated Hebrew-Egyptian system.

10. The Absence of the Promised Land

Without the Exodus, the concept of the "Promised Land" changes. Instead of a specific geographic location, the Promised Land becomes a metaphor for spiritual fulfillment and moral righteousness within the Egyptian state. The Hebrews, settled and prosperous in Egypt, focus on creating a just and harmonious society rather than seeking a physical homeland. The absence of a territorial Promised Land has profound implications for Jewish,

Christian, and Islamic theology. The idea of a chosen people destined to inhabit a specific land is replaced with a more universal concept of spiritual fulfillment. This leads to a more inclusive religious tradition, where the focus is on ethical living rather than territorial claims. Future conflicts over land are less about divine mandate and more about political and economic concerns, resulting in a more peaceful and stable region. The idea of Zion becomes a spiritual ideal rather than a physical place, shaping the development of monotheistic religions in a way that emphasizes unity and coexistence over division.

Conclusion

If the Hebrews had never left Egypt, the course of Jewish history—and by extension, the histories of Christianity and Islam—would have been radically different. The blending of Hebrew and Egyptian cultures would have created a unique civilization that shaped the development of religion, philosophy, and governance in the ancient world. The absence of the Exodus would have led to a more integrated and unified Mediterranean region, where religious and cultural diversity flourished under the influence of a shared Hebrew-Egyptian heritage. The legacy of the Hebrews, instead of being defined by a journey to a Promised Land, would be remembered for their role in forging one of history's most remarkable and harmonious civilizations. And somewhere in this alternate history, Moses, now an elderly statesman in the court of Pharaoh, might look back on his decision to stay in Egypt and think, "Maybe this wasn't such a bad idea after all."

What If the Assyrian Empire Had Survived Longer?

The Background

The Assyrian Empire, known for its military prowess, administrative efficiency, and a penchant for flaying enemies alive, was one of the ancient world's most formidable powers. At its height, the empire controlled vast territories across the Near East, from Egypt to the Persian Gulf. But like many empires before and after, it eventually crumbled under the weight of internal strife, rebellions, and external pressures. By the late 7th century BCE, the once-mighty Assyrian Empire had been reduced to ruins, its cities sacked and its people scattered. But what if the Assyrian Empire had managed to survive longer? What if, through a mix of reforms, military victories, and perhaps a few strategic marriages, the Assyrians had kept their grip on power for centuries more?

Let's imagine that Ashurbanipal, the last great king of Assyria, manages to crush the coalition of Babylonians, Medes, and Scythians that historically brought his empire to its knees. Perhaps he institutes a series of reforms that stabilize the empire, or maybe he discovers a cache of mystical artifacts that give his armies an edge—hey, this is alternate history, after all. The point is, the Assyrian Empire doesn't fall. Instead, it weathers the storm and continues to dominate the Near East for generations.

The 10 Possible Things That Would Happen

1. The Assyrian Pax: A Brutal Peace

With the survival of the Assyrian Empire, the ancient Near East enters a period of relative stability—provided you're okay with a bit of bloodshed here and there. The Assyrians, masters of psychological warfare, keep the peace through a combination of fear, heavy taxation, and the occasional public display of impalement. The region enjoys a level of order, though it's the kind of order that comes from knowing your head could end up on a pike if you step out of line. The Assyrian Pax (as historians would later dub it) leads to an unprecedented period of economic and cultural exchange across the empire. Roads are built, cities flourish, and trade routes stretch from the Mediterranean to the Indus Valley. The downside? Every so often, the Assyrians decide that one city or another needs a good sacking to remind everyone who's in charge. The phrase "peace through strength" takes on a whole new meaning, as does "strength through sheer terror."

2. Assyrian Cultural Renaissance (With a Dash of Intimidation)

The Assyrians, known for their love of libraries and massive stone carvings, continue to foster a rich cultural life. Ashurbanipal's famous library in Nineveh grows to become the largest collection of knowledge in the ancient world, rivaling the later Library of Alexandria. The Assyrians also develop their own distinct architectural style, characterized by towering ziggurats, fearsome winged bulls, and inscriptions that mostly say, "Don't even think about it." The continued influence of Assyrian culture leads to the spread of their art, literature, and language across the Near East. Babylonian and Persian scholars flock to Nineveh to study Assyrian science, mathematics, and astronomy. The arts flourish under the watchful eye of the Assyrian elite, though artists learn quickly that it's best to include at least one flattering depiction of the king in any major work. Future historians marvel at the sophistication of Assyrian culture, though they note that most surviving texts seem to be heavily censored.

3. The Assyrian Legal Code: Justice with a Heavy Hand

As the Assyrian Empire stabilizes, its rulers develop a more codified legal system to manage their vast territories. This legal code, known as the *Code of Ashurbanipal*, is a mix of brutal punishments and surprisingly progressive policies. Theft? You lose a hand. But women's rights? Surprisingly robust, with laws ensuring property rights and protections against abuse—because an empire that survives needs strong families, right? The *Code of Ashurbanipal* becomes the standard for law across the empire, influencing the legal systems of neighboring states. Future civilizations borrow heavily from Assyrian legal practices, though they often tone down the more draconian punishments. The Assyrian legal code also sparks the development of early forensic science, as judges try to avoid punishing the wrong person (because no one wants to explain that mistake to the king). The phrase "an eye for an eye" is taken literally, but so is "a fair trial."

4. The Expansion of the Assyrian Military Machine

With their empire secure, the Assyrians continue to innovate in the art of war. They develop new siege technologies, more advanced chariots, and a professional standing army that's the envy (and fear) of the ancient world. The Assyrian military becomes an unstoppable force, conquering new territories and keeping old ones in line with ruthless efficiency. The Assyrian dominance in military technology leads to an arms race across the ancient Near East. Neighboring kingdoms scramble to develop their own versions of Assyrian innovations, but they always seem to be one step behind. The constant pressure from Assyria forces these kingdoms to band together in increasingly desperate coalitions, none of which last very long. The Assyrian Empire expands its borders to include parts of Asia Minor, Arabia, and even pushes into Egypt once more, creating a vast empire that future historians call "Assyria Major" (with a side of "Minor Threats Crushed Quickly").

5. The Survival of Israel and Judah (Under Assyrian Rule)

In this alternate timeline, the Kingdoms of Israel and Judah don't fall to the Babylonians but remain vassal states under Assyrian control. The Hebrews are allowed to maintain their religious practices, as long as they pay their tribute and don't cause trouble. The Assyrians, pragmatic rulers that they are, find the Hebrew monotheism intriguing and perhaps even useful as a way to unify their territories. The survival of Israel and Judah under Assyrian rule leads to a different development of Judaism. The influence of Assyrian culture and religion shapes Hebrew theology, leading to a unique blend of monotheism with some Assyrian elements. The concept of an all-powerful, vengeful God resonates well with the Assyrian ethos, and future generations of Hebrews adopt some Assyrian customs into their own practices. The Hebrew Bible (Tanakh) includes stories of Assyrian kings who were feared and respected but also shows how God protected the faithful from their wrath. The phrase "fear of God" has a distinctly Assyrian flavor in this timeline.

6. Assyrian Influence on Greek Civilization

With the Assyrian Empire continuing to expand and influence the region, the nascent Greek city-states find themselves increasingly drawn into the Assyrian orbit. Greek mercenaries serve in Assyrian armies, and Assyrian emissaries bring their culture, art, and legal codes to the Greek mainland. Greek traders bring back Assyrian goods and ideas, leading to a significant cultural exchange. The influence of Assyria on Greek culture leads to a more militaristic and centralized Greek civilization. Greek city-states adopt Assyrian-style governance, with powerful kings who rule with an iron fist. Greek art and architecture take on a more grandiose, imposing style, with statues of winged bulls and ziggurat-inspired temples dotting the landscape. The philosophical schools of Greece are more focused on order and discipline than on abstract ideals, and Greek democracy, if it ever emerges, is heavily influenced by the hierarchical, top-down structure of Assyrian rule. The Parthenon ends up looking a bit more like an Assyrian palace, complete with intimidating reliefs of mythical creatures.

7. The Assyrian Language: Lingua Franca of the Ancient World

With their empire extending across the Near East and beyond, the Assyrians impose their language, Akkadian, as the official language of administration, trade, and diplomacy. Scribes across the empire are trained in Akkadian cuneiform, and the language becomes the unifying factor for the diverse peoples under Assyrian rule. Akkadian becomes the lingua franca of the ancient world, much like Latin did in Europe centuries later. As a result, future empires and civilizations adopt Akkadian as the language of learning, science, and literature. The great works of later civilizations, from Persian epic poetry to Greek philosophy, are written in Akkadian, which becomes the language of educated elites across the Near East and Mediterranean. The Rosetta Stone, when it's discovered millennia later, features Akkadian, Greek, and a much-abbreviated version of hieroglyphics, confusing archaeologists who wonder why everyone seemed to need to learn cuneiform.

8. The Birth of the Assyrian Religion

The continued dominance of the Assyrian Empire leads to the development of a state religion centered around the worship of Ashur, the chief god of the Assyrian pantheon. Ashur, portrayed as a warrior god, becomes the unifying deity of the empire, with temples dedicated to him in every major city. The Assyrian kings are seen as his earthly representatives, ruling by divine right and enforcing Ashur's will. The spread of the Assyrian religion influences the development of other religious traditions across the region. The idea of divine kingship, already present in many cultures, is further solidified by the Assyrian model, leading to a more theocratic approach to governance.

The worship of Ashur becomes widespread, with elements of his cult being absorbed into local religions. The later emergence of monotheistic religions is heavily influenced by the Assyrian emphasis on a single, all-powerful god who demands absolute loyalty. Religious syncretism becomes the norm, with temples to Ashur featuring altars to local deities, creating a unique blend of worship practices that confuses future theologians.

9. The Assyrian Academy: A Center of Learning and Terror

The survival of the Assyrian Empire leads to the establishment of an official academy in Nineveh, where the brightest minds of the empire are trained in everything from military strategy to engineering to the fine art of psychological warfare. The Assyrian Academy becomes the ancient world's most prestigious institution of learning, though the entrance exams are rumored to be brutal—literally. The Assyrian Academy becomes the model for later institutions of higher learning across the ancient world. Scholars and engineers trained in Nineveh spread Assyrian knowledge and techniques to the far corners of the empire, leading to advancements in architecture, medicine, and technology. The academy's influence ensures that Assyrian methods of governance, warfare, and cultural production become the standard for centuries to come. The curriculum includes courses like "Advanced Siege Warfare," "Introduction to Torture Techniques," and "Political Manipulation 101," making it the ancient equivalent of both Harvard and the CIA's training school.

10. The Legacy of Assyrian Brutality: A Reputation That Endures

The long-lasting Assyrian Empire, with its efficient but harsh rule, leaves a lasting mark on the ancient world. While the empire itself eventually falls (no empire lasts forever), the memory of Assyrian dominance and brutality persists in the cultural consciousness of the Near East. The Assyrians are both admired and feared, their legacy a complex mix of cultural achievement and ruthless power. Future empires, from Persia to Rome, look to the

Assyrians as a model of how to build and maintain power—but also as a cautionary tale. The Assyrian reputation for cruelty becomes legendary, influencing everything from later laws of war to the way rulers justify their actions. The Assyrian approach to governance—mixing fear with administrative efficiency—becomes a template for autocrats throughout history. The phrase "to Assyrianize" enters the lexicon, meaning to enforce order through terror and strict control, and is used by future historians to describe any regime that rules with an iron fist (and an occasional public execution).

Conclusion

If the Assyrian Empire had survived longer, the history of the ancient Near East—and by extension, the world—would have been dramatically different. The brutal yet advanced Assyrian state would have continued to shape the politics, culture, and religion of the region, leaving a legacy that mixed terror with innovation. The Assyrian Pax would have brought stability, but at a cost, with the empire's influence extending far beyond its borders. The survival of the Assyrian Empire would have created a world where fear and efficiency went hand in hand, where cultural achievements were often overshadowed by the ever-present threat of Assyrian retribution. And somewhere in this alternate history, an Assyrian scribe, writing in cuneiform, might have summed it up best: "The strong survive, but the brutal thrive."

What If the Indus Valley Civilization Had Not Collapsed?

The Background

The Indus Valley Civilization, one of the world's earliest urban cultures, flourished in what is now Pakistan and northwest India from around 3300 BCE to 1300 BCE. Known for its advanced city planning, impressive drainage systems, and undeciphered script, this civilization was a beacon of early human ingenuity. However, around 1900 BCE, the civilization began to decline, likely due to a combination of environmental changes, shifting river patterns, and possibly overexploitation of resources. By 1300 BCE, the once-great cities like Harappa and Mohenjo-Daro were largely abandoned, and the civilization faded into obscurity. But what if the Indus Valley Civilization had not collapsed? What if, instead of declining, it had adapted and thrived, continuing to shape the course of history in South Asia?

Let's imagine that the leaders of the Indus Valley Civilization, recognizing the environmental challenges and changing river courses, undertake a massive public works project to redirect water flow, improve irrigation, and sustain their agricultural base. Simultaneously, they develop new agricultural techniques, perhaps even domesticating a wider variety of crops, ensuring food security for their population. The civilization doesn't collapse; instead, it adapts, evolves, and continues to flourish for centuries.

The 10 Possible Things That Would Happen

1. *The Indus Renaissance*

With the Indus Valley Civilization surviving and thriving, a period of cultural and technological renaissance occurs. The cities, already advanced in urban planning, continue to grow, with new innovations in architecture, water management, and trade networks. Harappa and Mohenjo-Daro become the ancient world's equivalents of New York and Tokyo—bustling metropolises that set the standard for urban living. The Indus Valley's continued dominance leads to a significant spread of its cultural and technological advancements across the Indian subcontinent and beyond. Neighboring regions adopt Indus building techniques, leading to the development of vast urban centers throughout South Asia. Future historians refer to this era as the "Golden Age of the Indus," characterized by flourishing arts, sophisticated governance, and unprecedented urban development. The phrase "Indus Style" becomes synonymous with luxury, efficiency, and innovation.

2. *A Writing System Decoded*

In this alternate timeline, the undeciphered script of the Indus Valley Civilization doesn't remain a mystery. Instead, it evolves into a fully developed writing system that becomes the administrative and literary language of the region. This script, known as "Harappan," is used to record everything from trade transactions to epic poetry, and its influence spreads across South Asia. The Harappan script becomes one of the most important writing systems in the ancient world, influencing the development of later scripts in South Asia and beyond. As trade expands, merchants and scholars from other civilizations learn Harappan to engage in commerce and diplomacy with the Indus cities. Ancient libraries and schools dedicated to Harappan texts are established, preserving knowledge that would have been lost in our timeline. The ability to read and write in Harappan becomes a mark of prestige, much like Latin in medieval Europe.

3. Indus Maritime Dominance

With their cities thriving, the Indus Valley Civilization turns its attention to the seas. They develop advanced shipbuilding techniques, creating a fleet of sturdy, ocean-going vessels that dominate trade routes across the Arabian Sea and Indian Ocean. The Indus people establish trading colonies along the coast of the Arabian Peninsula, East Africa, and even Southeast Asia, spreading their influence far and wide. The Indus Valley becomes the premier maritime power of the ancient world, controlling trade routes that link the East and West. This early form of globalization leads to the exchange of goods, ideas, and technologies between distant regions. The Indus cities become melting pots of culture, where African, Arabian, and Southeast Asian influences blend with local traditions. The wealth generated from trade allows the Indus Valley to fund even more ambitious public works and cultural projects, further solidifying its status as a global superpower.

4. A Polytheistic Empire

The religious practices of the Indus Valley Civilization, which likely included the worship of nature deities and fertility symbols, continue to evolve into a complex polytheistic system. This religion, known as "Harappanism," becomes the state religion of the Indus Valley and spreads across the region. Temples dedicated to a pantheon of gods and goddesses dot the landscape, and priests play a central role in both religious and political life. The spread of Harappanism influences the development of other religious traditions in South Asia. The Vedic religion, which historically emerged after the decline of the Indus Valley Civilization, is shaped by Harappan practices and beliefs, leading to a unique fusion of religious ideas. The caste system, if it emerges at all, is less rigid, with social mobility possible through religious merit and service to the gods. Future religions, including Buddhism and Jainism, also bear the mark of Harappan influence, with rituals and symbols borrowed from the ancient civilization's traditions.

5. Technological Advancements Beyond Their Time

The continued prosperity of the Indus Valley Civilization leads to a series of technological breakthroughs. The Harappans develop early forms of metallurgy, creating stronger tools and weapons that give them a military advantage over neighboring regions. They also make significant advances in medicine, mathematics, and astronomy, laying the groundwork for future scientific discoveries. The technological innovations of the Indus Valley Civilization accelerate the development of science and engineering in South Asia. By the time the Greeks are building the Parthenon, the Harappans have already constructed massive observatories to chart the stars and predict eclipses with remarkable accuracy. The Indus Valley becomes a hub for inventors and scholars, attracting talent from across the known world. The knowledge preserved and expanded in Harappan universities influences later civilizations, including those in the Middle East, Persia, and Greece, setting the stage for the scientific revolutions of the future.

6. Indus Political Structure: A Bureaucratic Powerhouse

The survival of the Indus Valley Civilization leads to the development of a sophisticated political system, characterized by a highly organized bureaucracy. The civilization's rulers, known as "Harappan Administrators," govern through a network of officials who oversee everything from tax collection to public works. The Indus political model emphasizes efficiency, meritocracy, and the rule of law. The Harappan model of governance becomes a blueprint for other states in South Asia and beyond. The emphasis on bureaucracy and meritocratic principles spreads to neighboring civilizations, influencing the development of government institutions across the region. The concept of centralized administration, with officials accountable to the state rather than to individual rulers, becomes a defining feature of later empires, including the Maurya and Gupta Empires. The phrase "Harappan efficiency" becomes shorthand for effective governance, though critics argue that it's just a fancy way of saying "bureaucratic red tape."

7. The Indus-Aryan Fusion

As the Indus Valley Civilization thrives, it eventually encounters the Indo-Aryan peoples, who historically migrated into the Indian subcontinent around 1500 BCE. However, in this timeline, instead of conflict and cultural displacement, the two groups engage in a peaceful synthesis. The Indo-Aryans bring their language and Vedic traditions, which blend with Harappan culture to create a rich, hybrid civilization. The fusion of Indus and Aryan cultures leads to the development of a new language, "Harappan Sanskrit," which becomes the lingua franca of the region. The Rigveda, one of the oldest sacred texts of the Indo-Aryans, is written in Harappan Sanskrit and incorporates elements of Harappan religion and philosophy. The blending of cultures creates a more inclusive society, where Indo-Aryan and Harappan traditions coexist and enrich each other. The epic tales of the Mahabharata and Ramayana, when they are eventually composed, feature heroes who embody both Harappan wisdom and Aryan valor, creating a new mythology that shapes the spiritual and cultural identity of the Indian subcontinent.

8. The Indus Code: Early Legal System

With their civilization enduring, the Harappans develop one of the world's first comprehensive legal codes, known as the "Indus Code." This set of laws governs everything from property rights to criminal justice, with a focus on fairness and communal harmony. The Indus Code is inscribed on stone tablets and displayed in public spaces throughout the civilization's cities. The Indus Code becomes the foundation for legal systems across South Asia and influences the development of law in other ancient civilizations. The emphasis on written laws and legal transparency spreads to neighboring regions, leading to the codification of laws in Mesopotamia, Persia, and beyond. The idea of equal justice under the law takes root in the ancient world, though historians note that the Harappans were still pretty harsh when it came to enforcing their rules—stealing a cow was still a fast track to a life of forced labor. The legacy of the Indus Code endures for centuries, with later rulers citing it as the inspiration for their own legal reforms.

9. Harappan Art and Literature: A Lasting Legacy

The continued prosperity of the Indus Valley Civilization leads to a flourishing of art and literature. Harappan artists develop unique styles of sculpture, pottery, and jewelry that become highly sought after across the ancient world. Harappan literature, written in the now-deciphered script, includes epic poems, philosophical treatises, and detailed histories of the civilization's achievements. The artistic and literary traditions of the Harappans influence the cultural development of South Asia and beyond. Harappan motifs and techniques appear in the art of later civilizations, from the intricate patterns of Persian carpets to the geometric designs of Greek pottery. Harappan literature becomes a cornerstone of education in the region, with students studying the works of Harappan poets and philosophers alongside those of later Indian and Persian authors. The influence of Harappan aesthetics is so pervasive that even centuries later, rulers from distant lands commission Harappan artisans to create works for their palaces and temples.

10. A Unified South Asia

With the Indus Valley Civilization acting as a cultural and economic powerhouse, South Asia sees an earlier unification under a centralized state. The Harappan rulers, known for their administrative acumen, manage to bring the disparate regions of the Indian subcontinent under a single political entity, creating the first pan-Indian empire long before the Maurya Dynasty. The early unification of South Asia under Harappan rule leads to a more cohesive and stable region, where trade, culture, and technology flourish. The unified state becomes a major player on the global stage, rivaling the great empires of the ancient world, such as Persia, Egypt, and Rome. The capital city, Harappa, becomes one of the most important cities in history, known for its grand architecture, vibrant markets, and intellectual achievements. The unified South Asian state also plays a crucial role in the spread of Buddhism, Hinduism, and other religious traditions, with Harappan philosophy and ethics forming the backbone of these spiritual teachings. The phrase "Harappan Empire" is synonymous with peace, prosperity, and the enduring legacy of one of history's greatest civilizations.

Conclusion

If the Indus Valley Civilization had not collapsed, the history of South Asia—and the world—would have been profoundly different. A thriving, ancient urban culture in the region could have led to earlier technological and societal advancements, shaping the development of civilizations across Asia, the Middle East, and beyond. The legacy of the Harappans, instead of being a lost chapter in history, would have become a defining influence on the cultural, religious, and political landscape of the ancient world. The Indus Valley Civilization's continued existence would have set the stage for a more unified, prosperous, and interconnected South Asia, leaving a legacy that resonates through the ages. And somewhere in this alternate history, an ancient Harappan scribe, writing in the now-famous script, might have noted with satisfaction, "We built this city on trade, ingenuity, and a really solid drainage system."

What If Sparta Had Won the Peloponnesian War?

The Background

The Peloponnesian War, fought between Athens and Sparta from 431 to 404 BCE, was one of the most significant conflicts in ancient Greek history. Athens, with its powerful navy, thriving arts, and democratic government, squared off against Sparta, the militaristic and oligarchic powerhouse known for its disciplined warriors and austere lifestyle. Historically, the war ended with a Spartan victory, but the fragile peace that followed didn't last, and Athens eventually regained much of its influence. But what if Sparta's victory had been more decisive? What if, instead of a temporary setback for Athens, the war had ended with Sparta firmly in control of Greece, reshaping the entire course of Western civilization?

Let's imagine that Sparta, instead of just winning the war, completely crushes Athens, dismantling its navy, occupying the city, and imposing a harsh oligarchic government that stifles any hope of democratic resurgence. The Athenian Golden Age of art, drama, and philosophy is snuffed out as Spartan rule extends over Greece. With Athens subdued, Sparta asserts its dominance, creating a Spartan-led Greece that values military discipline, austerity, and order above all else.

The 10 Possible Things That Would Happen

1. *The Spartan Empire: Greece Under the Hoplon*

With Athens out of the picture, Sparta establishes itself as the uncontested leader of Greece. The city-state's strict militaristic values become the foundation of a new Spartan Empire, where discipline, obedience, and martial prowess are the highest virtues. All other Greek city-states are brought into line, either through force or intimidation, and a Spartan-led coalition governs the region. The Spartan Empire's focus on military discipline leads to the creation of a professional standing army that becomes the most formidable fighting force in the ancient world. The Spartans enforce a rigid social order across Greece, suppressing any cultural or intellectual movements that don't align with their values. The phrase "Spartan simplicity" becomes a euphemism for "boring and terrifying," and art critics lament that the only acceptable form of sculpture now involves chiseled abs and spears.

2. *The Decline of Athenian Culture: No More Philosophers*

With Sparta in control, the rich cultural and intellectual life of Athens is systematically dismantled. Philosophers like Socrates, who encourage free thinking and question authority, are viewed as dangerous subversives. The Academy and the Lyceum are shut down, and the great works of drama, art, and literature that Athens is famous for are either destroyed or banned as "decadent." The suppression of Athenian culture leads to a massive brain drain as philosophers, playwrights, and artists flee Greece for more hospitable environments. Those who remain in Greece are forced to keep their thoughts to themselves—or risk a one-way trip to the Spartan equivalent of a gulag. Western philosophy takes a hit as the free exchange of ideas is stifled, and future generations look back on this period as the "Great Silence," when the cradle of Western thought was rocked to sleep by Spartan fists. The phrase "thinking outside the box" is replaced by "don't think, just march."

3. The Spartan Arts and Crafts Movement: All Bronze, No Brains

With Spartan values dominating Greece, the arts take a sharp turn toward the utilitarian. Sculpture, painting, and poetry are stripped of any ornamental or abstract qualities. Instead, art becomes a tool for glorifying the state and the military. Spartan sculpture is dominated by images of soldiers in perfect battle formation, while poetry consists mainly of odes to discipline, bravery, and how great it is to have no material possessions. The Spartan arts movement influences the development of art across the ancient world. Roman and later Renaissance art is less focused on beauty and more on strength and utility. The Renaissance becomes known as the "Bronze Age Revival," where artists spend most of their time sculpting perfectly symmetrical, expressionless warriors. Michelangelo's *David* is replaced by *Leonidas,* a statue of a grim-faced Spartan king holding a spear, with the phrase "Art is for the weak" carved into the pedestal. Art museums become much less interesting places to visit, unless you're really into statues that look like they're about to punch you.

4. Spartan Education: The Agoge Goes National

The Spartan system of education, known as the *Agoge,* becomes the standard for all Greek city-states. Boys are taken from their families at a young age and subjected to rigorous physical training, discipline, and indoctrination into Spartan ideals. Education is no longer about philosophy or the arts but about creating the perfect soldier-citizen who obeys orders without question. The widespread adoption of the *Agoge* leads to a generation of Greeks who are physically fit, mentally tough, and completely uninterested in intellectual pursuits. Universities and academies are repurposed as training grounds for the military, and the only form of debate allowed is whether spears or swords are the superior weapon. The phrase "A sound mind in a sound body" is revised to "A sound body, and that's all you need." As a result, scientific and mathematical advancements stall, and Greek contributions to fields like medicine and astronomy fade into obscurity.

5. The Spartan Economic Model: All Work, No Pay

Sparta's disdain for wealth and luxury spreads throughout Greece, leading to a new economic model based on communal ownership and subsistence living. Private property is heavily restricted, and trade is controlled by the state. Citizens are expected to contribute to the common good, with no expectation of personal wealth or material gain. The Spartan economic model stifles innovation and trade, leading to a stagnant economy across Greece. The merchant class, once vibrant in cities like Athens and Corinth, is reduced to a shadow of its former self, with most economic activity centered around supporting the military. Currency is replaced by iron bars, making transactions cumbersome and discouraging trade with non-Greek states. Future historians refer to this period as the "Iron Age of Commerce," where the only things moving in the marketplace were spears and scowls.

6. The Spread of Spartan Governance: Democracies on the Run

Sparta's victory in the Peloponnesian War leads to the widespread adoption of its oligarchic system of government across Greece. Democratic institutions, once the pride of Athens, are dismantled and replaced with councils of elders and military leaders who enforce Spartan law. The idea of democracy is ridiculed as a foolish experiment that weakens the state. The fall of democracy in Greece has far-reaching consequences for the development of Western political thought. The concept of citizen participation in government is suppressed, and future civilizations are less likely to experiment with democratic forms of governance. The Roman Republic, if it emerges at all, does so with a strong emphasis on oligarchy and military rule, drawing inspiration from the Spartan model. When historians write about democracy, they describe it as "that thing the Athenians tried, and we all know how that turned out."

7. The Spartan League: A Greek NATO (Without the Diplomacy)

Under Spartan dominance, Greece forms a powerful military alliance known as the "Spartan League." This league is less about cooperation and more about enforcing Spartan rule across the Greek world. Member states are required to contribute soldiers to the Spartan army and adhere to Spartan laws, with any sign of dissent being crushed swiftly and brutally. The Spartan League's aggressive expansionism leads to a series of conflicts with neighboring powers, including Persia and later Rome. However, unlike the Delian League under Athens, the Spartan League's lack of diplomatic finesse leads to constant warfare, as Sparta refuses to negotiate or compromise. The result is a perpetually militarized Greece, where the borders are constantly shifting, and peace is a rare and fleeting thing. The phrase "Greek diplomacy" becomes an oxymoron, replaced by "Greek threat assessment."

8. Spartan Colonization: Austerity Abroad

With Greece under their control, the Spartans turn their attention to expanding their influence abroad. Spartan colonies are established throughout the Mediterranean, from Sicily to Asia Minor. However, unlike the Athenian colonies, which spread art, philosophy, and commerce, Spartan colonies are focused solely on military and agricultural production. The cultural influence of these colonies is minimal—unless you count the spread of really, really strict boot camps. The Spartan approach to colonization leads to a more militarized Mediterranean world, where the primary exports are soldiers and grain. The cultural exchange that historically occurred through Athenian colonies is significantly diminished, leading to a less vibrant and diverse Mediterranean culture. Future generations look back on this period as the "Spartanization of the Mediterranean," where cities became little more than fortified camps, and festivals were just excuses to practice spear-throwing. The term "Spartan hospitality" becomes synonymous with "sleeping on a stone slab and being up at dawn for drills."

9. Spartan Religion: The Cult of Ares

With the Spartans in charge, the Greek pantheon undergoes a bit of a reshuffle. The war god Ares, once considered a bit of a brute by the other gods, becomes the chief deity of Greece, with temples dedicated to him in every city-state. Other gods, like Athena and Apollo, are still worshipped but take a back seat to the god of war. Religious festivals are rebranded as military parades, and priests double as drill sergeants. The Spartanization of Greek religion leads to a more austere and martial spiritual life. The elaborate rituals and ceremonies associated with the worship of gods like Dionysus and Demeter are replaced by solemn oaths of loyalty to the state and Ares. The Eleusinian Mysteries, once a celebrated rite of initiation, are transformed into a grueling endurance test that few survive. The phrase "divine inspiration" is replaced by "divine intimidation," and the only acceptable form of worship is to serve in the army.

10. The Decline of Innovation: A World Stuck in the Bronze Age

Sparta's emphasis on tradition and stability stifles innovation across Greece. The Spartans, suspicious of anything new or untested, discourage experimentation in all fields, from technology to philosophy. As a result, the Greek world becomes stagnant, with little progress in science, medicine, or the arts. The lack of innovation in Greece has a ripple effect across the ancient world. The technological and scientific advancements that historically emerged from Greece are delayed by centuries, and the Roman Empire, when it rises, inherits a world still stuck in the Bronze Age. Future civilizations struggle to break free from the Spartan legacy of conservatism, leading to a slower pace of development in everything from engineering to astronomy. The phrase "If it ain't broke, don't fix it" becomes a Spartan mantra, and the world moves at a pace that even a tortoise would find frustrating.

Conclusion

If Sparta had decisively won the Peloponnesian War, the course of Western civilization would have been profoundly altered. A Spartan-led Greece would have been more militaristic, less focused on arts and philosophy, and far more concerned with maintaining order and discipline. The cultural and intellectual legacy of Athens would have been suppressed, leading to a world where the arts, sciences, and democratic ideals were stifled in favor of a rigid, militaristic society. The influence of Sparta would have cast a long shadow over the ancient world, shaping the development of Western culture in ways that future generations would struggle to overcome. And somewhere in this alternate history, a Spartan poet—assuming one ever existed—might have written, "We conquered the world, but lost our souls in the process. Also, can someone please invent a more comfortable bed?"

What If the Etruscans Had Maintained Control Over Rome?

The Background

Before Rome became the mighty empire that would dominate the ancient world, it was just another small city-state on the Italian peninsula, one that fell under the influence of the Etruscans. The Etruscans, a sophisticated and enigmatic civilization from northern Italy, ruled over Rome during its early days, shaping its urban layout, religious practices, and even its political institutions. However, around 509 BCE, the Romans rebelled against their Etruscan kings, establishing the Roman Republic and setting the stage for their eventual empire. But what if that rebellion never happened? What if the Etruscans had maintained control over Rome, infusing the city with their own distinct culture and values, and preventing the rise of the Roman Republic as we know it?

Let's imagine that the last Etruscan king, Tarquinius Superbus, manages to quell the Roman revolt with a mix of political savvy and military might. Perhaps he enacts reforms that placate the Roman aristocracy, or maybe he just deploys a particularly effective army of Etruscan hoplites who remind the Romans that rebellion is not worth the trouble. Either way, the Etruscans maintain their grip on Rome, and the city develops under their influence rather than breaking away to chart its own course.

The 10 Possible Things That Would Happen

1. The Etruscanization of Rome: A Different Kind of Urbanization

Under continued Etruscan rule, Rome develops not into the stark, militaristic city of marble we know, but into a thriving, culturally rich metropolis infused with Etruscan aesthetics. The city's architecture reflects Etruscan tastes, with elaborate tombs, vibrant frescoes, and grand temples dedicated to Etruscan gods like Tinia, Uni, and Menrva. The Roman Forum, instead of being the center of political life, becomes more of a ceremonial space, filled with Etruscan festivals and religious rites. The Etruscanization of Rome leads to a unique blend of cultures in the Italian peninsula, where Etruscan, Latin, and other Italic traditions mix more freely. As a result, Rome becomes a cultural melting pot rather than the militaristic powerhouse it historically was. The phrase "All roads lead to Rome" is replaced by "All roads lead to a really good Etruscan feast," as the city becomes known for its art, cuisine, and religious diversity. The famous Roman toga is replaced by the more colorful and elaborate Etruscan *tebenna*, and the city's residents pride themselves on their sophisticated, if somewhat indulgent, way of life.

2. The Senate: Still Powerful, But Not as We Know It

The Roman Senate, under Etruscan influence, develops differently. Instead of becoming the central authority in a republic, it remains an advisory body to the Etruscan kings, who continue to rule with significant power. The Senate is composed of both Etruscan and Roman nobles, creating a hybrid aristocracy that blends the two cultures. Senators spend more time debating religious rituals and city planning than plotting political coups. The lack of a true republic in Rome leads to a slower development of democratic institutions across the Italian peninsula. The idea of citizen participation in government remains limited, with most power concentrated in the hands of a few Etruscan elites. The concept of *SPQR* (Senatus Populusque Romanus) never takes off, and future generations view Rome as a city-state dominated by an aristocratic oligarchy rather than a beacon of republicanism. The phrase "Vox Populi" is replaced by "Vox Etrusci," and political life in Rome is seen as an exercise in ceremonial pomp rather than active governance.

3. Religion: Etruscan Gods Rule the Pantheon

Under Etruscan rule, Rome's religious landscape is dominated by Etruscan deities. The Roman gods, while not entirely forgotten, take a backseat to the Etruscan pantheon. Tinia becomes the chief god, worshipped in a grand temple on the Capitoline Hill, while Uni, the goddess of fertility and marriage, is venerated in elaborate public festivals that outshine anything dedicated to Juno or Venus. The dominance of Etruscan religion influences the development of Roman spiritual life. Augury and divination, central to Etruscan religious practices, become even more deeply embedded in Roman culture. The Roman priesthood is filled with Etruscan soothsayers, who hold significant political power by interpreting the will of the gods through the flight patterns of birds and the entrails of sacrificial animals. The phrase "All roads lead to Rome" is expanded to "All roads lead to Rome, where you'll find out if the gods are in a good mood today." The blending of Etruscan and Roman religious practices creates a spiritual tradition that is more mystic and ritualistic, with less emphasis on the legalistic approach that historically characterized Roman religion.

4. The Military: Still Strong, But More Defensive

The Etruscans, known for their formidable but defensive military strategies, influence the development of Rome's military. Instead of the aggressive expansionist policies that defined the Roman Republic, Rome under Etruscan rule focuses on protecting its territories and building formidable defenses. The Roman legions, while still respected, are primarily used to guard the borders and maintain internal order rather than conquer new lands. The lack of Roman expansionism significantly alters the history of the Mediterranean. Without the drive to conquer and assimilate other cultures, Rome does not build an empire stretching across Europe, North Africa, and the Middle East. The Mediterranean remains a patchwork of competing city-states and kingdoms, with no single power dominating the region. Future historians refer to this period as the "Great Stalemate," where regional powers jostle for influence without any clear victor. The phrase "Pax Romana" never enters the lexicon, and the idea of a unified Roman Empire becomes a distant fantasy shared by only the most ambitious Etruscan dreamers.

5. Roman Law: More Etruscan, Less Universal

Under Etruscan rule, Roman law develops along more localized and less universal lines. The Etruscan kings impose legal systems that vary from city to city, reflecting the diverse cultures and traditions of the Italian peninsula. While the Roman legal code remains respected, it lacks the universal application that it historically achieved under the Republic and Empire. The fragmented legal landscape of Etruscan-controlled Rome leads to a less cohesive Italian peninsula. Each region maintains its own laws and customs, making trade, governance, and diplomacy more complex and cumbersome. The concept of "Roman law" as a cornerstone of Western legal tradition never fully develops, and future legal systems across Europe evolve in a more decentralized manner. The phrase "When in Rome, do as the Romans do" is replaced by "When in Rome, check with the local magistrate first, because the laws might be completely different from the next town over."

6. Arts and Culture: The Etruscan Golden Age

With the Etruscans firmly in control, Rome becomes a center of Etruscan art and culture. The city is adorned with elaborate frescoes, intricate pottery, and grand tombs that celebrate the afterlife. Etruscan culture, with its love of music, dance, and banquets, flourishes in Rome, making it a hub of artistic expression and hedonistic celebration. The Etruscan influence leads to a distinct cultural identity for Rome that is more focused on the pleasures of life than the stoic virtues of the historical Roman Republic. The Roman Forum becomes a place not just for political discourse but also for elaborate public festivals featuring music, dance, and theatrical performances. The Roman Colosseum, if it's ever built, is used more for ceremonial banquets and Etruscan religious rituals than for gladiatorial games. The phrase "bread and circuses" is replaced by "wine and dances," as the people of Rome indulge in the finer things in life under Etruscan rule.

7. Technology and Infrastructure: Advanced, But Not Expansive

The Etruscans, known for their engineering prowess, continue to develop Rome's infrastructure, but with a focus on enhancing the quality of life within the city rather than building roads and aqueducts that stretch across an empire. Rome under the Etruscans boasts advanced drainage systems, beautiful public baths, and impressive city walls, but the grand infrastructure projects that historically characterized the Roman Empire are limited in scope. The lack of expansive infrastructure projects under Etruscan rule limits Rome's ability to project power across the Italian peninsula and beyond. The famous Roman roads, known for connecting the far reaches of the empire, are reduced to well-paved city streets that don't extend far beyond the city's immediate surroundings. The Roman aqueducts, while still impressive, only serve the city and its environs, leaving other regions to fend for themselves. Future generations see Rome as a well-developed city-state but not the center of a vast network of territories connected by engineering marvels. The phrase "All roads lead to Rome" is taken quite literally—because there aren't that many roads to begin with.

8. Diplomacy Over Conquest: A Peaceful Italy

With the Etruscans in charge, Rome adopts a more diplomatic approach to its neighbors, focusing on alliances and treaties rather than outright conquest. The Etruscan kings, skilled in negotiation and statecraft, build a network of allied city-states across Italy, creating a loose confederation where Rome is the first among equals. The emphasis on diplomacy over conquest leads to a more stable and peaceful Italian peninsula. The city-states of Italy, united under Etruscan leadership, cooperate on matters of trade, defense, and culture, creating a regional alliance that is more collaborative than imperial. The lack of Roman expansionism means that the Italian peninsula remains a collection of independent states, each with its own identity and traditions. The phrase "divide and conquer" is replaced by "unite and prosper," and future historians look back on this period as the "Italian Renaissance" that occurred centuries earlier than in our timeline.

9. Education and Philosophy: The Etruscan Curriculum

Education in Etruscan-controlled Rome focuses on practical knowledge, religious training, and the arts rather than the abstract philosophy that later characterized the Roman Republic. The Etruscans place a strong emphasis on teaching their youth the skills needed for public service, religious rituals, and the management of estates, rather than encouraging the exploration of new ideas or scientific inquiry. The Etruscan emphasis on practical education leads to a society that values tradition and social order over innovation and intellectual curiosity. The great philosophical schools that historically emerged in Athens and later influenced Rome never take root in Etruscan Rome. Instead, Roman education remains focused on maintaining the status quo, with little room for the kind of philosophical debate that shaped Western thought. The phrase "Cogito, ergo sum" ("I think, therefore I am") is replaced by "Ago, ergo sum" ("I act, therefore I am"), reflecting the Etruscan belief in the importance of deeds over ideas.

10. The Etruscan Diaspora: A Lasting Influence

Over time, the Etruscans' control over Rome leads to the spread of Etruscan culture throughout the Mediterranean. Etruscan traders, artisans, and mercenaries travel far and wide, bringing their art, religion, and social customs to other parts of the ancient world. Etruscan influence can be seen in the art and architecture of Carthage, the religious practices of the Phoenicians, and even in the legal codes of the Iberian Peninsula. The Etruscan Diaspora spreads their culture far beyond the borders of Italy, creating a lasting legacy that influences future civilizations. The distinctive Etruscan art style, with its vibrant colors and intricate designs, becomes a sought-after commodity across the ancient world. Etruscan religious practices, particularly their emphasis on augury and divination, are adopted by other cultures, leading to a more mystic and ritualistic form of spirituality in the Mediterranean. Future historians marvel at the reach of Etruscan culture, wondering how a relatively small civilization managed to leave such a lasting impact on the world. The phrase "Etruscan heritage" is spoken with reverence, and the study of Etruscan influence becomes a major field of academic inquiry in universities from Alexandria to Athens.

Conclusion

If the Etruscans had maintained control over Rome, the history of the Italian peninsula—and the broader Mediterranean—would have been dramatically different. Rome, instead of becoming the center of a vast, militaristic empire, would have developed into a culturally rich but politically conservative city-state under Etruscan influence. The legacy of the Etruscans would have shaped the development of art, religion, law, and governance in ways that future generations would struggle to understand. The world might have been more peaceful, but also less innovative, with a focus on tradition and order over exploration and conquest. And somewhere in this alternate history, a Roman noble might have looked out over the city and thought, "It's good to be in charge—but wouldn't it be nice to have just a little more marble?"

What If the Celtic Tribes Had Successfully Unified Against Rome?

The Background

The Celts, known for their fierce warriors, vibrant culture, and, let's be honest, a general disdain for keeping written records, were a collection of tribes spread across much of Europe. While they shared common language roots and cultural traits, they were famously divided, often more interested in fighting each other than uniting against a common enemy. Enter Rome, the juggernaut of the ancient world, with its disciplined legions and insatiable appetite for expansion. Historically, the Celts' lack of unity made them easy pickings for the Romans, who chipped away at their territories piece by piece. But what if, in a moment of unprecedented cooperation, the Celtic tribes had managed to set aside their differences and unify against Rome? What if, instead of being conquered, they had stood together as a united Celtic nation?

Let's imagine that a charismatic Celtic leader—let's call him "Vercingetorix the Great"—emerges at just the right moment. Perhaps inspired by a particularly motivating bardic tune or the realization that Rome won't stop until every last Celtic warrior is under their sandal, he manages to unite the major tribes across Gaul, Britannia, and even parts of Iberia and Central Europe. Through a combination of diplomacy, clever alliances, and maybe a few strategic marriages, the Celts form a unified confederation that is strong enough to challenge Roman expansion.

The 10 Possible Things That Would Happen

1. The Celtic Confederation: A New Power in Europe

With the tribes united, the Celts form a powerful confederation that stretches from the British Isles to the Alps. This new entity, known as the "Celtic Confederation," operates more like a loose alliance than a centralized state, but it's enough to present a formidable challenge to Rome. The Celts maintain their tribal identities but cooperate on matters of defense, trade, and diplomacy. The creation of the Celtic Confederation shifts the balance of power in Europe. Rome, previously unstoppable in its expansion, suddenly faces a well-organized and highly motivated enemy. The Celts, known for their guerrilla tactics and deep knowledge of their own lands, begin to push back against Roman advances. The phrase "Divide and conquer" loses its relevance in Roman strategy meetings, replaced by "Unite and worry."

2. The Battle of Alesia: A Different Outcome

The historical Battle of Alesia, where Julius Caesar famously defeated Vercingetorix and the Gauls, becomes a decisive Celtic victory instead. With reinforcements from across the confederation, the Celts break the Roman siege, forcing Caesar to retreat in what becomes one of Rome's most humiliating defeats. Caesar's defeat at Alesia severely dents his reputation and political standing in Rome. The Senate, seeing him as a liability rather than a hero, strips him of his command and sends him into exile—likely to some quiet villa where he spends his days writing bitter memoirs. Without Caesar's rise to power, the Roman Republic doesn't transition into the Roman Empire. Instead, Rome remains a republic, struggling to maintain its territories in the face of Celtic resistance. The phrase "Veni, vidi, vici" is replaced by "Veni, vidi, currit"—"I came, I saw, I ran away."

3. A Celtic Renaissance: Culture Over Conquest

With their newfound unity, the Celts experience a cultural renaissance. The arts, music, and craftsmanship flourish as the tribes focus on building a strong and vibrant society rather than just fighting off invaders. Druids, now with more influence than ever, oversee the construction of massive stone circles, impressive hill forts, and intricately designed metalwork. The Celtic Confederation becomes known for its cultural achievements as much as its military prowess. The bards, who historically sang of battles and heroes, now celebrate the peace and prosperity brought by unity. The Celts develop a written language, finally putting their myths, laws, and histories to parchment (or more likely, decorated bark scrolls). Future historians marvel at the "Celtic Golden Age," where art and knowledge spread across Europe, influencing other cultures from Iberia to the Balkans. The term "Celtic knot" becomes synonymous not just with intricate designs but also with the complex and sophisticated society that produced them.

4. The Fall of Rome: A New World Order

With a united Celtic front pushing back, Rome finds itself overextended and struggling to maintain control of its European territories. The Roman legions, stretched thin, face increasing resistance not just from the Celts but from other "barbarian" groups emboldened by Celtic success. Eventually, the Western Roman Empire collapses much earlier than in our timeline, with the Celts playing a significant role in its downfall. The early fall of Rome leads to a different power structure in Europe. Instead of the rise of Germanic kingdoms, the Celtic Confederation emerges as the dominant force in Western Europe. The Celts, now free from Roman oppression, spread their influence across the former Roman territories, integrating with other cultures and establishing a network of allied kingdoms. The phrase "Pax Romana" is replaced by "Pax Celtica," though it's more of a boisterous peace filled with festivals, feasting, and the occasional friendly brawl.

5. Celtic Technology: Innovation by Necessity

Facing off against the might of Rome, the Celts are forced to innovate. They develop advanced ironworking techniques, superior metallurgy, and even early forms of siege technology to counter Roman fortifications. Their guerrilla tactics evolve into more sophisticated military strategies, making them not just formidable in battle but also in engineering and construction. The technological advancements of the Celts lead to a more rapid development of European technology. The Celts, once known primarily for their warriors, become renowned for their blacksmiths, engineers, and architects. Roman roads are replaced by Celtic paths, which are less direct but have better scenery and more pubs along the way. Future technological revolutions in Europe are attributed to the foundations laid by Celtic innovators, and the Industrial Revolution is moved up by a few centuries, spurred by Celtic ingenuity. The phrase "As strong as a Celtic blade" becomes a common compliment, and Celtic engineering becomes the gold standard.

6. The Celtic Religion: Druids and Deities Rule the Day

With their victory over Rome, the Celts are free to spread their religious practices across Europe. The Druids, respected for their wisdom and spiritual authority, become the unifying force behind the Celtic Confederation. They establish schools of learning and centers of worship that attract students and pilgrims from across Europe. The spread of Celtic religion influences the development of spiritual practices across the continent. Instead of the rise of Christianity, Europe experiences a prolonged era of pagan worship, where nature deities, ancestor veneration, and seasonal festivals dominate religious life. The Druids, known for their knowledge of astronomy and the natural world, develop a proto-scientific approach to understanding the universe. Stonehenge becomes the center of a vast religious network, where the Celtic calendar is used to mark the seasons, and the solstice celebrations rival any modern-day New Year's Eve party. The phrase "In the name of the

Father, the Son, and the Holy Spirit" is replaced by "In the name of the Oak, the Yew, and the Holly."

7. Celtic Trade Networks: A Booming Economy

With Rome no longer dictating trade across Europe, the Celts establish their own extensive trade networks. They trade iron, tin, and silver mined from their territories, as well as crafted goods like swords, jewelry, and pottery. The Celts also establish maritime routes across the English Channel, the North Sea, and even into the Mediterranean, creating a thriving economy that connects Europe's distant corners. The Celtic trade networks lead to greater economic integration across Europe, with Celtic traders becoming the dominant mercantile class. Ports like Massilia (modern-day Marseille) and Londinium (London) become bustling trade hubs where Celtic goods are exchanged for spices, silk, and other luxuries from the East. The Celts develop a monetary system based on intricately designed coins, which become highly valued for their artistic and material worth. The phrase "All that glitters is not gold" is replaced by "All that glitters is probably Celtic silver."

8. A Unified Language: The Rise of Celtiberian

With the Celtic Confederation holding sway over much of Europe, a common language begins to emerge, known as "Celtiberian." This language, a blend of various Celtic dialects with influences from Latin and other local tongues, becomes the lingua franca of the confederation, used in trade, diplomacy, and law. The spread of Celtiberian leads to a more unified cultural identity across Europe. The language facilitates communication and cooperation among the various Celtic tribes and their allies, creating a sense of shared identity that transcends regional differences. Future European languages, including English, French, and Spanish, are heavily influenced by Celtiberian, leading to a more Celtic-sounding linguistic heritage. The phrase "It's all Greek to me" is replaced by "It's all Celtiberian to me," as the language becomes the cornerstone of European communication.

9. Celtic Law and Governance: A Different Political Model

The Celts, known for their tribal councils and chieftains, develop a unique system of governance that blends their traditional practices with some of the administrative techniques borrowed from Rome. This system, known as the "Celtic Assembly," consists of elected representatives from each tribe who meet regularly to discuss matters of war, trade, and law. The Druids play a key role as advisors and mediators, ensuring that decisions are made in harmony with the gods and nature. The Celtic Assembly creates a more decentralized but cooperative political structure across Europe. Power is shared among the tribes, with no single ruler dominating the confederation. This model of governance influences the development of later European political systems, leading to a tradition of federalism and regional autonomy that persists into the modern era. The phrase "Absolute power corrupts absolutely" is less relevant in this world, where power is deliberately distributed to prevent any one tribe from becoming too dominant.

10. The Celtic Renaissance: A Legacy of Art, Knowledge, and Freedom

With their victory over Rome and the establishment of a strong, unified confederation, the Celts usher in a new era of cultural flourishing. This "Celtic Renaissance" sees advancements in the arts, literature, and sciences, as well as the preservation of Celtic traditions and knowledge. The Druids, as custodians of this knowledge, establish centers of learning that rival the great libraries of the ancient world. The Celtic Renaissance influences the cultural development of Europe for centuries to come. The Celts become known not only as fierce warriors but also as patrons of the arts and sciences. Their achievements in metallurgy, astronomy, and medicine are celebrated and passed down through generations. The European Enlightenment, when it eventually arrives, is built on the foundations laid by the Celtic Renaissance, with thinkers and artists drawing inspiration from ancient Celtic texts and traditions. The phrase "Renaissance man" is replaced by "Druidic scholar," as the legacy of the Celts endures in the hearts and minds of future generations.

Conclusion

If the Celtic tribes had successfully unified against Rome, the history of Europe—and by extension, the world—would have taken a radically different path. A united Celtic nation would have posed a formidable challenge to Roman expansion, potentially leading to the early collapse of the Roman Empire and the rise of a new cultural and political power in Europe. The legacy of the Celts would have shaped the development of European civilization in profound ways, from language and law to art and religion. The world might have been more decentralized, with a greater emphasis on cultural diversity and regional autonomy, but also more unified in its resistance to domination and conquest. And somewhere in this alternate history, a Celtic bard, strumming a harp in a grand stone hall, might sing of a world where the Celts didn't just survive—but thrived, leaving a legacy that echoes through the ages.

What If Buddhism Had Spread Widely in the West Instead of Christianity?

The Background

Buddhism, founded by Siddhartha Gautama in the 5th century BCE, spread across Asia, shaping the spiritual landscape of India, China, Japan, and Southeast Asia. Meanwhile, Christianity, originating in the 1st century CE, spread through the Roman Empire and eventually became the dominant religion in Europe and the Americas, profoundly influencing Western culture, art, and politics. But what if, instead of Christianity, it was Buddhism that took root and spread widely in the West? What if, through a twist of fate—perhaps an enthusiastic Roman emperor converting to Buddhism or the Buddhist missionaries outshining their Christian counterparts—Europe and the Americas embraced the teachings of the Buddha?

Let's imagine that around the 1st century CE, a charismatic Buddhist monk—let's call him "Mahindra the Tireless"—arrives in Rome, carrying scrolls of the Dhammapada and a remarkably calm demeanor. His teachings of peace, compassion, and mindfulness resonate with the Roman populace, weary of war and political strife. Emperor Marcus Aurelius, intrigued by this Eastern philosophy, converts to Buddhism and promotes it as the official religion of the Roman Empire. Over the next few centuries, Buddhism spreads across Europe, shaping the spiritual and cultural landscape of the West.

The 10 Possible Things That Would Happen

1. The Roman Empire: From Gladiators to Meditation Halls

With the Roman Empire officially embracing Buddhism, the Colosseum is repurposed not as a venue for blood sports but as a massive meditation hall. The once-savage gladiatorial games are replaced by peaceful retreats, where Romans gather to practice mindfulness and discuss the Four Noble Truths. The Via Sacra, the sacred road of Rome, becomes a path lined with stupas and monasteries, where monks offer teachings on the nature of suffering and the path to enlightenment. The shift in Roman values from conquest to compassion leads to a more peaceful society, but also one that is less interested in expanding its borders. The Roman legions, now more focused on inner peace than on military discipline, see fewer battles and more retreats to monasteries. The phrase "All roads lead to Rome" takes on a new meaning, as pilgrims from across the empire travel to the Eternal City not for conquest, but for spiritual guidance. The Roman Empire, now more introspective, becomes a center of learning and spiritual practice rather than military power.

2. The Council of Bodhgaya: The Western Canon of Buddhism

Just as Christianity had its Councils of Nicaea to formalize doctrine, the Western world under Buddhism holds its own series of councils to establish the Western Canon of Buddhism. The Council of Bodhgaya (held in Rome, with a nod to the Buddha's enlightenment) decides on the official texts, practices, and interpretations of Buddhism that will be followed in the Western world. Debates are held on whether to include the Pali Canon or to create a new, Romanized version of Buddhist teachings. The decisions made at the Council of Bodhgaya lead to the creation of a uniquely Western form of Buddhism, one that incorporates Roman and Greek philosophical ideas into the teachings of the Buddha. Stoicism blends with the Eightfold Path, and the concept of *logos* (reason) is integrated into Buddhist thought. This hybrid philosophy, known as "Helleno-Buddhism," becomes the dominant spiritual framework in the West. The phrase "When in Rome, do as the Romans do" is replaced by "When in Rome, meditate like a monk."

3. Art and Architecture: Pagodas and Frescoes

The spread of Buddhism across Europe leads to a dramatic shift in art and architecture. Instead of Gothic cathedrals, Europe is dotted with grand pagodas and monasteries, each adorned with intricate carvings of the Buddha, bodhisattvas, and scenes from the Jataka tales. Frescoes in public buildings depict the life of the Buddha, from his birth to his enlightenment under the Bodhi tree. The focus on inner peace and the impermanence of life leads to a more serene and contemplative aesthetic in Western art. The dramatic, emotion-laden scenes of Christian art are replaced by peaceful images of meditation, nature, and the cyclical nature of life. The Renaissance, when it arrives, is less about humanism and more about the exploration of spiritual and philosophical ideas through art. Michelangelo's *David* is replaced by *Siddhartha*, a statue of the Buddha in serene meditation, while Leonardo da Vinci's *The Last Supper* becomes *The First Teaching*, depicting the Buddha delivering his first sermon to the five ascetics.

4. The Crusades: The Great Pilgrimages of Compassion

Without Christianity, there are no Crusades as we know them. Instead, Europe embarks on a series of "Great Pilgrimages of Compassion," where armies of monks and laypeople set out not to conquer the Holy Land, but to spread the teachings of Buddhism and offer aid to those in need. These pilgrimages, led by charismatic Buddhist leaders, are peaceful missions to establish monasteries, schools, and hospitals across the Mediterranean and the Near East. The absence of the Crusades leads to a more peaceful relationship between the West and the Islamic world. The "Great Pilgrimages" foster cultural exchange rather than conflict, leading to a blending of Buddhist, Islamic, and Greco-Roman traditions in the Mediterranean.

The cities of the Levant become centers of learning where scholars from different cultures study and debate philosophy, science, and spirituality. The phrase "Holy War" is replaced by "Holy Walk," as the Western world embraces the idea of spreading peace and compassion through pilgrimage.

5. The Protestant Reformation: The Great Schism of Mindfulness

Just as the Protestant Reformation challenged the authority of the Catholic Church, the Western world under Buddhism experiences its own schism. A group of reform-minded monks, dissatisfied with the growing complexity and ritualism of Western Buddhism, advocate for a return to the simplicity of the original teachings of the Buddha. This "Great Schism of Mindfulness" leads to the creation of new sects, each emphasizing different aspects of Buddhist practice. The Great Schism of Mindfulness creates a diversity of Buddhist traditions in the West, from the austere practices of the "Theravada Reformed" to the more mystical "Zen of the West." These new sects spread across Europe and the Americas, leading to a rich tapestry of spiritual practices that coexist, often peacefully, but sometimes with heated debates over the "correct" path to enlightenment. The phrase "Thou shalt not" is replaced by "Thou should consider," reflecting the more contemplative approach to spiritual guidance in this alternate world.

6. Education and Philosophy: Universities of Wisdom

With Buddhism as the dominant religion, Western education takes on a more philosophical and introspective focus. The great universities of Europe, such as Oxford and the Sorbonne, become centers for the study of Buddhist philosophy, ethics, and meditation. Students learn not only the classics of Greek and Roman thought but also the teachings of the Buddha and the principles of mindfulness. The focus on wisdom and inner peace in education leads to a society that values contemplation over competition. Western philosophy evolves with a strong emphasis on ethics, the nature of the mind, and the pursuit of enlightenment. The scientific method, while still developed, is approached with a more holistic perspective, integrating spirituality and morality into the exploration of the natural world. The phrase "Knowledge is power" is replaced by "Knowledge is the path to wisdom," reflecting the integration of spiritual growth into the pursuit of education.

7. Colonization: Compassionate Conquest?

As European nations begin to explore and colonize the Americas and other parts of the world, they do so under the influence of Buddhist principles. The drive for material wealth and territorial expansion is tempered by the teachings of compassion, non-violence, and respect for all living beings. Colonization still happens, but it takes on a very different form—more about cultural exchange and mutual benefit than exploitation. The approach to colonization based on Buddhist principles leads to a more equitable and less destructive interaction between European colonizers and indigenous peoples. While there are still power dynamics and conflicts, the emphasis on compassion and non-harm prevents the worst atrocities of historical colonization. The Americas develop as a patchwork of diverse cultures, where indigenous traditions blend with European and Asian influences. The phrase "Manifest Destiny" is replaced by "Manifest Compassion," as the guiding principle of expansion is not domination, but the spread of wisdom and understanding.

8. The Industrial Revolution: Mindfulness and Machines

The Industrial Revolution still occurs, but in a society shaped by Buddhism, it takes on a different character. The drive for innovation and progress is balanced by a concern for the environment, the well-being of workers, and the spiritual impact of technology. Factories and cities are designed with meditation spaces, green areas, and strict regulations to prevent harm to people and the planet. The Industrial Revolution in this world is slower, more sustainable, and less exploitative. The focus on mindfulness leads to innovations in technology that prioritize efficiency and harmony with nature. The great inventors of the age are celebrated not just for their machines but for their commitment to reducing suffering and promoting well-being. The phrase "Time is money" is replaced by "Time is mindfulness," as society values balance and reflection over relentless productivity.

9. The Enlightenment: The Age of Enlightenment—Literally

The Western Enlightenment, historically focused on reason and individualism, is instead an age where the pursuit of enlightenment (in the spiritual sense) becomes the dominant intellectual movement. Philosophers and scientists alike seek to understand the nature of the mind, the causes of suffering, and the path to Nirvana. The teachings of the Buddha are studied alongside those of Aristotle and Newton, leading to a unique blend of spiritual and rational inquiry. The Age of Enlightenment in this timeline leads to a society that values both science and spirituality as complementary paths to understanding the world. The philosophical discussions of the time revolve around the integration of reason and compassion, with great debates on how best to reduce suffering in society. The concept of human rights is deeply influenced by the Buddhist principle of compassion for all beings, leading to early movements for social justice, environmental protection, and animal rights. The phrase "Cogito, ergo sum" ("I think, therefore I am") is replaced by "Medito, ergo sum" ("I meditate, therefore I am").

10. Modern Western Society: A Culture of Mindfulness

In the modern era, Western society is deeply influenced by Buddhist principles. Mindfulness practices are integrated into daily life, from schools and workplaces to politics and healthcare. The Western world is less materialistic and more focused on mental and emotional well-being, with meditation and mindfulness being as common as coffee breaks. Compassion, non-violence, and sustainability are the guiding values of society. The cultural landscape of Europe and the Americas is vastly different from our timeline. Consumerism is less rampant, with a focus on simplicity and minimalism. The advertising industry is more likely to promote inner peace than luxury goods, and the phrase "Keeping up with the Joneses" is replaced by "Finding contentment with the Joneses." The mental health crisis is less severe, with widespread access to mindfulness-based therapies and community support. The political discourse is more civil, with leaders who emphasize compassion, wisdom, and the well-being of all citizens. The Western world, while technologically advanced, is also deeply connected to spiritual practices that promote harmony and balance.

Conclusion

If Buddhism had spread widely in the West instead of Christianity, the spiritual and cultural landscape of Europe and the Americas would be profoundly different. A society shaped by Buddhist principles would prioritize compassion, mindfulness, and non-violence over conquest, competition, and material wealth. The Western world would develop a unique blend of spiritual and rational inquiry, leading to a more peaceful, equitable, and sustainable civilization. And somewhere in this alternate history, a wise monk, sitting in meditation on a serene hilltop, might smile and say, "Perhaps the greatest conquest is not of lands or people, but of the mind itself."

What If the Silk Road Had Never Been Established?

The Background

The Silk Road, that legendary network of trade routes connecting the East and West, wasn't just a highway for silk, spices, and precious gems; it was a conduit for ideas, religions, technologies, and cultures. Stretching from China through Central Asia to the Mediterranean, it facilitated the exchange of goods and knowledge that shaped the civilizations of Europe, the Middle East, and Asia for centuries. But what if this crucial artery of global exchange had never been established? Perhaps harsh deserts and impassable mountains deterred all but the most foolhardy travelers, or maybe local rulers never realized the benefits of opening their borders to merchants. Without the Silk Road, the world would be a much different place—less connected, less advanced, and possibly much more boring.

Let's imagine that early attempts to establish trade routes between the East and West were thwarted by natural barriers, hostile tribes, and a general lack of interest in what other cultures had to offer. The Chinese emperors, satisfied with their own riches, decide against venturing westward, while the Roman Empire, more interested in conquering Gaul than in acquiring silk, never extends its reach into Asia. The great cities of Central Asia remain isolated, and the cultures of East and West develop in parallel but separate paths.

The 10 Possible Things That Would Happen

1. *East and West: Strangers in the Night*

Without the Silk Road, the civilizations of East and West remain largely ignorant of each other. The Chinese might hear vague rumors about a distant land where people wear togas and eat grapes, while the Romans might dismiss tales of an empire where dragons fly (actually just decorative motifs) as fanciful stories told by sailors who had too much wine. There's no Marco Polo to bridge the gap, so Europe and Asia develop without any significant interaction. The lack of cultural exchange means that many of the innovations that historically spread via the Silk Road—like papermaking, gunpowder, and the compass—remain confined to their regions of origin. Europe struggles with clunky parchment while the Chinese use paper to write their poetry. The Romans try to perfect their siege warfare without gunpowder, resorting to increasingly elaborate catapults that never quite hit the mark. The phrase "The world is getting smaller" never enters the lexicon, and everyone's maps remain hilariously inaccurate.

2. The Great Wall of Isolation

With no Silk Road to protect, the Chinese emperors decide to double down on their isolationist policies. The Great Wall, historically built to keep out invaders, becomes a symbol of China's desire to remain aloof from the chaotic and uncultured Western world. Instead of being a beacon of civilization, China becomes a "mystery wrapped in an enigma"—or at least that's what the few European travelers who manage to sneak past the guards write in their poorly translated accounts. China's isolation leads to a slower pace of technological and cultural development. Without the stimulus of foreign ideas, Chinese society becomes more insular, focusing on perfecting its existing traditions rather than innovating. Confucianism remains the dominant philosophy, unchallenged by the influence of Buddhism or Christianity. The lack of external threats or opportunities also means that

China remains a vast, stable, but inward-looking empire for much longer, while the rest of the world moves on without it. The phrase "Made in China" is replaced by "What's China?"

3. Rome: All Roads Lead... Nowhere

Rome, without the lure of Eastern luxuries like silk and spices, remains focused on its internal affairs and its endless conflicts with the barbarian tribes. The lack of foreign trade means that Roman merchants are less wealthy, and the economy is more dependent on agriculture and local production. The empire, without the influx of exotic goods to fuel its luxury markets, becomes less cosmopolitan and more provincial. The absence of Eastern trade stifles the Roman economy, leading to slower urban development and a less vibrant cultural life. The famous Roman baths, instead of being places where people debate philosophy while soaking in imported perfumes, become simpler and more functional. Roman fashion remains stuck in a toga-based rut, and the phrase "All roads lead to Rome" becomes more of a statement of despair than pride. The Roman Empire might still fall, but it does so with fewer silk cushions to soften the blow.

4. No Silk, No Spice: A Bland World

Without the Silk Road, the culinary world remains tragically limited. The West never discovers the delights of Chinese silk or Indian spices, so European cuisine stays as bland as boiled potatoes (though potatoes aren't there yet either, but you get the idea). The wealthy Romans continue to flavor their food with local herbs, never knowing the joys of cinnamon, pepper, or cloves. Chinese cuisine, meanwhile, remains rich in spices, but no one in the West knows about it, leading to a global divide where the East enjoys flavorful feasts while the West... doesn't. The lack of spices in European cuisine means that meals are functional but uninspired. The culinary arts in Europe develop slowly, with innovation stifled by the limited availability of ingredients. The Renaissance chefs, without access to exotic flavors, focus on perfecting bread and cheese, leaving the world's foodies feeling a bit let down. The phrase "Variety is the spice of life" is replaced by "Variety is overrated," and future historians lament the centuries of blandness that followed.

5. Religion Without Borders

Without the Silk Road, the spread of religions like Buddhism, Christianity, and Islam is significantly slower and more localized. Buddhism remains largely confined to India and Southeast Asia, never reaching China, Japan, or the West. Christianity struggles to move beyond the Roman Empire, and Islam, without the cultural exchange facilitated by trade routes, has a more limited reach. The world's major religions develop in isolation, leading to a more fragmented spiritual landscape. The lack of religious exchange leads to a world where spiritual practices are more diverse but also more insular. There's less chance for syncretism, and religious conflicts are more localized, with each region developing its own distinct traditions. The idea of a global religious community never takes hold, and missionaries, without trade caravans to join, have to travel on foot, leading to much slower conversions. The phrase "All paths lead to the same destination" is replaced by "Stay on your own path," and the world's religions remain more provincial and less interconnected.

6. Technology in Slow Motion

The absence of the Silk Road means that technological advancements spread at a snail's pace, if at all. Innovations like papermaking, the stirrup, and the compass, which historically spread along trade routes, remain confined to their regions of origin. Europe continues to rely on cumbersome scrolls and inefficient plows, while China's inventions, like the printing press, never reach the West. The result is a world where technological progress is uneven and regional rather than global. The slower spread of technology leads to a more fragmented world, where different regions develop at vastly different paces. The Industrial Revolution, if it happens at all, is delayed by centuries, with each region having to reinvent the wheel (literally) rather than building on shared knowledge. The lack of cross-cultural exchange means that innovations are often rediscovered independently, leading to a world where technological progress is more isolated and less collaborative. The phrase "Necessity is the mother of invention" is replaced by "Necessity is the mother of frustration," as inventors in different parts of the world struggle to solve the same problems without knowing that others have already done it.

7. Fashion Faux Pas: The Global Style Divide

Without the Silk Road, the exchange of fashion trends between East and West is virtually nonexistent. The iconic silk robes of Chinese nobility remain unknown in Europe, while Roman togas never influence Eastern attire. Fashion in the West remains dominated by wool, linen, and basic designs, with little variation or innovation. The East, meanwhile, continues to develop its own rich textile traditions, but without the influence of Western styles. The global divide in fashion leads to a world where regional styles are more pronounced and less influenced by external trends. The East becomes known for its elaborate and colorful attire, while the West is seen as drab and conservative. The phrase "Fashion knows no borders" never comes into existence, and instead, regional fashion weeks become events where people from different cultures are shocked by how different everyone else looks. The fashion industry, without the influence of cross-cultural exchange, develops more slowly, and the world misses out on centuries of sartorial innovation.

8. Economic Stagnation: The Cost of Isolation

The lack of the Silk Road stifles economic growth on a global scale. Without the influx of exotic goods from the East, European economies are more insular and less dynamic. Trade remains localized, with less opportunity for wealth accumulation and economic diversification. The great trading cities of the Mediterranean, like Venice and Constantinople, never achieve their historical prosperity, and the concept of global trade never takes off. The slower economic growth leads to a world where wealth is more evenly distributed, but also where poverty is more widespread. Without the booming trade that historically fueled the growth of cities and empires, urbanization is slower, and rural economies remain dominant. The lack of economic opportunity means that social mobility is limited, and the development of a middle class is delayed. The phrase "The rich get richer" is replaced by "The rich stay the same," and the world's economies are more stagnant and less interconnected.

9. Cultural Echo Chambers: Art Without Influence

Without the Silk Road, the cultural exchange between East and West is minimal, leading to a world where art and literature develop in isolation. The great works of Eastern art, like Chinese landscape painting and Indian sculpture, never influence Western artists, who continue to focus on Greco-Roman styles. Similarly, Eastern artists remain uninfluenced by Western techniques and ideas, leading to a more conservative and less dynamic artistic landscape. The lack of cultural exchange leads to a world where art is more traditional and less innovative. Without the cross-pollination of ideas, artistic movements are slower to develop, and the world misses out on the vibrant fusion of styles that historically occurred as a result of the Silk Road. The Renaissance, if it happens at all, is a more muted affair, with fewer groundbreaking innovations and more emphasis on perfecting existing techniques. The phrase "Art imitates life" is replaced by "Art imitates itself," as artists draw inspiration from their own traditions rather than from the wider world.

10. The Americas: An Isolated Continent

Without the Silk Road, the exploration and colonization of the Americas might be significantly delayed. The drive to explore and find new trade routes is less urgent without the allure of Eastern goods, and European explorers might not venture across the Atlantic as early as they did in our timeline. The indigenous cultures of the Americas continue to develop in isolation, without the disruptive influence of European colonization. The delayed contact between Europe and the Americas leads to a different trajectory for both continents. The indigenous civilizations, like the Aztecs and the Inca, continue to thrive and develop their own advanced societies without interference from European powers. When contact eventually does occur, it is more likely to be a mutual exchange rather than a one-sided conquest, leading to a world where the Americas are more integrated into the global community from a position of strength rather than subjugation. The phrase "New World" is replaced by "The Other World," as the Americas are seen as a distant but equally advanced region of the globe.

Conclusion

If the Silk Road had never been established, the world would be a much different place—less connected, less culturally rich, and significantly less advanced. The lack of trade and cultural exchange between East and West would have stunted global development, leading to a more fragmented and isolated world where each region developed in its own bubble. The great civilizations of Europe, the Middle East, and Asia would have remained strangers, with fewer opportunities to learn from one another and fewer shared achievements. And somewhere in this alternate history, a frustrated Roman merchant, looking at a pile of unsold togas, might mutter, "If only there were a way to sell these to the people on the other side of the world... if only."

What If Sargon of Akkad's Empire Had Lasted Longer?

The Background

Sargon of Akkad, often hailed as the world's first emperor, forged the Akkadian Empire around 2334 BCE, uniting the diverse city-states of Mesopotamia under a single rule. His empire was remarkable for its centralized administration, a professional standing army, and the spread of the Akkadian language. However, like many empires, it was short-lived, crumbling under the weight of internal strife, invasions, and environmental challenges after only about two centuries. But what if the Akkadian Empire had not only survived these early challenges but also thrived, becoming a lasting political and cultural force in the ancient Near East?

Let's imagine that Sargon's successors, instead of succumbing to the pressures that historically led to the empire's collapse, managed to implement reforms that stabilized the empire. Perhaps they developed more sustainable agricultural practices, better defense strategies against the Gutians (a pesky group of mountain tribes), and even instituted a clearer line of succession to prevent the kind of power struggles that often plague early empires. With these changes, the Akkadian Empire doesn't just survive—it flourishes, becoming a dominant force in Mesopotamia for centuries.

The 10 Possible Things That Would Happen

1. The Akkadian Golden Age: Mesopotamia's Superpower

With the empire's longevity, Akkad becomes the cultural, political, and economic heart of Mesopotamia. The city of Akkad itself is transformed into a grand metropolis, rivaling even Babylon in later years. The Akkadian language becomes the lingua franca of the entire region, cementing its influence over trade, diplomacy, and culture across the Near East. The Akkadian language and culture spread far beyond Mesopotamia, influencing the development of other civilizations in the region, including the Hittites, Elamites, and even the Egyptians. Future generations of rulers from various cultures adopt Akkadian titles and styles to legitimize their own reigns. The phrase "All roads lead to Akkad" becomes a common saying, as the city becomes synonymous with power and prosperity. The Akkadian cuneiform script remains the standard for record-keeping and literature for centuries, ensuring that Akkadian myths and legal codes have a lasting impact on the ancient world.

2. The Akkadian Bureaucracy: A Model for Governance

The enduring Akkadian Empire develops a highly sophisticated bureaucracy, building on Sargon's centralized administration. This system becomes the model for governance in the ancient world, with an efficient network of provincial governors, tax collectors, and scribes. The empire's administration is so well-organized that future empires, including the Assyrians and Babylonians, base their own governments on Akkadian principles. The Akkadian model of governance influences not just Mesopotamia but also other emerging empires, including those in the Mediterranean and beyond. The idea of a centralized state with a professional bureaucracy spreads, leading to more stable and enduring governments across the ancient world. The phrase "Bureaucracy is the backbone of empire" is coined by an Akkadian scribe, and it becomes the motto for countless rulers who realize that while armies win battles, bureaucrats win empires.

3. The Akkadian Religion: A Pantheon for the Ages

With the Akkadian Empire's longevity, the Akkadian pantheon, led by gods like Enlil, Ishtar, and Marduk, becomes deeply entrenched in the religious practices of the region. The Akkadian myths and religious rituals spread throughout the empire and influence the spiritual beliefs of neighboring peoples. Temples dedicated to Akkadian deities dot the landscape from the Persian Gulf to the Mediterranean. The Akkadian religious influence leads to a more uniform pantheon across the Near East, with local deities being assimilated into the Akkadian framework. This shared religious tradition fosters a sense of unity within the empire and even with neighboring cultures, reducing the likelihood of religious conflicts. The phrase "In the name of Marduk" becomes a common invocation, used by everyone from soldiers going into battle to merchants haggling over prices. The later Babylonian and Assyrian empires, rather than introducing new gods, simply expand on the existing Akkadian pantheon, creating a continuous religious tradition that lasts for millennia.

4. Military Prowess: The Invincible Akkadian Legions

Sargon's successors, building on the empire's military traditions, maintain and expand a powerful standing army that is the envy (and fear) of the ancient world. The Akkadian legions are known for their discipline, organization, and innovative tactics, making them virtually unbeatable on the battlefield. The empire uses its military might to secure its borders and exert influence over neighboring regions. The Akkadian military becomes the standard by which all other ancient armies are measured. Neighboring states, in a bid to protect themselves or compete with Akkad, develop their own professional armies modeled after the Akkadian legions. This arms race leads to a more militarized ancient world, where conflicts are larger in scale but also more strategically sophisticated. The phrase "Akkadian discipline" enters the military lexicon, and future generals study Akkadian tactics as the pinnacle of ancient warfare.

5. The Akkadian Trade Network: Connecting the Ancient World

With the empire's stability, Akkad becomes the hub of a vast trade network that stretches from the Indus Valley to the Mediterranean. Akkadian merchants, protected by the empire's military and supported by its infrastructure, facilitate the exchange of goods, ideas, and technologies across the ancient world. The empire's wealth grows as it becomes the center of international commerce. The Akkadian trade network leads to increased cultural and technological exchange across the ancient world. Innovations such as metallurgy, writing, and agricultural techniques spread more rapidly, accelerating the development of civilizations along these trade routes. The phrase "All wealth flows to Akkad" becomes a truism, as the empire's coffers swell with the profits of trade. The wealth generated by trade also funds public works, leading to the construction of grand temples, roads, and irrigation systems that further enhance the empire's power and prestige.

6. Cultural Dominance: Akkadian Literature and Art

The long-lasting Akkadian Empire becomes a cultural beacon, producing literature, art, and architecture that set the standard for the ancient world. The epic of Gilgamesh, already one of the oldest known literary works, becomes a cornerstone of Akkadian culture, and its themes of heroism, mortality, and the quest for wisdom resonate across generations. Akkadian art, characterized by its detailed carvings and monumental architecture, influences artistic traditions throughout Mesopotamia and beyond. The cultural achievements of the Akkadian Empire are preserved and revered by later civilizations. Akkadian literature, including the epic of Gilgamesh, is studied and adapted by scribes in Babylon, Assyria, and even distant Greece. The phrase "As wise as Gilgamesh" becomes a common compliment, and Akkadian art styles influence everything from Persian reliefs to Hellenistic sculpture. The Akkadian cultural legacy endures for millennia, with future archaeologists uncovering Akkadian tablets and marveling at the sophistication of this ancient civilization.

7. Political Stability: A Lasting Dynasty

Sargon's dynasty, bolstered by successful reforms and military victories, remains in power for centuries. The Akkadian rulers, known for their administrative acumen and strategic marriages, create a stable and enduring line of succession that prevents the internal conflicts and power struggles that historically plagued ancient empires. The political stability of the Akkadian Empire creates a model for later dynasties, both within Mesopotamia and in other regions. The idea of a strong, centralized authority with a clear line of succession becomes the ideal for future rulers, reducing the frequency of coups and civil wars. The phrase "As stable as Akkad" becomes synonymous with political longevity, and the Akkadian Empire is remembered as the gold standard of ancient governance. This stability allows the empire to focus on long-term projects, such as grand architectural endeavors and the codification of laws, further cementing its legacy.

8. The Spread of Akkadian Science: Early Advancements

The Akkadian Empire, with its emphasis on administration and record-keeping, fosters an environment where science and technology can flourish. Akkadian scholars, working in the empire's great cities, make early advancements in mathematics, astronomy, and medicine. These scientific achievements are recorded on clay tablets and disseminated throughout the empire's vast territory. The early spread of Akkadian scientific knowledge accelerates the development of these fields in neighboring civilizations. The Akkadian number system, based on a sexagesimal (base-60) system, becomes the standard for mathematical calculations in the ancient world, influencing everything from engineering to timekeeping. The phrase

"Akkadian precision" is used to describe everything from astronomical observations to architectural measurements, and the empire's contributions to science are remembered as foundational to the later advancements of the Greeks, Persians, and others.

9. Religious Syncretism: A Unified Pantheon

As the Akkadian Empire expands, it encounters a diverse array of cultures and religious practices. Rather than imposing a single state religion, the Akkadian rulers adopt a policy of religious syncretism, blending their own gods with those of the conquered peoples. This creates a unified pantheon that reflects the empire's multicultural nature, fostering a sense of unity and shared identity among its diverse population. The Akkadian approach to religion influences the development of religious practices in the ancient world. The concept of a unified pantheon, where gods from different cultures are worshipped together, spreads to other empires, including the Hittites, Persians, and Greeks. This leads to a more inclusive and flexible approach to religion, where the gods are seen as manifestations of a single divine order rather than as separate, competing entities. The phrase "One empire, many gods" becomes a motto for the Akkadian rulers, and their religious policies are remembered as a model of tolerance and integration.

10. The Akkadian Legacy: The Birthplace of Civilization

With its long-lasting influence, the Akkadian Empire becomes known as the birthplace of civilization in the ancient world. Later empires, from Babylon to Persia, look back on Akkad as the model of imperial governance, cultural achievement, and military might. The Akkadian language, literature, and legal codes are studied and revered for centuries, shaping the development of later civilizations. The enduring legacy of the Akkadian Empire influences the course of history for millennia. The Akkadian model of empire-building, with its emphasis on centralization, bureaucracy, and cultural integration, becomes the blueprint for future empires. The phrase "All empires begin in

Akkad" is often used by historians to describe the influence of the Akkadian Empire on later civilizations. The empire's achievements in governance, culture, and science are celebrated as the foundations of the ancient world, and its legacy continues to be felt long after the empire itself has faded into history.

Conclusion

If Sargon of Akkad's empire had lasted longer, the course of history in Mesopotamia and beyond would have been profoundly altered. A more enduring Akkadian Empire would have influenced the political structures, cultures, and technologies of later civilizations, creating a legacy that shaped the ancient world in ways we can only imagine. The Akkadian Empire, with its sophisticated bureaucracy, cultural achievements, and military prowess, would have set the standard for what it meant to be an empire in the ancient world. And somewhere in this alternate history, an Akkadian scribe, writing on a clay tablet, might have mused, "The empire endures, and with it, so do we."

What If the Mycenaean Civilization Had Not Collapsed?

The Background

The Mycenaean civilization, flourishing in the late Bronze Age (circa 1600-1100 BCE), was the cradle of what we now recognize as ancient Greek culture. Known for their impressive palatial complexes, intricate Linear B script, and epic tales that would later inspire Homer's *Iliad* and *Odyssey*, the Mycenaeans were the dominant force in the Aegean world. However, around 1200 BCE, their civilization mysteriously collapsed, ushering in a "Dark Age" that lasted for several centuries. This period of decline saw the loss of literacy, the fall of palaces, and a general regression in societal complexity. But what if the Mycenaean civilization had not collapsed? What if they had weathered the storms—whether those were natural disasters, invasions, or internal strife—and continued to develop uninterrupted?

   Let's imagine that the Mycenaean rulers, instead of succumbing to the pressures that historically led to their downfall, manage to fortify their cities, maintain social cohesion, and innovate their agricultural practices to prevent famine. Whether through luck, leadership, or a particularly effective set of policies (perhaps involving fewer human sacrifices and more grain storage), the Mycenaean civilization not only survives but thrives, evolving without interruption into a more complex and enduring society.

The 10 Possible Things That Would Happen

1. The Continuity of Bronze Age Culture: Palaces and Power

With the Mycenaean civilization enduring, the grand palatial centers like Mycenae, Pylos, and Tiryns remain hubs of political power, culture, and economic activity. The powerful *wanax* (king) system continues, with local rulers maintaining control over their territories from these fortified centers. The Linear B script, used for bureaucratic record-keeping, evolves into a more sophisticated written language, ensuring that literacy never fades from Greek society. The preservation of palatial culture leads to a continuous tradition of centralized governance and state-controlled economies in the Greek world. Future city-states, instead of developing independently, remain under the influence of these powerful palatial centers. The phrase "All roads lead to Mycenae" becomes a common saying, reflecting the centralized nature of the Mycenaean state. The later rise of democratic ideals in Greece is delayed, as the hierarchical structure of Bronze Age society remains dominant for much longer.

2. The Mycenaean Military: Unstoppable Sea Raiders

The Mycenaeans, known for their warrior culture and seafaring prowess, continue to dominate the Aegean and Mediterranean through their naval power. The tradition of launching raids on neighboring lands for resources and glory persists, with Mycenaean fleets becoming the scourge of the ancient world. They maintain control over trade routes, ensuring a steady flow of wealth into their palatial centers. The Mycenaean naval dominance stifles the rise of other maritime powers in the Mediterranean, such as the Phoenicians and later, the Greeks of the Archaic period. The Mediterranean remains a Mycenaean lake, with other cultures paying tribute or facing the wrath of the Mycenaean warships. The phrase "Beware of Mycenaeans bearing gifts" becomes a warning across the ancient world, as the Mycenaeans' reputation for both trade and treachery spreads. The development of a more peaceful, trade-oriented Mediterranean culture is delayed, as the Mycenaean penchant for conquest remains unchecked.

3. The Mycenaean Pantheon: Gods of the Bronze Age

The Mycenaean religion, which already featured early versions of the gods that would later populate the Greek pantheon, continues to evolve in a more structured and ritualistic direction. Temples dedicated to Zeus, Poseidon, and other deities are expanded and enriched with offerings from across the empire. The religious practices of the Mycenaeans become more elaborate, with state-sponsored festivals and rituals that reinforce the power of the ruling class. The continuity of Mycenaean religion leads to a more rigid and hierarchical religious structure in the Greek world. The gods are seen as distant and powerful beings, closely tied to the state, rather than the more relatable, anthropomorphic deities of later Greek mythology. The phrase "As the gods will" becomes a justification for the absolute power of the Mycenaean kings, who are seen as divine intermediaries. The later development of personal piety and philosophical questioning of the gods is delayed, as religion remains a tool of statecraft and social control.

4. The Preservation of Linear B: A Literate Society

With the Mycenaean civilization enduring, the use of the Linear B script continues and evolves into a more comprehensive writing system, perhaps merging with or influencing the Phoenician alphabet. Literacy spreads beyond the scribes of the palaces to the broader population, leading to an early tradition of written literature, law codes, and historical records in the Greek world. The early spread of literacy in Greece accelerates the development of literature, philosophy, and science. The epic tales of the Mycenaean kings, such as those of Agamemnon and Odysseus, are written down much earlier, preserving them in their original Bronze Age context. The phrase "It's written in stone" takes on a literal meaning, as the Mycenaeans carve their laws and histories into the walls of their palaces.

The later flowering of Greek literature in the Classical period is built on a much older, more continuous tradition, leading to a richer and more diverse cultural heritage.

5. The Mycenaean Economy: A Mediterranean Powerhouse

The Mycenaean civilization, with its control over trade routes and access to vast resources, becomes the economic powerhouse of the ancient Mediterranean. The Mycenaeans develop advanced techniques in agriculture, metallurgy, and crafts, exporting luxury goods such as fine pottery, textiles, and weapons to neighboring regions. Their wealth allows them to invest in grand public works, including roads, bridges, and monumental architecture. The dominance of the Mycenaean economy delays the rise of other economic centers in the Mediterranean, such as the Phoenician city-states and later, the Greek polis. The phrase "As rich as a Mycenaean" becomes synonymous with unimaginable wealth, as the Mycenaean elite continue to amass fortunes from trade and conquest. The economic strength of the Mycenaean state also supports the development of a more complex and stratified society, with a clear division between the ruling class, the artisans, and the laborers. The later emergence of a more egalitarian economic structure in Greece is delayed, as the Mycenaean model of wealth accumulation and centralized control remains dominant.

6. The Trojan War: A Historical Event

In this alternate timeline, the Mycenaean civilization endures long enough to witness and document the events of the Trojan War. The war, rather than being a semi-mythical tale passed down through oral tradition, is recorded in detail by Mycenaean scribes. The conflict, sparked by trade rivalries and political intrigue, becomes a major historical event, shaping the course of Mycenaean politics and society. The documentation of the Trojan War as a historical event rather than a mythic legend changes the way it is remembered and interpreted by future generations. The phrase "The face that launched a thousand ships" is still used, but with a more literal understanding of the political and economic motivations behind the war. The mythologization of Greek history is less pronounced, as the Mycenaeans leave behind a rich body of historical records that provide a more nuanced view of their civilization. This leads to a different development of Greek literature, with a greater emphasis on historical accuracy and less on mythic exaggeration.

7. A Continuous Bronze Age: Delayed Iron Age

The survival of the Mycenaean civilization means that the transition to the Iron Age is delayed. The Mycenaeans, with their advanced bronze-working techniques and access to tin and copper, see little need to adopt the new metal. The Bronze Age continues, with incremental improvements in technology and warfare, but without the revolutionary changes that the Iron Age would bring. The delayed adoption of iron technology leads to a slower pace of military and economic change in the ancient world. Neighboring cultures, influenced by the Mycenaeans' continued use of bronze, also delay their transition to iron, leading to a more stable but less dynamic period of history. The phrase "Iron sharpens iron" is replaced by "Bronze shapes the world," as the Mycenaeans continue to dominate the technological landscape. The eventual transition to the Iron Age, when it does occur, is more gradual and less disruptive, leading to a smoother evolution of society and warfare.

8. The Evolution of Greek Identity: Mycenaean Heritage

With the Mycenaean civilization enduring, the Greek identity evolves with a strong emphasis on Mycenaean heritage. The epic tales of heroes like Achilles, Agamemnon, and Odysseus are not just myths but are celebrated as the foundational legends of a still-living culture. The Mycenaean language, art, and religious practices continue to shape Greek society, creating a sense of continuity and tradition that spans centuries. The emphasis on

Mycenaean heritage leads to a more cohesive and unified Greek identity, with a shared cultural and historical foundation. The phrase "In the shadow of the heroes" becomes a popular saying, as the Greeks view themselves as the inheritors of a grand and ancient legacy. This strong sense of continuity also influences Greek politics, with future city-states aligning themselves with Mycenaean traditions and seeking to emulate the glory of the Bronze Age. The later development of Greek democracy is influenced by this heritage, with a greater emphasis on the role of the elite and the preservation of tradition.

9. Art and Architecture: Mycenaean Influence on the Classical World

The continued development of Mycenaean art and architecture leads to a distinct and enduring style that influences later Greek and even Roman aesthetics. The monumental architecture of the Mycenaean palaces, with their massive stone walls and intricate reliefs, sets the standard for public buildings and temples in the ancient world. Mycenaean pottery and jewelry, known for their fine craftsmanship, become highly prized throughout the Mediterranean. The influence of Mycenaean art and architecture leads to a more uniform and less diverse artistic tradition in the ancient world. The phrase "Built to last" is often used to describe Mycenaean-inspired structures, which are known for their durability and grandeur. The later development of Greek art, particularly during the Classical period, is shaped by Mycenaean styles, leading to a more conservative and less experimental approach to aesthetics. The iconic Doric and Ionic orders of Greek architecture may evolve differently, with a stronger emphasis on the monumental and the heroic.

10. The Mycenaean Legacy: A Bronze Age Empire

With the Mycenaean civilization enduring, it becomes the first true empire of the ancient Greek world. The Mycenaeans, through a combination of military power, economic strength, and cultural influence, establish a hegemony over the Aegean and beyond. This Mycenaean Empire, with its vast territories and centralized administration, becomes the model for future empires in the ancient world. The Mycenaean Empire sets the precedent for the later empires of the ancient world, including those of Alexander the Great and the Romans. The phrase "All empires begin in Mycenae" is often used to describe the influence of the Mycenaean state on subsequent imperial ambitions. The later development of the Greek polis, with its emphasis on city-state independence, is delayed or altered, as the Mycenaean model of centralized power remains influential. The concept of empire, with its focus on unity and central authority, becomes a defining feature of the ancient Greek world, leading to a different trajectory for the development of Western civilization.

Conclusion

If the Mycenaean civilization had not collapsed, the course of Greek and, by extension, Western history would have been profoundly different. The continuity of Bronze Age traditions would have shaped the development of Greek culture, politics, and identity in ways that might have delayed or altered the rise of democracy, philosophy, and the arts. The Mycenaeans, as a dominant force in the ancient world, would have left a lasting legacy that influenced the development of later civilizations, creating a world where the shadow of the Bronze Age loomed large over the Classical period. And somewhere in this alternate history, a Mycenaean bard, standing in the grand hall of a still-thriving palace, might sing, "The heroes never fell, and their kingdom endures, shining as bright as bronze in the eternal sun."

What If the Roman Empire Had Never Adopted Christianity?

The Background

The Roman Empire's adoption of Christianity under Emperor Constantine in the early 4th century CE was a pivotal moment in world history. Prior to this, Christianity was just one of many religions vying for followers in the diverse and polytheistic Roman Empire. Constantine's conversion, followed by the Edict of Milan in 313 CE, which legalized Christianity, set the stage for the faith to become the dominant religion of Europe and eventually the Western world. But what if the Roman Empire had never adopted Christianity? What if Constantine had remained a worshiper of Sol Invictus, or if the Roman Senate had decided to stick with Jupiter and the pantheon of Roman gods? The consequences for the religious and cultural development of Europe and beyond would have been profound.

Let's imagine that Constantine, after a different vision or perhaps a particularly successful pagan ritual, decides not to embrace Christianity. Instead, he reaffirms his commitment to the traditional Roman pantheon, perhaps even revitalizing it with a state-sponsored religious reform that incorporates popular Eastern deities like Mithras or Isis. The Edict of Milan, in this scenario, legalizes all religions but does not give Christianity any special favor. Without imperial support, Christianity remains a minority religion, struggling for acceptance in a sea of competing beliefs.

The 10 Possible Things That Would Happen

1. Christianity: A Minor Cult Among Many

Without the Roman Empire's endorsement, Christianity struggles to gain the widespread appeal it historically achieved. It remains one of many mystery religions practiced in the empire, alongside the cults of Mithras, Isis, and Cybele. Christians continue to meet in secret, more out of necessity than persecution, and the religion develops in isolation from mainstream Roman society. The lack of imperial support for Christianity means that it remains a minor sect, largely confined to small communities in the Eastern Mediterranean. The phrase "Render unto Caesar" takes on a different meaning, as Christians have little influence on the politics or culture of the empire. Future generations may view Christianity as an obscure and somewhat eccentric belief system, much like how we today regard the cult of Dionysus or Orphism. The Bible, if it's compiled at all, is a niche religious text, read by few outside the faith.

2. The Persistence of Paganism: Jupiter Reigns Supreme

Without the rise of Christianity, the traditional Roman pantheon remains central to Roman life. Temples to Jupiter, Mars, and Venus continue to dominate the landscape, and state-sponsored rituals ensure that the gods' favor is sought for every important decision, from military campaigns to harvests. The Vestal Virgins remain a respected institution, and the College of Pontiffs retains its influence over Roman society. The persistence of paganism means that Europe's cultural and religious landscape remains deeply polytheistic. Future rulers, whether Roman, Gothic, or Frankish, see their legitimacy as tied to their ability to maintain the favor of the gods. The phrase "By the will of the gods" is commonly invoked in political discourse, and the concept of monotheism remains a fringe idea. The later development of European philosophy and science is shaped by a worldview that sees the universe as governed by multiple divine forces, rather than a single omnipotent deity.

3. The Fate of the Church: A Struggle for Survival

Without the backing of the Roman state, the Christian Church lacks the resources and influence to become a centralized institution. Bishops continue to operate independently, with little coordination between different regions. The Church's influence is confined to small, localized communities, and its ability to attract converts is limited by competition from other religions that have the backing of the state or wealthy patrons. The lack of a unified Church means that Christianity remains fragmented, with different interpretations and practices emerging in various regions. The phrase "One true faith" never takes hold, as there is no central authority to define orthodoxy. Future historians may speak of "Christianities" rather than "Christianity," noting the diverse and often conflicting beliefs that fall under the same general banner. The development of Christian theology is less systematic, with fewer resources devoted to the study and codification of doctrine.

4. The Byzantine Empire: Pagan Continuity

In the Eastern Roman Empire, known as Byzantium, the continuity of pagan traditions means that the cultural and religious landscape remains closely tied to the Greco-Roman past. The emperors continue to see themselves as divine or semi-divine figures, with their authority bolstered by the support of the gods. The Hagia Sophia, instead of becoming a Christian basilica, is constructed as a grand temple to Athena, reflecting the Byzantine Empire's connection to its Hellenistic roots. The preservation of pagan traditions in Byzantium leads to a stronger emphasis on classical education and the arts. The Byzantine Empire becomes a bastion of Greco-Roman culture, with a thriving tradition of philosophy, rhetoric, and the visual arts. The phrase "All roads lead to Athens" gains renewed significance, as the study of Plato and Aristotle remains central to intellectual life. The later Renaissance in Western Europe may be less about rediscovering ancient texts and more about continuing an unbroken tradition of classical scholarship.

5. The Dark Ages: A Different Kind of Darkness

Without the unifying influence of Christianity, the collapse of the Western Roman Empire leads to a more fragmented and chaotic post-Roman world. Local warlords and chieftains vie for power, often invoking the favor of various gods and goddesses to legitimize their rule. The concept of a Christianized "Christendom" never emerges, and the political landscape of early medieval Europe is a patchwork of competing pagan kingdoms. The absence of a unifying religion like Christianity means that Europe's Dark Ages are marked by a more pronounced cultural and religious diversity. The phrase "Every man for himself" becomes a common refrain, as the lack of a central religious authority leads to a more anarchic and individualistic society. The spread of literacy is slower, as there is no Church to preserve and promote learning. The development of European languages and cultures is more varied, with regional differences becoming even more pronounced over time.

6. No Holy Roman Empire: A Pagan Europe

The idea of a Holy Roman Empire, with its emphasis on a Christianized European identity, never takes hold. Instead, Europe's political landscape is dominated by pagan kingdoms and empires, each with its own pantheon and religious traditions. Charlemagne, if he exists at all, is a warrior-king who claims descent from Wotan or Mars, and his empire is built on the worship of the old gods rather than the Christian cross. The lack of a Holy Roman Empire leads to a more fragmented and decentralized Europe. The phrase "Holy Roman Emperor" is replaced by "High King of the Gods," as rulers claim divine ancestry rather than religious sanction. The later development of European politics is shaped by a tradition of localism and polytheism, with no single religion or empire dominating the continent. The Crusades, if they occur at all, are less about reclaiming the Holy Land and more about expanding the influence of a particular deity or pantheon.

7. The Renaissance: A Return to the Gods

The Renaissance, instead of being a rediscovery of classical texts through the lens of Christianity, becomes a full-blown revival of Greco-Roman culture and religion. Artists, writers, and philosophers of the Renaissance draw directly on the myths and traditions of the ancient world, celebrating the gods and heroes of old in their work. Michelangelo sculpts Zeus instead of David, and Raphael's *School of Athens* is a temple scene with the gods lounging around discussing the finer points of divinity. The Renaissance becomes a more overt celebration of paganism, with the arts and sciences developing in the context of a polytheistic worldview. The phrase "Man is the measure of all things" takes on a more literal meaning, as the human form is celebrated as a reflection of the divine in all its varied aspects. The later development of humanism is closely tied to the idea of emulating the gods, rather than seeking divine grace or salvation. The Catholic Church, never having risen to prominence, plays no role in the period, and Europe's intellectual elite embrace a vision of the world that is both deeply classical and proudly pagan.

8. The Reformation: A Schism Among the Gods

Without Christianity's dominance, the Reformation never occurs. Instead, religious conflicts in Europe are marked by rivalries between different cults and traditions within the pagan pantheon. Various regions develop their own interpretations of the gods, leading to a series of religious wars and schisms that are more about which gods to worship than how to worship them. The absence of the Reformation means that Europe's religious landscape remains fluid and diverse, with no single tradition holding sway for long. The phrase "As fickle as the gods" becomes a popular way to describe the shifting allegiances of European rulers, who frequently change their patron deities to suit political needs. The concept of religious tolerance develops differently, with a focus on accommodating multiple gods and practices within a single society. The later development of secularism is influenced by the need to manage this diversity, leading to a more pluralistic and less dogmatic Europe.

9. The Americas: Gods of the New World

When European explorers eventually reach the Americas, they do so without the Christian missionary zeal that historically accompanied them. Instead of seeking to convert the indigenous peoples to Christianity, they see the gods of the New World as potential allies or rivals to their own deities. The encounter between Old World and New World religions leads to a complex and often uneasy blending of traditions. The religious landscape of the Americas develops as a fusion of indigenous and European traditions, with new pantheons emerging that combine elements from both worlds. The phrase "In the name of the gods" becomes a common invocation in treaties and alliances, as both sides seek to honor their deities in their interactions. The later development of the Americas is shaped by this religious syncretism, leading to a society that is more spiritually diverse and less dominated by a single religious tradition. The cultural exchange between Europe and the Americas is more balanced, with indigenous beliefs influencing European practices as much as the other way around.

10. The Modern World: A Polytheistic Legacy

In the modern era, the legacy of a non-Christian Roman Empire is a world that is religiously diverse and deeply influenced by the gods and myths of the ancient world. Polytheism remains a common religious framework, with different cultures maintaining their own pantheons and practices. The idea of a single, universal truth is less prevalent, replaced by a more pluralistic and relativistic worldview. The modern world is characterized by a greater acceptance of religious diversity, with multiple gods and traditions coexisting in most societies. The phrase "All gods are welcome here" becomes a common sentiment, reflecting the widespread belief that no single deity has a monopoly on truth or power. The development of modern science and philosophy is influenced by this pluralism, leading to a more open-ended and exploratory approach to knowledge. The secularization of society takes a different path, as it emerges not from the rejection of a single dominant religion but from the need to navigate a world filled with many competing beliefs.

Conclusion

If the Roman Empire had never adopted Christianity, the religious and cultural landscape of Europe and the world would have been drastically different. The persistence of paganism would have shaped the development of Western civilization, leading to a more pluralistic and diverse society with multiple religious traditions coexisting. The absence of a unified Christian Church would have meant a different trajectory for European history, with less emphasis on monotheism and more on the polytheistic traditions of the ancient world. And somewhere in this alternate history, a Roman philosopher, sitting in a temple dedicated to a dozen gods, might have mused, "The gods are many, and so are the truths we seek. Let us honor them all, for in their diversity lies our strength."

What If Socrates Had Never Been Executed?

The Background

Socrates, the quintessential philosopher of ancient Athens, was sentenced to death in 399 BCE for allegedly corrupting the youth and impiety—charges that, in hindsight, seem more like a convenient way for the Athenian authorities to rid themselves of a perpetual gadfly. His execution, by consuming a cup of hemlock, has been immortalized as a symbol of the conflict between free thought and political power. But what if the Athenian jury had shown leniency? What if Socrates had been fined, exiled, or simply allowed to continue his philosophizing unabated? The effects of his continued presence in Athens could have profoundly shaped not only Athenian politics and philosophy but the trajectory of Western thought.

Let's imagine that the Athenian jury, perhaps swayed by one of Socrates' more persuasive arguments—or simply growing tired of his relentless questioning—decides not to condemn him to death. Instead, they sentence him to a fine, which his wealthy friends gladly pay, or maybe they just tell him to shut up and stay out of trouble. Socrates, undeterred, continues to roam the streets of Athens, engaging in his famous dialogues with anyone who will listen (or who can't escape his probing questions).

The 10 Possible Things That Would Happen

1. The Continued Influence of Socratic Thought: Philosophy on Every Corner

With Socrates still alive and philosophizing, the streets of Athens become even more intellectually vibrant. Socratic dialogues are no longer confined to Plato's writings; they happen in real-time, as Socrates engages with citizens, students, and politicians daily. His persistent questioning of everything—from the nature of justice to the meaning of virtue—continues to challenge the status quo, forcing Athenians to confront their own ignorance. The continued presence of Socrates leads to a more reflective and self-critical Athenian society. The phrase "Know thyself" becomes more than just a maxim; it's a civic duty. The Athenians, always eager to avoid the embarrassment of being publicly outsmarted by Socrates, develop a culture of rigorous debate and intellectual humility. This culture influences other Greek city-states, leading to a more philosophical approach to governance and daily life across the Hellenic world. Future philosophers, inspired by Socrates' relentless questioning, push the boundaries of thought even further, leading to advancements in ethics, politics, and metaphysics.

2. Socrates the Politician: An Unlikely Career

With his life spared, Socrates might eventually be persuaded (or perhaps coerced) into taking a more active role in Athenian politics. While he had always avoided public office, preferring to question rather than govern, his continued influence could lead to a shift in his approach. Perhaps he's appointed as a special advisor or, in a twist of irony, elected to the very assembly that once condemned him. Socrates' involvement in politics would introduce a new level of philosophical rigor to Athenian decision-making. Policies and laws are subjected to endless scrutiny, with Socrates challenging every assumption and dissecting every argument. The phrase "Socratic dialogue" becomes synonymous with a grueling but necessary part of the legislative process. While some Athenians grow frustrated with the endless debates, others appreciate the depth of consideration now given to every issue. The city-state of Athens, known for its democracy, becomes equally famous for its philosophical governance—a place where no idea goes unexamined.

3. The Preservation of Athenian Democracy: A Philosophical Renaissance

Socrates' survival and influence might help stave off the decline of Athenian democracy. His insistence on virtue, wisdom, and the examined life could inspire a new generation of leaders who are more concerned with the public good than personal gain. Athens, instead of spiraling into internal strife and eventual conquest by Macedon, might experience a philosophical renaissance, where democracy is strengthened by a commitment to ethical governance. The strengthening of Athenian democracy leads to a more resilient political structure, capable of weathering the challenges that historically led to its decline. The phrase "Athens, the School of Hellas" takes on a new meaning, as the city-state becomes a beacon of enlightened governance and philosophical thought. Other Greek city-states, and later the Hellenistic kingdoms, look to Athens as a model for how to balance power, wisdom, and civic responsibility. The eventual spread of democracy in the ancient world is more robust, with the Athenian model serving as a lasting influence on political thought.

4. Plato's Career: A Different Path

Without the drama of Socrates' trial and execution to inspire him, Plato's philosophical journey might take a different course. Perhaps he remains more grounded in the here and now, rather than retreating into the realm of abstract Forms. Instead of founding the Academy, he might collaborate with Socrates on a series of public debates and dialogues, or even take a more active role in politics himself. Plato's philosophical works, while still profound, are less focused on the metaphysical and more concerned with practical ethics and political theory. The phrase "Platonic ideal" is less associated with otherworldly perfection and more with the ideal of the philosopher-statesman. Future philosophy, while still grappling with the nature of reality, places greater emphasis on the application of philosophical principles to everyday life. The development of Western thought is more pragmatic and less speculative, with a stronger focus on ethics, politics, and the improvement of society.

5. Aristotle's Education: A More Direct Line to Socrates

With Socrates alive and still teaching, Aristotle might have the opportunity to study directly under him, rather than just under Plato. This direct mentorship could lead Aristotle to develop a more Socratic approach to inquiry, with an even greater emphasis on questioning assumptions and exploring a wide range of topics through dialogue. Aristotle's philosophical system, already known for its breadth and depth, becomes even more expansive and inclusive of Socratic methods. The phrase "Socratic logic" becomes a key part of the Aristotelian corpus, influencing everything from ethics to biology. Aristotle's works are infused with a greater emphasis on dialectical reasoning, leading to a more dynamic and interactive approach to learning in the Lyceum. The development of the scientific method is accelerated by this fusion of Socratic questioning and Aristotelian empiricism, laying the groundwork for future advancements in both philosophy and science.

6. Socrates and the Sophists: The Ultimate Rivalry

With Socrates alive and well, his rivalry with the Sophists—those itinerant teachers of rhetoric and relativism—continues to flourish. Socratic dialogues become increasingly focused on debunking Sophist teachings, with public debates between Socrates and prominent Sophists becoming the hottest ticket in town. Athenians flock to these intellectual showdowns, eager to see Socrates dismantle his opponents' arguments with his characteristic wit and irony. The ongoing rivalry between Socrates and the Sophists leads to a more public and vigorous debate about the nature of truth, morality, and education. The phrase "Sophistry vs. Socracy" becomes a popular way to describe any fierce intellectual rivalry. Over time, the Sophists are forced to refine their arguments, leading to a more rigorous and sophisticated tradition of rhetoric and logic in Athens. This intellectual ferment influences later philosophers, who build on both Socratic and Sophist methods to develop new theories of knowledge, ethics, and communication.

7. The Alcibiades Problem: A More Virtuous Athenian Leader?

Alcibiades, the brilliant but notoriously unscrupulous Athenian general and politician, was one of Socrates' most famous protégés. Historically, Socrates failed to temper Alcibiades' ambition and recklessness, leading to disastrous consequences for Athens. But with Socrates around to continue guiding him, could Alcibiades have become a more virtuous and stable leader? If so, his influence on Athenian politics—and the outcome of the Peloponnesian War—might have been very different. A more virtuous Alcibiades, tempered by Socratic wisdom, leads Athens with greater prudence and integrity. The phrase "Socratic virtue" becomes associated with a new generation of leaders who prioritize the common good over personal ambition. The Peloponnesian War, if it still occurs, may end more favorably for Athens, or be avoided altogether through more skillful diplomacy. The survival and prosperity of Athens under Alcibiades' leadership set a precedent for future Greek leaders, who see the value of combining political power with philosophical wisdom. The notion of the "philosopher-king," later popularized by Plato, becomes a practical reality rather than a distant ideal.

8. The Macedonian Challenge: A Stronger Greek Response

With Athens more unified and philosophically robust under Socratic influence, the Greek city-states may present a stronger and more coordinated response to the rise of Macedon under Philip II and Alexander the Great. Socrates' teachings on virtue, justice, and the importance of collective action could inspire a renewed sense of Greek unity, leading to more effective resistance against Macedonian domination. The Greek city-states, united by a shared commitment to Socratic ideals, mount a more formidable defense against Macedon. The phrase "United we stand, divided we fall" becomes a rallying cry for a new coalition of Greek cities. While the military might of Macedon is still formidable, the philosophical and political cohesion of the Greeks allows them to hold their own, leading to a longer and more evenly matched struggle. The later spread of Hellenistic culture is still influenced by Alexander's conquests, but the Greek heartland remains more autonomous and less subject to Macedonian control, preserving its philosophical traditions.

9. The Socratic Method in Education: A New Greek Curriculum

With Socrates alive and continuing his teaching, the Socratic Method becomes even more deeply ingrained in the educational systems of Athens and beyond. Schools and academies across the Greek world adopt this method of questioning and dialogue as the foundation of their curricula, leading to a more dynamic and interactive approach to learning. The widespread adoption of the Socratic Method revolutionizes education in the ancient world. The phrase "To Socratize" becomes a common term for engaging in deep, critical discussions. Future generations of students, trained in this method, become more adept at critical thinking, debate, and ethical reasoning. This educational revolution spreads beyond Greece to the Hellenistic world and eventually to Rome, influencing the development of Western education for centuries to come. The emphasis on dialogue and inquiry leads to a more innovative and intellectually vibrant society, where the pursuit of knowledge is both a personal and communal endeavor.

10. The Legacy of Socrates: A World Shaped by Questioning

The survival of Socrates and his continued influence lead to a world where questioning assumptions, challenging authority, and seeking truth through dialogue become the hallmarks of Western thought. Socrates' legacy is not just preserved through the writings of his students but through the very fabric of Greek and, later, Western civilization. His teachings influence everything from politics and education to science and art, creating a culture that values wisdom, humility, and the relentless pursuit of truth. The lasting influence of Socratic thought leads to a Western world where philosophy is not just an academic discipline but a way of life. The phrase "The unexamined life is not worth living" becomes a guiding principle for generations of thinkers, leaders, and citizens. The Renaissance, when it occurs, is fueled by a continuous tradition of Socratic inquiry, leading to even greater advancements in science, philosophy, and the arts. The Enlightenment, too, is deeply shaped by this legacy, with philosophers like Descartes and Kant building on the foundations laid by Socrates. The modern world, in this timeline, is characterized by a deep commitment to critical thinking, dialogue, and the search for meaning—a world where the spirit of Socrates lives on in every classroom, courtroom, and public square.

Conclusion

If Socrates had never been executed, the trajectory of Western civilization would have been profoundly different. His continued influence in Athens could have strengthened democracy, shaped political leadership, and inspired a culture of rigorous intellectual inquiry that would resonate through the ages. The philosophical traditions of the West, built on the foundations of Socratic questioning, would have developed in ways both familiar and unexpectedly new. And somewhere in this alternate history, an Athenian citizen, after yet another exhausting debate with Socrates, might have sighed and said, "The man just won't quit, will he? But perhaps that's exactly what we need."

What If the Phoenicians Had Established a Dominant Mediterranean Empire?

The Background

The Phoenicians, those ancient seafaring merchants from the Levant, were the masters of trade and navigation in the Mediterranean. Known for their purple dye, cedar wood, and the creation of the alphabet, they established colonies from Carthage in North Africa to Cádiz in Spain. However, despite their influence, they never unified into a single dominant empire, preferring instead a loose confederation of city-states like Tyre, Sidon, and Byblos. But what if the Phoenicians had gotten tired of just trading goods and decided to trade up to empire-building? What if, instead of letting the Greeks and Romans have all the fun, they established a dominant Mediterranean empire that shaped the course of history?

Let's imagine that one particularly ambitious and charismatic Phoenician leader—let's call him "King Punik the Persistent"—manages to unify the scattered city-states of Phoenicia under a single banner. Through a combination of strategic marriages, clever diplomacy, and a few well-timed naval victories, Punik establishes a centralized Phoenician Empire with its capital at Tyre. This empire doesn't just trade across the Mediterranean; it dominates it, spreading Phoenician culture, language, and influence far and wide.

The 10 Possible Things That Would Happen

1. The Phoenician Alphabet: The ABCs of Empire

With a dominant Phoenician Empire controlling the Mediterranean, their alphabet, the precursor to most modern alphabets, becomes the standard script across the region. Forget Latin or Greek—if you want to write something down in this world, you're doing it in Phoenician script. Scribes from Iberia to Anatolia learn to craft those beautiful Phoenician letters, spreading literacy and standardizing communication. The spread of the Phoenician alphabet accelerates the development of written languages across the Mediterranean, creating a more literate and interconnected world. The phrase "It's all Greek to me" is replaced by "It's all Phoenician to me," as everyone from Roman senators to Egyptian scribes struggles with their Phoenician penmanship. Future alphabets, including Greek and Latin, evolve from Phoenician in even more direct ways, leading to a script that looks vaguely familiar but with a twist of the Levant. In this world, you're not just writing—you're *writing Phoenician*.

2. Carthage: The Capital of the Mediterranean

Instead of just being a powerful city-state, Carthage becomes the shining jewel of the Phoenician Empire—a bustling, cosmopolitan capital that makes Rome look like a provincial backwater. With its strategic position and a fleet that puts others to shame, Carthage becomes the hub of trade, politics, and culture in the Mediterranean. It's not just where deals are made; it's where empires rise and fall. Carthage's prominence reshapes the power dynamics of the ancient world. The phrase "All roads lead to Carthage" replaces "All roads lead to Rome," as everyone from Greek philosophers to Egyptian priests travels there to debate, trade, and be seen. The Punic Wars never happen, because why fight the empire that everyone wants to be part of? Instead, Rome, if it exists at all, is just another Carthaginian province, famous for its olives and somewhat tedious senators.

3. The Phoenician Pantheon: Gods of the Mediterranean

With the Phoenician Empire comes the spread of their religion. Baal, Astarte, and Melqart become household names across the Mediterranean, with temples dedicated to them in every major city. Sacrifices are made, festivals are held, and everyone knows that if you want to appease the gods, you'd better do it the Phoenician way. The spread of the Phoenician pantheon leads to a more uniform religious landscape in the Mediterranean. The phrase "By the beard of Baal!" becomes the go-to exclamation for sailors, merchants, and warriors alike. The influence of the Phoenician gods means that other deities, like the Greek Olympians or the Roman pantheon, either get absorbed into the Phoenician system or are relegated to the religious equivalent of a historical footnote. Future religious traditions, including early Christianity, have to navigate a landscape dominated by Phoenician deities, leading to a blend of religious practices that confuses future historians and amuses the gods.

4. Phoenician Trade Networks: The Silk Road of the Sea

The Phoenician Empire's dominance ensures that their trade networks become even more extensive, stretching from the British Isles to the Indian Ocean. Their ships, famous for their speed and durability, carry everything from tin and amber to spices and silk. The Mediterranean becomes a Phoenician lake, and their merchants are the undisputed masters of maritime commerce. The Phoenician trade networks create a level of economic integration across the ancient world that rivals the later Silk Road. The phrase "Phoenician gold" becomes synonymous with wealth, as their traders bring back riches from every corner of the known world. This economic dominance leads to the development of a Mediterranean-wide currency system, with Phoenician coins accepted everywhere from Gaul to Persia. The concept of a "global market" emerges centuries earlier, laying the groundwork for future economic systems.

5. The Phoenician Navy: Ruling the Waves

With their empire dependent on maritime power, the Phoenicians build a navy that is unmatched in the ancient world. Their triremes patrol the seas, protecting trade routes and enforcing the empire's will. Pirates, once a nuisance, now find themselves either serving the Phoenician Empire or being swiftly dealt with by its well-organized navy. The dominance of the Phoenician navy ensures that the Mediterranean remains a safe and prosperous region for trade and travel. The phrase "Safe as a Phoenician harbor" becomes a popular saying among sailors and merchants. This naval power also deters other would-be empires, as no one dares challenge Phoenician control of the seas. The Phoenician approach to naval warfare, combining speed, strategy, and superior shipbuilding, becomes the gold standard for future maritime powers. Even in the distant future, historians and naval officers study the "Punic Sea Tactics" as the pinnacle of ancient naval warfare.

6. Language and Literature: The Phoenician Influence

The spread of the Phoenician Empire brings with it the spread of their language and literature. The epic tales of Tyre and Sidon, the heroic exploits of Carthaginian warriors, and the philosophical musings of Phoenician sages become the foundation of Mediterranean literature. Homer's *Iliad* is still composed, but in Phoenician, and the tales of the Trojan War include a few more Phoenician heroes than we remember. The literary landscape of the Mediterranean is dominated by Phoenician stories, myths, and philosophies. The phrase "Sing, O goddess, of the wrath of Melqart" opens the Phoenician *Iliad*, while the *Odyssey* becomes a tale of a Carthaginian sailor trying to find his way back to Tyre. Greek and Latin literature, if they exist at all, are heavily influenced by Phoenician themes and motifs. The later development of Western literature is shaped by this Phoenician foundation, leading to a literary tradition that celebrates maritime adventure, clever merchants, and the favor of the gods.

7. The Phoenician Colonies: A Mediterranean Network

The Phoenician Empire's dominance leads to the establishment of even more colonies across the Mediterranean and beyond. Cities like Carthage, Cádiz, and Utica become thriving hubs of commerce, culture, and political power, each contributing to the strength of the empire. These colonies maintain strong ties to Tyre and Sidon, creating a network of cities that share language, culture, and governance. The network of Phoenician colonies ensures that the empire remains stable and prosperous for centuries. The phrase "As connected as Carthage and Tyre" becomes synonymous with strong political and economic ties. This colonial network also spreads Phoenician culture and influence to regions that historically developed independently, leading to a more unified and cohesive Mediterranean world. Future empires, including those of Alexander the Great and the Romans, have to contend with the enduring legacy of Phoenician colonies, which remain loyal to their mother cities and resistant to foreign domination.

8. Technological Innovation: Phoenician Ingenuity

The Phoenician Empire, with its wealth and resources, becomes a center of technological innovation. Their engineers and craftsmen develop new ship designs, advanced navigation techniques, and even early forms of automation for their workshops and temples. The empire's emphasis on trade and efficiency drives the development of technologies that make them the envy of the ancient world. The technological advancements of the Phoenicians lead to a more rapid development of industry and commerce across the Mediterranean. The phrase "As innovative as a Phoenician" becomes a compliment among inventors and entrepreneurs. This culture of innovation influences later civilizations, including the Greeks and Romans, who adopt and build upon Phoenician technologies. The early development of mechanical devices, navigation tools, and efficient production methods leads to a more advanced and interconnected ancient world, setting the stage for future technological revolutions.

9. The Fall of Rome: Carthage's Victory

With a dominant Phoenician Empire, Carthage remains the most powerful city in the Mediterranean, outlasting and eventually defeating its historical rival, Rome. The Punic Wars, if they occur at all, end in a decisive Carthaginian victory, with Rome reduced to a client state or vassal of Carthage. The famous Roman Empire, if it exists, is just another chapter in the history of the Phoenician Empire's dominance. The fall of Rome leads to a very different trajectory for European history. The phrase "Carthago Delenda Est" is never uttered, as it is Rome that faces destruction or subjugation. The spread of Roman culture, law, and language is curtailed, with Phoenician traditions taking their place. The later development of Western civilization is heavily influenced by Phoenician rather than Roman ideas, leading to a Mediterranean world that is more maritime, mercantile, and multilingual. Future historians write about the "Carthaginian Empire" as the greatest civilization of antiquity, with Rome playing a supporting role at best.

10. The Legacy of the Phoenician Empire: A Mediterranean World

The enduring legacy of the Phoenician Empire shapes the cultural, political, and economic development of the Mediterranean for millennia. Their emphasis on trade, navigation, and cultural exchange creates a world that is more interconnected and cosmopolitan. The Phoenician language, culture, and innovations continue to influence later civilizations, from the Greeks and Romans to the Byzantines and Arabs. The phrase "We are all Phoenicians" becomes a popular saying in the ancient world, reflecting the widespread influence of Phoenician culture. The later development of the Mediterranean world is characterized by a fusion of Phoenician, Greek, and Roman traditions, with Phoenician elements often taking precedence. The Renaissance, when it occurs, is influenced by the rediscovery of Phoenician texts, art, and ideas, leading to a revival of maritime exploration and mercantile values. The modern world, in this timeline, owes much of its character to the enduring legacy of the Phoenician Empire, with its emphasis on trade, innovation, and cultural exchange shaping the course of history.

Conclusion

If the Phoenicians had established a dominant Mediterranean empire, the course of history would have been dramatically altered. The spread of Phoenician culture, language, and influence would have created a world that was more interconnected, innovative, and maritime-focused. The legacy of the Phoenician Empire would have shaped the development of Western civilization, with Carthage, not Rome, as the center of the ancient world. And somewhere in this alternate history, a Phoenician merchant, gazing out at a sea dotted with ships bearing the symbol of Baal, might have chuckled and said, "Who needs Rome when you have the whole Mediterranean in your pocket?"

What If the Minoans Had Not Been Destroyed by the Volcanic Eruption at Thera?

The Background

The Minoans, those ancient masters of the seas and creators of labyrinthine palaces, were the pride of Crete and the envy of the Aegean. They built a civilization so advanced that their frescoes depicted dolphins frolicking and bull-leapers doing, well, dangerous acrobatics over large animals. However, around 1600 BCE, the volcanic eruption at Thera (modern-day Santorini) sent shockwaves—both literal and metaphorical—throughout the region, contributing to the collapse of Minoan civilization. But what if this catastrophic eruption never happened? What if the Minoans, with their love of peaceful trade and elaborate art, continued to dominate the Aegean and beyond?

Let's imagine that the volcano at Thera never erupts, or if it does, it's just a minor burp rather than a civilization-ending cataclysm. The Minoans, spared from disaster, continue to flourish on Crete, expanding their influence throughout the Aegean. Their palaces remain intact, their trade routes secure, and their civilization continues to thrive for centuries longer than in our timeline.

The 10 Possible Things That Would Happen

1. Minoan Dominance: The Aegean's Unchallenged Superpower

Without the catastrophic eruption, the Minoans maintain their status as the dominant power in the Aegean. Their fleet, already the envy of the Mediterranean, grows even larger, ensuring that their influence extends from Asia Minor to mainland Greece. The Minoans, with their knack for diplomacy and trade, create a vast network of alliances, bringing peace (and Minoan pottery) to the entire region. The phrase "All roads lead to Knossos" becomes the Aegean equivalent of "All roads lead to Rome." The Greeks, instead of developing independently, find themselves heavily influenced by Minoan culture. This influence permeates everything from architecture to fashion—goodbye, chiton, hello, flowing Minoan robes! Future Greek city-states are more like Minoan colonies, adopting Minoan laws, customs, and, of course, their love of bull-leaping (because who wouldn't want to try their luck with a massive, angry bull?).

2. The Greek Language: A Minoan Twist

With the Minoans dominating the region, their language, Linear A, becomes the lingua franca of the Aegean. Greek, as we know it, evolves with a heavy Minoan influence, resulting in a language that's a curious blend of Linear A and early Greek dialects. Imagine Homer's *Iliad* being written in a script that looks more like Minoan hieroglyphs than the familiar Greek alphabet. Future scholars scratch their heads trying to decipher ancient Greek texts that look suspiciously Minoan. The phrase "It's all Greek to me" becomes "It's all Minoan to me," as everyone from archaeologists to schoolchildren struggles with this hybrid script. The later development of the Greek alphabet is delayed, leading to a world where writing systems are more varied and less standardized across the Mediterranean. Literacy rates in Greece are lower, but those who can read and write are considered the elite of the elite—like the ancient version of tech-savvy coders.

3. Minoan Religion: Goddess Power

Minoan religion, with its emphasis on goddess worship and nature deities, spreads throughout the Aegean, supplanting or blending with local Greek religious practices. The Minoan Great Goddess, often depicted with snakes in her hands (because why not?), becomes the dominant deity in the region, worshipped from Crete to the Cyclades. Greek mythology, instead of revolving around the Olympian gods, takes on a distinctly Minoan flavor. The phrase "By the grace of the Great Goddess" becomes a common invocation, and Zeus, if he exists at all, plays second fiddle to the powerful Minoan goddesses. Future myths feature heroic deeds done in honor of the goddess rather than the whims of the more capricious Olympians. The later development of Greek religion is marked by a strong matriarchal influence, leading to a society where women hold more power and religious rituals are centered around fertility, nature, and, occasionally, snake handling.

4. Minoan Architecture: Palaces and Labyrinths Everywhere

With the Minoans continuing to thrive, their architectural style becomes the blueprint for buildings across the Aegean. Grand palaces, inspired by the labyrinthine complexity of Knossos, spring up on every island and mainland city-state. These palaces, adorned with colorful frescoes and intricate columns, become symbols of power and prestige. The architectural legacy of the Minoans leads to a more unified and cohesive aesthetic across the Aegean. The phrase "Living in a palace" becomes synonymous with living in a Minoan-inspired home, complete with central courtyards, elaborate drainage systems, and enough corridors to get lost in. Future Greek architects, instead of developing the Doric and Ionic orders, focus on perfecting the Minoan style, leading to a world where temples look more like luxurious palaces than the austere structures we know today. Athens' Parthenon, in this timeline, would be less about imposing columns and more about bright colors, intricate murals, and a touch of labyrinthine mystery.

5. Minoan Navy: Ruling the Waves

With their fleet untouched by natural disasters, the Minoans continue to rule the Mediterranean waves. Their ships, renowned for their speed and agility, patrol the seas, ensuring safe passage for traders and discouraging piracy. The Minoan navy becomes the most feared and respected force in the ancient world, deterring would-be conquerors and securing the empire's far-flung trade routes. The dominance of the Minoan navy leads to a more peaceful and prosperous Mediterranean. The phrase "Minoan peace" replaces "Pax Romana" as the go-to term for an era of stability and trade. Without the threat of piracy, commerce flourishes, and the Minoans grow even wealthier. Other civilizations, seeing the benefits of naval power, attempt to emulate the Minoan fleet, but none can quite match their prowess. This naval supremacy also means that the Minoans play a key role in shaping the geopolitics of the region, often intervening in disputes between other states or establishing protectorates in exchange for trade privileges.

6. Minoan Art and Culture: A Lasting Legacy

Minoan art, known for its vibrant colors and dynamic scenes, becomes the standard for artistic expression in the Aegean. Frescoes, pottery, and jewelry all bear the unmistakable Minoan style, with its emphasis on nature, movement, and the human form. This artistic dominance influences not only the visual arts but also music, dance, and literature across the region. The cultural influence of the Minoans leads to a more colorful and expressive artistic tradition in the ancient world. The phrase "As lively as a Minoan fresco" becomes a compliment for anything that exudes energy and vibrancy. Greek art, instead of evolving into the more formal and idealized forms of the Classical period, remains rooted in the dynamic and naturalistic style of the Minoans. This emphasis on movement and life extends to other aspects of culture, with Minoan-style festivals, dances, and performances becoming central to social life in the Aegean. The later development of Greek theater, for example, might be more focused on dance and spectacle than on dialogue and tragedy.

7. The Mycenaean Question: Who's Really in Charge?

The rise of the Mycenaeans on the Greek mainland is significantly altered by the continued dominance of the Minoans. Instead of emerging as a powerful rival, the Mycenaeans find themselves in a more subservient position, heavily influenced by Minoan culture and politics. They adopt Minoan practices, from writing to architecture, and become more of an extension of the Minoan world than a separate civilization. The subjugation of the Mycenaeans leads to a more homogenized Aegean culture, where Minoan influences dominate. The phrase "Mycenaean power" becomes a joke, as everyone knows it's the Minoans who are really pulling the strings. This dominance delays or even prevents the later rise of Mycenaean power, leading to a world where the Trojan War, if it happens at all, is fought not between Greeks and Trojans but between two factions of Minoan-influenced states. The later development of Greek culture, particularly the epic tradition, is heavily influenced by Minoan themes, leading to tales of diplomacy, trade, and peaceful coexistence rather than the more warlike stories of the Homeric epics.

8. The Minoan Economy: A Trade Empire

With their trade routes unimpeded by natural disasters, the Minoans continue to expand their economic influence throughout the Mediterranean. They establish colonies and trading posts from Egypt to Italy, controlling the flow of goods and resources across the ancient world. The Minoan economy, already robust, becomes the driving force behind the wealth of the entire Aegean region. The economic dominance of the Minoans leads to a more integrated and prosperous Mediterranean economy. The phrase "Rich as a Minoan" becomes synonymous with unimaginable wealth. This prosperity allows the Minoans to invest in public works, education, and the arts, leading to a golden age of Minoan civilization. Other cultures, recognizing the benefits of trade with the Minoans, seek to align themselves with Crete, creating a network of allies and partners that ensures the stability and longevity of the Minoan Empire. The later development of economic systems in the Mediterranean is heavily influenced by Minoan practices, leading to a world where trade and commerce are central to political power.

9. The Delayed Greek Renaissance: A Minoan-Led Revival

With the Minoans in control, the Greek Renaissance, which historically occurred in the Archaic period, is delayed. The Minoans, with their emphasis on peace, prosperity, and trade, maintain a stable and culturally rich society that leaves little room for the kind of upheaval that spurs innovation. When the Renaissance finally arrives, it is a Minoan-led revival of art, architecture, and philosophy, heavily influenced by centuries of Minoan dominance. The delayed Greek Renaissance leads to a world where the cultural flowering of the Aegean is more gradual and less dramatic. The phrase "Better late than never" is often applied to the Minoan-led Renaissance, which, while rich in beauty and innovation, lacks the revolutionary spirit of the historical Greek Renaissance. This more gradual development results in a civilization that is more conservative and less prone to radical change. Future philosophers, scientists, and artists are influenced by this tradition, leading to a world where progress is steady but slower, with fewer dramatic leaps and more careful refinements.

10. The Legacy of the Minoan Empire: An Enduring Civilization

The continued dominance of the Minoans leads to an enduring legacy that shapes the course of Mediterranean history for millennia. The Minoan civilization, with its emphasis on trade, culture, and diplomacy, becomes the foundation upon which future empires are built. The Minoans, known for their peaceful coexistence and cultural achievements, are remembered as the progenitors of Western civilization. The phrase "In the footsteps of the Minoans" becomes a popular saying for those who seek to build a prosperous and enlightened society. The later development of Western civilization is heavily influenced by Minoan ideals, leading to a world that values peace, trade, and cultural exchange over conquest and domination. The Renaissance, when it eventually occurs, is marked by a revival of Minoan art and philosophy, leading to a cultural rebirth that celebrates the beauty and harmony of the natural world. The modern world, in this timeline, owes much of its character to the enduring legacy of the Minoans, with their influence visible in everything from architecture and art to philosophy and politics.

Conclusion

If the Minoans had not been destroyed by the volcanic eruption at Thera, the course of history in the Aegean and beyond would have been profoundly different. The Minoans, with their advanced culture, peaceful trade, and love of art, would have continued to dominate the region, shaping the development of Greek civilization and leaving a lasting legacy that influenced the entire Mediterranean world. And somewhere in this alternate history, a Minoan merchant, sipping wine from a beautifully crafted goblet, might have chuckled and said, "It's good to be the king—or at least the civilization that keeps the kings in check."

What If the Chinese Han Dynasty Had Not Fallen?

The Background

The Han Dynasty, often regarded as one of the golden ages of Chinese history, ruled from 206 BCE to 220 CE. During its reign, China saw tremendous advances in technology, culture, and trade, not to mention the solidification of the Silk Road. However, like all good things, the Han Dynasty eventually came to an end, succumbing to internal strife, corruption, and the inevitable power struggles that tend to ruin a good empire. But what if the Han Dynasty had managed to stick around? What if the cracks in their bureaucratic armor were patched up, the eunuchs kept in check, and the Yellow Turban Rebellion was just a bad day in the history books rather than the beginning of the end?

Let's imagine that Emperor Ling of Han, instead of being a pawn to palace intrigues, suddenly develops a backbone and a keen sense of statecraft—perhaps after an intense meditation session or a particularly insightful fortune cookie. He institutes sweeping reforms that curb the power of corrupt officials, rejuvenate the imperial bureaucracy, and restore confidence in the dynasty. The Han Dynasty, instead of limping to a tragic end, charges forward, expanding its influence and solidifying its legacy for centuries to come.

The 10 Possible Things That Would Happen

1. The Han Technological Renaissance: Faster, Higher, Stronger

With the Han Dynasty continuing its reign, the pace of technological innovation accelerates. The Han were already responsible for advancements like the seismograph, paper, and the compass, but now, freed from the distractions of rebellion and collapse, their scholars and inventors have time to really go wild. Steam power? Sure, why not. Early industrialization? Absolutely. The Han Dynasty becomes a hotbed of invention, with new gadgets and gizmos popping up faster than you can say "Confucian ethics." The phrase "It's all about who you know" becomes "It's all about what you invent," as everyone from peasants to princes scrambles to create the next big thing. The Han Chinese start sending delegations to the Roman Empire, not to beg for peace, but to show off their new steam-powered toys. The Industrial Revolution kicks off centuries early, with Han steamships patrolling the Yangtze while Europeans are still figuring out how to boil water. The Silk Road becomes a superhighway of tech exchange, with caravans carrying blueprints alongside silk and spices. The world gets a head start on the whole "modern civilization" thing, thanks to a dynasty that just wouldn't quit.

2. The Confucian Empire: More Harmony, Less Mayhem

With the Han Dynasty continuing, Confucianism becomes even more deeply embedded in Chinese society, and by extension, the rest of East Asia. The Confucian values of hierarchy, respect, and social harmony become the bedrock of not just government but everyday life. Instead of the chaos that often followed dynastic collapses, China enjoys centuries of relative stability under the guiding hand of Confucian scholars who really know how to keep things in order (and how to guilt trip you if you step out of line). The phrase "Respect your elders" becomes a literal survival strategy, as Confucian ethics dictate every aspect of life, from how you eat your noodles to how you overthrow a rival warlord (politely, of course). East Asian geopolitics becomes a lot less bloody and a lot more about who can quote Confucius better. Neighboring states, eager to stay on the Han Dynasty's good side, adopt Confucianism with gusto, leading to a more harmonious and less war-torn East Asia. Even in the distant future, political leaders around the world look to Confucian texts for guidance, and "What would Confucius do?" becomes the go-to question in every tricky situation.

3. The Expansion of the Han: A Pan-Asian Empire

Without the distraction of internal collapse, the Han Dynasty turns its attention outward, expanding its borders even further. They solidify control over Central Asia, push deeper into Korea, and even make significant inroads into Southeast Asia. The Han Empire becomes a sprawling behemoth, encompassing a vast swath of Asia and bringing a wide array of cultures under its umbrella. The phrase "The sun never sets on the Han Empire" becomes a common boast in the imperial court, as the Han territory stretches across multiple time zones. With all this expansion, the Han also bring their culture, language, and administrative systems to their new territories, creating a Pan-Asian empire that influences everything from language to cuisine. Future historians marvel at how the Han managed to unite such a diverse region under a single banner, and the term "Hanification" becomes a well-known concept, as the Han way of life spreads across Asia. The idea of a unified Asia becomes a reality centuries earlier, with the Han Dynasty leading the charge.

4. No Three Kingdoms: A Less Romantic Era

Without the collapse of the Han, the period of the Three Kingdoms—a time of legendary battles, epic heroes, and endless warfare—never happens. While this spares millions from the horrors of war, it also deprives future generations of one of the most romanticized periods in Chinese history. The novel *Romance of the Three Kingdoms* never gets written, and instead, poets and writers focus on the glory of a united and stable Han Empire. The phrase "It's like something out of the Three Kingdoms" never enters the lexicon, and instead, people use "As boring as Han stability" to describe periods of peace and prosperity. Future dynasties look back on this period not as a time of turmoil and heroism, but as a golden age of bureaucracy, where the most exciting thing that happened was the introduction of a new tax code. Without the romanticized tales of warlords and strategists, future Chinese literature takes a different turn, focusing more on the virtues of good governance and less on the drama of civil war. Strategy games are a lot less exciting too, with players competing to manage taxes and infrastructure rather than leading armies into battle.

5. Han Diplomacy: The Great Game of Thrones

With a stable empire at home, the Han Dynasty becomes a master of diplomacy abroad. They forge alliances, manipulate rivals, and generally play the game of thrones on a grand scale, ensuring that no foreign power can challenge their supremacy. The Han court becomes the place where the world's rulers come to seek favor, negotiate treaties, and occasionally engage in some good old-fashioned intrigue. The phrase "All roads lead to Luoyang" becomes the diplomatic mantra of the ancient world, as everyone from Roman envoys to Indian princes makes the journey to the Han capital. The Han court becomes a melting pot of cultures, languages, and ideas, with foreign dignitaries vying for the favor of the emperor. The concept of diplomacy as a high-stakes game of strategy and cunning takes root, with the Han setting the standard for how to outmaneuver rivals without ever drawing a sword. Future generations of diplomats study Han tactics, leading to a world where "soft power" is just as important as military might.

6. The Silk Road: An Even Bigger Deal

With the Han Dynasty in full swing, the Silk Road—already a major trade route—becomes the lifeblood of the empire's economy. The Han invest heavily in infrastructure, security, and trade, ensuring that the Silk Road is safer, faster, and more profitable than ever. Goods, ideas, and technologies flow freely between East and West, with the Han reaping the benefits of their position at the crossroads of the ancient world. The phrase "All that glitters is gold" becomes "All that glitters is silk," as the Han silk trade becomes the envy of the world. The influx of wealth from the Silk Road allows the Han to fund even more grand projects, from monumental architecture to scientific research. The exchange of ideas along the Silk Road leads to an early form of globalization, with cultures from across Eurasia influencing each other in ways that accelerate technological and cultural development. The Han also become known as the patrons of a new, more interconnected world, where trade and communication are the keys to prosperity.

7. Cultural Integration: A Han Melting Pot

The continued expansion and stability of the Han Dynasty lead to a more integrated and multicultural society. As the Han Empire grows, it absorbs people from all over Asia, creating a melting pot of cultures, languages, and traditions. The Han are masters of cultural synthesis, blending different practices into a cohesive and harmonious society. The phrase "We're all Han here" becomes the unofficial motto of the empire, as people from diverse backgrounds adopt Han customs and contribute to the rich tapestry of imperial culture. The integration of different cultures leads to a flourishing of the arts, with new styles of music, dance, and visual art emerging from the fusion of traditions. The Han language, already a unifying force, becomes even more dominant, serving as the lingua franca for a vast and diverse population. Future historians marvel at how the Han managed to create such a cohesive and vibrant society, leading to the idea of "Han multiculturalism" as a model for successful empires.

8. The Han Military: An Unstoppable Force

With no internal collapse to weaken them, the Han military becomes an even more formidable force. They continue to innovate in terms of tactics, weaponry, and logistics, ensuring that they remain the dominant military power in Asia. The Han army, already famous for its discipline and organization, becomes an unstoppable force, capable of defending the empire's vast borders and expanding them even further. The phrase "As tough as Han steel" becomes the go-to compliment for anything or anyone that is particularly resilient. The Han military's prowess deters would-be invaders and rebels, leading to a period of unprecedented peace and stability across Asia. The continued success of the Han army also means that other empires, from Rome to Parthia, think twice before challenging the might of the Han. Future generations study Han military tactics, leading to a world where the principles of discipline, strategy, and innovation are the keys to victory on the battlefield.

9. Han Science and Innovation: The Age of Enlightenment

The continued stability of the Han Dynasty allows for an explosion of scientific and intellectual inquiry. With resources and time to spare, Han scholars delve into the mysteries of the natural world, making groundbreaking discoveries in medicine, astronomy, engineering, and more. The Han Dynasty becomes known not just for its political and military power, but for its contributions to human knowledge and progress. The phrase "The Han Enlightenment" becomes a historical term, referring to this golden age of science and innovation. The advances made during this period influence everything from agriculture to medicine, leading to a healthier, more prosperous population. The Han's scientific achievements spread along the Silk Road, influencing other cultures and accelerating the pace of global development. Future generations look back on this period as the foundation of modern science, with Han scholars being celebrated as the pioneers of their fields.

10. The Legacy of the Han: A New World Order

The continued reign of the Han Dynasty leaves an indelible mark on world history. The Han Empire becomes the template for future empires, with its emphasis on cultural integration, technological innovation, and strong governance serving as a model for centuries to come. The Han way of life, from their language to their administrative practices, spreads far beyond China, influencing civilizations across Asia and beyond. The phrase "The Han Way" becomes synonymous with good governance, cultural sophistication, and economic prosperity. The legacy of the Han Dynasty shapes the development of future empires, from the Mongols to the British, with each one looking to the Han as a model of success. The idea of a "Han World Order" takes root, with the principles of the Han Dynasty influencing everything from international diplomacy to economic systems. The modern world, in this timeline, is deeply shaped by the enduring legacy of the Han, with their influence visible in everything from architecture and art to politics and philosophy.

What If the Macedonian Phalanx Had Been Defeated by the Persian Immortals?

The Background

The Macedonian Phalanx, a tight-knit formation of spear-wielding soldiers, was the brainchild of Philip II of Macedon and perfected by his son, Alexander the Great. This military innovation allowed the Macedonians to steamroll their way across the ancient world, from Greece to Egypt, and ultimately to the doorstep of India. However, their most famous victory came at the expense of the mighty Persian Empire, which had dominated the ancient Near East for centuries. But what if, instead of the Macedonian Phalanx slicing through Persian lines like a hot knife through butter, they were met with an unexpected and overwhelming defeat at the hands of the Persian Immortals, those elite warriors of the Persian Empire?

Let's imagine that at the Battle of Gaugamela in 331 BCE, instead of the Macedonian Phalanx crushing the Persian forces, Alexander the Great's tactical genius meets its match. The Persian Immortals, rather than being just a fancy name for some heavily armored dudes, live up to their reputation as invincible warriors. Through a combination of superior strategy, reinforcements, and maybe a little divine intervention from Ahura Mazda, the Immortals not only halt the Macedonian advance but decisively defeat Alexander's forces, sending the young conqueror scrambling back to Macedon with his tail between his legs.

The 10 Possible Things That Would Happen

1. Alexander the Not-So-Great: A Tarnished Legacy

With his once-invincible phalanx shattered by the Persian Immortals, Alexander's reputation takes a nosedive. Instead of being remembered as the conqueror of the known world, he becomes "Alexander the What-Could-Have-Been." His dreams of a vast empire are dashed, and he returns to Macedon with far fewer soldiers and a lot more humility. The phrase "Don't be an Alexander" becomes the ancient world's equivalent of "Don't bite off more than you can chew." Future generations of Macedonian kings focus on domestic issues, avoiding the tempting but dangerous lure of eastward expansion. Greece, deprived of the spoils of conquest, remains a collection of squabbling city-states, never achieving the unified empire that Alexander had envisioned. Meanwhile, the story of Alexander's defeat becomes a cautionary tale, teaching future leaders the dangers of overconfidence and underestimating one's enemies.

2. The Persian Empire Strikes Back: Reasserting Dominance

With Alexander's forces in disarray, the Persian Empire seizes the opportunity to reassert its dominance over Greece. The Persian king, instead of fleeing for his life, marches triumphantly back into the Greek city-states, reestablishing Persian control over the region. The Persians become the undisputed masters of the eastern Mediterranean, with Greece falling firmly back under their control. The phrase "As Persian as democracy" becomes the ancient equivalent of an oxymoron, as the Persian Empire imposes its autocratic rule over Greece. The idea of Greek freedom and democracy, already fragile, is crushed under the weight of Persian bureaucracy and imperial control. Athens becomes a Persian satrapy, with the Parthenon repurposed as a temple to Ahura Mazda. Future historians marvel at the strange hybrid culture that emerges, where Persian satraps rule over Greek philosophers who are forced to praise the virtues of Zoroastrianism instead of discussing the latest Socratic paradox.

3. The Decline of Hellenism: No Spread of Greek Culture

Without Alexander's conquests, the spread of Hellenistic culture across the Near East and beyond never occurs. The Persian Empire, victorious and reinvigorated, actively suppresses Greek culture, viewing it as a threat to their dominance. Instead of Greek becoming the lingua franca of the eastern Mediterranean, Persian and Aramaic remain the dominant languages, and the cultural exchange that defined the Hellenistic era is stifled. The phrase "It's all Greek to me" never enters the lexicon because, well, Greek culture never gets the chance to spread far enough for it to be misunderstood. Instead, the world gets a heavy dose of Persian literature, philosophy, and art. Zoroastrianism spreads as the dominant religion, with fire temples dotting the landscape from Greece to India. The later development of Western civilization is markedly different, with far less emphasis on Greek ideals of democracy, philosophy, and art, and a greater influence from Persian concepts of kingship, order, and divine justice. Future scholars puzzle over the lost potential of Greek culture, speculating about what might have been if those Persians hadn't been so darn good at fighting.

4. The Roman Empire: A Different Kind of Expansion

Without the Hellenistic kingdoms as a buffer and inspiration, Rome's expansion into the eastern Mediterranean takes a different turn. Instead of encountering a mix of Greek and Eastern cultures, the Romans face a more unified and formidable Persian Empire that controls the entire region. Rome's ambitions are checked, and they are forced to find other avenues for expansion, perhaps focusing more on consolidating power in Europe and Africa. The phrase "Rome wasn't built in a day" is replaced with "Rome didn't cross the Hellespont," as Roman expansion eastward is blocked by a resurgent Persian Empire. The famous clashes between Rome and Persia become the central drama of Roman history, with a series of costly wars that drain Roman resources and prevent them from ever fully conquering the eastern Mediterranean. Instead of spreading Roman law and culture across the known world, the Romans become more insular, focusing on maintaining control over their European territories. The future development of Europe is more isolated, with less influence from the East and a stronger emphasis on indigenous traditions and cultures.

5. Philosophy and Science: A Persian Twist

With the Persian Empire reestablished as the dominant power in the ancient world, Persian philosophy and science take center stage. Instead of the works of Plato and Aristotle, it is Zoroastrian scholars and Persian scientists who lead the intellectual charge, influencing the development of thought across the Mediterranean and beyond. Greek philosophy, while not entirely suppressed, is relegated to the margins, overshadowed by the teachings of the Persian magi. The phrase "Know thyself" is replaced by "Follow the light," as Zoroastrian teachings about the duality of good and evil become the dominant philosophical framework. Persian advancements in astronomy, mathematics, and medicine spread across the empire, laying the groundwork for future scientific developments in the Islamic world. The Renaissance, when it occurs, is less about rediscovering Greek philosophy and more about a renewed interest in ancient Persian thought. The modern world, in this timeline, is deeply influenced by Zoroastrian concepts of morality, dualism, and the eternal struggle between light and darkness, leading to a very different intellectual and cultural landscape.

6. The Silk Road: A Persian Superhighway

With the Persian Empire stronger than ever, they take full control of the Silk Road, turning it into a well-maintained superhighway of trade and culture. The flow of goods between East and West becomes even more pronounced, with Persian cities like Susa and Persepolis becoming major centers of commerce. The Persians capitalize on this by establishing a network of trade routes that connect the Mediterranean with China, India, and Central Asia. The phrase "All roads lead to Persepolis" becomes the ancient world's equivalent of a corporate slogan, as the Persians rake in wealth from the vast trade networks they control. Persian luxury goods—silks, spices, perfumes—flood the Mediterranean markets, leading to an obsession with all things Persian in Europe and Africa. The influence of Persian culture spreads far and wide, shaping everything from fashion to cuisine. The later development of global trade is heavily influenced by Persian innovations in logistics, finance, and infrastructure, making the Persian Empire the world's first true global economic power.

7. A Zoroastrian World: The Rise of Dualism

With the Persian victory, Zoroastrianism spreads far beyond its original borders, becoming the dominant religion in the ancient world. The dualistic teachings of Ahura Mazda and Angra Mainyu (the forces of good and evil) permeate the religious and philosophical landscape of the Mediterranean, challenging the polytheistic beliefs of the Greeks and Romans. Temples to Ahura Mazda are built across Greece and Asia Minor, with Zoroastrian fire altars becoming a common sight. The phrase "The eternal flame" takes on a whole new meaning, as Zoroastrian fire temples become the center of religious life in the Mediterranean. The spread of Zoroastrianism leads to a greater emphasis on moral dualism in Western thought, influencing everything from ethics to law. The later development of Christianity and Islam is shaped by this Zoroastrian influence, with concepts like heaven, hell, and the final judgment becoming central to these religions. The world's major religious traditions, while still diverse, share a common thread of dualistic belief, leading to a more unified and coherent religious landscape.

8. Art and Architecture: Persian Grandeur

Persian victory brings with it a surge of Persian art and architecture across the Mediterranean. The grand palaces, intricate reliefs, and monumental structures of the Persian Empire become the new standard for architectural excellence. Greek and Roman styles are heavily influenced by Persian aesthetics, leading to a fusion of artistic traditions that creates a unique and enduring cultural legacy. The phrase "Persian style" becomes synonymous with luxury, elegance, and grandeur, as architects and artists across the Mediterranean emulate the opulent designs of Persepolis and Susa. The Parthenon, instead of being a symbol of Greek classical architecture, becomes a hybrid structure, blending Greek columns with Persian reliefs and motifs. This fusion of styles influences the development of art and architecture for centuries to come, leading to a more eclectic and diverse cultural heritage. Future historians marvel at the rich tapestry of artistic traditions that emerge from this period, with Persian influence seen in everything from Renaissance painting to modern skyscrapers.

9. The Decline of Greek Democracy: A Persian Autocracy

With Persian influence dominating the political landscape, the ideals of Greek democracy take a backseat to Persian autocracy. The Persian model of centralized, divine kingship becomes the standard for governance across the Mediterranean, with local rulers adopting Persian titles and practices to legitimize their authority. The concept of democracy, already fragile in Greece, is further weakened by the Persian victory. The phrase "Power to the people" is replaced by "Power to the king," as the Persian model of governance spreads across the Mediterranean. Future political developments in Europe and Asia are shaped by this autocratic tradition, with fewer experiments in republicanism and more emphasis on centralized authority. The later development of democratic ideas is delayed, as autocratic rule becomes the norm for centuries. When democracy does eventually reemerge, it is seen as a radical and dangerous idea, met with suspicion and resistance by rulers who have grown accustomed to the Persian way of doing things.

10. The Legacy of the Persian Empire: A New World Order

The victory of the Persian Immortals at Gaugamela leads to the establishment of a new world order, with the Persian Empire as its undisputed leader. The empire's influence extends across the known world, shaping the development of civilizations for centuries to come. The Persian model of governance, culture, and religion becomes the foundation upon which future empires are built, leading to a world where Persian ideals and practices are deeply embedded in the fabric of global civilization. The phrase "All hail the Persian Empire" becomes the rallying cry of a new era, as the world looks to Persia for leadership and guidance. The later development of global politics is shaped by the Persian legacy, with future empires, from the Mongols to the Ottomans, adopting and adapting Persian practices to suit their needs. The modern world, in this timeline, is deeply influenced by Persian culture, with Persian art, philosophy, and governance leaving an indelible mark on global civilization. And somewhere in this alternate history, a Persian scholar, gazing out over a vast and prosperous empire, might have chuckled and said, "It turns out that the Immortals really were immortal—at least in the pages of history."

Conclusion

If the Macedonian Phalanx had been defeated by the Persian Immortals, the course of Western civilization would have been profoundly different. The Persian Empire, reasserting its dominance, would have shaped the cultural, political, and religious development of the Mediterranean and beyond, leading to a world where Persian ideals and practices were the foundation of global civilization. And somewhere in this alternate history, Alexander the Great might have been remembered not as a conqueror but as the young upstart who dared to challenge the might of Persia—and lost.

What If the Carthaginian Explorer Hanno Had Discovered the Americas?

The Background

Hanno the Navigator, a Carthaginian explorer from the 5th century BCE, is best known for his voyage along the west coast of Africa, where he claimed to have encountered strange creatures, massive forests, and perhaps even gorillas (which he thought were "hairy people"). But what if, instead of sticking to the African coastline, Hanno had gotten a bit more adventurous? Let's imagine that a particularly strong wind—or maybe the allure of glory and endless riches—pushed Hanno and his fleet far off course, across the Atlantic Ocean, and smack into the shores of the Americas. The consequences of this early transatlantic encounter would have been nothing short of world-changing.

Let's say that in 450 BCE, Hanno, after a particularly wild night of Carthaginian wine and overconfidence, decides to sail westward into the unknown, leaving behind the safety of the African coast. After weeks at sea, just as his crew is about to mutiny and feed him to the sea gods, they sight land—lush, green, and entirely unfamiliar. Hanno has just become the first Old World explorer to land in the Americas, specifically somewhere in what is now Brazil or the Caribbean.

The 10 Possible Things That Would Happen

1. Carthaginian Colonies in the New World: Welcome to Hannotown

With the Americas now on their radar, the Carthaginians—ever the enterprising merchants—immediately see the potential for profit. They establish a series of colonies along the coast, trading with the indigenous peoples and setting up Hannotown (because why not name it after the guy who found it?) as the capital of this New World enterprise. The Americas become a bustling hub of Carthaginian trade, with ships regularly crossing the Atlantic laden with exotic goods. The phrase "Go west, young man" is coined by a particularly adventurous Carthaginian merchant, as the lure of the New World draws settlers, traders, and opportunists from across the Mediterranean. The colonies thrive, and Carthage, flush with new wealth, begins to outshine even Rome in terms of power and influence. Future historians write about the "Punic Americas," where Carthaginian culture, language, and religion take root. The indigenous peoples, while still independent, begin to adopt Carthaginian technologies and practices, leading to a fusion of Old and New World cultures centuries before Columbus ever sets sail.

2. The Carthaginian-Mesoamerican Alliance: Friends in High Places

Hanno's discovery isn't just about trade; it's also about power. The Carthaginians, savvy as they are, quickly form alliances with powerful Mesoamerican civilizations like the Olmecs or early Mayans. These alliances bring mutual benefits: the Carthaginians gain access to Mesoamerican gold, silver, and other resources, while the Mesoamericans receive Carthaginian metalworking, shipbuilding, and military technologies. The phrase "Strange bedfellows" becomes the tagline of the Carthaginian-Mesoamerican alliance, as these two civilizations—separated by an ocean but united by a love of shiny things—reshape the balance of power in the

Americas. The Olmecs, now armed with Carthaginian iron weapons, expand their influence across Central America, creating a Mesoamerican empire that rivals anything the Old World has to offer. Future scholars scratch their heads over Olmec carvings of ships and elephants (because of course the Carthaginians brought some elephants along), leading to endless debates about early transoceanic contact.

3. Roman Jealousy: The Punic Wars Get a New Battleground

The Romans, never ones to sit back and let the Carthaginians have all the fun, quickly catch wind of Hanno's discovery. Rome, already eyeing Carthage as a rival, decides that it too should have a piece of this New World pie. The Punic Wars, instead of being confined to the Mediterranean, spill over into the Americas, with Roman legions landing on the shores of Hannotown, ready to "civilize" (read: conquer) the Carthaginian colonies. The phrase "All roads lead to Hannotown" becomes a sarcastic jab at the Romans' relentless pursuit of Carthaginian territories, as the Americas become the new front in the ongoing Punic conflict. The Romans, unused to the dense jungles and strange wildlife of the New World, struggle to adapt, leading to the infamous "Battle of the Mosquitoes," where more soldiers fall to disease than to enemy action. Eventually, the Romans establish their own colonies, leading to a complex and competitive patchwork of Punic and Roman territories across the Americas. Future historians refer to this period as the "Punic-American Wars," where the fate of the New World is decided not by indigenous peoples, but by bickering Old World empires.

4. Carthaginian Agriculture: The New World Meets the Old World

The Carthaginians, always keen to make the most of their colonies, begin to introduce Old World crops and agricultural practices to the Americas. Olive groves, vineyards, and wheat fields spring up alongside the indigenous maize, beans, and squash. This agricultural exchange isn't one-sided, either—Carthaginian merchants eagerly bring back potatoes, tomatoes, and cacao to the Old World, revolutionizing Mediterranean cuisine centuries ahead of schedule. The phrase "You say tomato, I say tomat" becomes a popular Carthaginian expression, as the Mediterranean diet is transformed by the influx of New World crops. Carthaginian cuisine, already renowned for its use of spices and herbs, now incorporates chocolate (cacao) and tomatoes, leading to a culinary revolution that leaves Rome's bread and circuses looking downright bland. The introduction of Old World crops to the Americas leads to an agricultural boom, with both continents enjoying unprecedented prosperity. The later Columbian Exchange, when it happens, is less about discovery and more about Carthaginian merchants smugly saying, "Been there, done that."

5. Carthaginian Religion: Baal and the New World Gods

The Carthaginians, known for their devotion to gods like Baal and Tanit, bring their religious practices to the Americas. They establish temples and altars in their colonies, while also interacting with the indigenous belief systems. The result is a fascinating blend of Carthaginian and Mesoamerican religions, where Baal shares the stage with Quetzalcoatl, and human sacrifice takes on some decidedly Punic overtones. The phrase "By the beard of Baal!" becomes a common exclamation in the Americas, as Carthaginian and Mesoamerican religious practices merge into a unique and complex belief system. Future archaeologists are left scratching their heads over altars adorned with both Punic and Mesoamerican symbols, leading to endless debates about the nature of religious syncretism. The fusion of these two religions results in a pantheon that is as terrifying as it is diverse, with gods demanding everything from elaborate rituals to the occasional sacrificial victim. The later spread of Christianity to the Americas faces stiff competition from this well-established and deeply entrenched belief system, leading to a religious landscape that is far more varied and complex than in our timeline.

6. A New Language: Punic-Maya Pidgin

With regular contact between Carthaginians and Mesoamericans, a new pidgin language emerges, blending elements of Punic (the Carthaginian language) and Mayan. This hybrid language becomes the lingua franca of trade, diplomacy, and daily life in the Carthaginian colonies, making it easier for both cultures to communicate and cooperate. The phrase "Lost in translation" takes on a whole new meaning as future linguists try to decipher the Punic-Maya pidgin. This new language spreads rapidly, becoming the dominant form of communication across the Americas and even influencing speech patterns back in the Old World. The blending of languages leads to a richer, more dynamic culture, with poetry, literature, and oral traditions that draw on both Carthaginian and Mesoamerican influences. The later development of written scripts in the Americas incorporates elements of Punic writing, leading to a unique and complex system that baffles future archaeologists.

7. Carthaginian Innovations: Engineering Marvels in the New World

The Carthaginians, known for their engineering prowess, bring their expertise to the Americas. They introduce aqueducts, advanced shipbuilding techniques, and large-scale construction projects, transforming the infrastructure of the New World. Carthaginian architects work alongside Mesoamerican builders to create impressive structures that blend Old World engineering with New World aesthetics. The phrase "As solid as a Carthaginian pyramid" becomes a mark of architectural excellence, as the Americas are dotted with structures that combine the grandeur of Mesoamerican pyramids with the engineering genius of Carthage. Future explorers marvel at the sight of Hannotown's Great Temple, a fusion of Carthaginian and Mesoamerican design that rivals the wonders of the Old World. The Americas, with their new infrastructure, become even more prosperous and interconnected, with trade routes crisscrossing the continent and linking the Punic colonies with the rest of the New World. The later arrival of European explorers is met with a continent that is far more developed and sophisticated than they could have imagined, leading to a very different outcome for the age of exploration.

8. The Atlantic Trade Route: A New World Economy

With the establishment of Carthaginian colonies in the Americas, a new trade route across the Atlantic becomes one of the most important economic corridors in the ancient world. Carthaginian ships regularly ply the waters between the Old and New Worlds, carrying goods, people, and ideas back and forth. The Americas become fully integrated into the global economy, centuries before anyone in Europe even dreams of crossing the Atlantic. The phrase "Atlantic crossing" becomes synonymous with wealth and opportunity, as merchants and adventurers from across the Mediterranean make the journey to the New World in search of fortune. The integration of the Americas into the global economy leads to unprecedented prosperity on both sides of the Atlantic, with Carthaginian ports buzzing with activity. The demand for New World goods in the Old World skyrockets, leading to the development of specialized industries and crafts that cater to this transatlantic trade. The later European colonization efforts are met with stiff competition from the well-established Carthaginian presence, leading to a more complex and contested struggle for control of the New World.

9. The Spread of Disease: An Early Plague

With contact between the Old and New Worlds comes the inevitable spread of diseases. However, in this timeline, the disease transmission works both ways. The Carthaginians bring Old World diseases like smallpox to the Americas, but they also carry back New World diseases to the Old World, leading to outbreaks that affect both continents. The phrase "What doesn't kill you makes you stronger" is tested to its limits as both the Old and New Worlds grapple with devastating pandemics. The spread of disease leads to significant population declines on both continents, but it also sparks advances in medicine and public health as the Carthaginians and their allies seek ways to combat these new threats. The pandemics slow the pace of colonization and expansion, leading to a more cautious and measured approach to exploration and settlement. The later development of global trade and exploration is shaped by this early encounter with disease, leading to stricter quarantine measures and a greater emphasis on medical knowledge.

10. The Carthaginian Golden Age: A New Superpower

With the wealth and resources of the Americas at their disposal, Carthage enters a golden age of prosperity and power. The Carthaginian Empire becomes the dominant superpower of the ancient world. Their influence extends across the Mediterranean and the Atlantic, with colonies and trade networks that span the globe. The Punic Empire becomes a beacon of cultural, economic, and military might. The phrase "Carthage must be admired" replaces "Carthage must be destroyed," as the Carthaginian Empire reaches its zenith. The Roman Republic, unable to compete with Carthage's wealth and power, remains a regional power, never achieving the imperial heights it did in our timeline. The Carthaginian influence on global culture, economy, and politics is profound, shaping the development of Western civilization in ways that are both familiar and entirely unexpected. The later history of Europe, Africa, and the Americas is marked by the enduring legacy of Carthage, with Punic culture, language, and traditions leaving an indelible mark on the world.

Conclusion

If the Carthaginian explorer Hanno had discovered the Americas, the course of history on both sides of the Atlantic would have been dramatically altered. The Carthaginians, ever the savvy merchants and empire-builders, would have established a thriving presence in the New World, reshaping the trajectory of Western civilization. The resulting cultural, economic, and political exchanges would have created a world that was far more interconnected and complex, with Carthage emerging as the dominant superpower of the ancient world. And somewhere in this alternate history, a Carthaginian merchant, gazing out over the bustling port of Hannotown, might have chuckled and said, "Who knew getting lost at sea would be the best thing that ever happened to us?"

What If the Ancient Egyptian Pharaoh Akhenaten's Religious Revolution Had Succeeded?

The Background

Pharaoh Akhenaten, formerly known as Amenhotep IV, was Egypt's most unorthodox ruler, to put it mildly. Around 1353 BCE, he decided that worshipping a plethora of gods just wasn't his style, so he upended centuries of tradition and declared Aten, the sun disk, as the one true god. He then moved the capital to a brand-new city, Akhetaten (modern-day Amarna), effectively telling the priests of Amun, "Take your statues and go home." Unsurprisingly, this religious revolution didn't sit well with the majority of Egyptians, who were rather attached to their old gods. After Akhenaten's death, the old ways were swiftly restored, and Akhenaten was largely erased from history—literally, with his statues and images chiseled away. But what if Akhenaten's monotheistic revolution had not only survived his death but flourished? What if the worship of Aten had become the cornerstone of Egyptian religion and influenced the world beyond the Nile?

Let's imagine that Akhenaten, instead of being succeeded by the boy-king Tutankhamun, is followed by a strong, devout successor—let's call him "Atenhotep," because why not keep it in the family? Atenhotep, a true believer in his father's monotheistic vision, consolidates power, keeps the priesthood of Aten firmly in control, and successfully quashes any attempts to restore the old gods. The cult of Aten becomes deeply entrenched in Egyptian society, spreading like wildfire across the land, with temples to Aten popping up faster than you can say "Amen" (or "Aten," in this case).

The 10 Possible Things That Would Happen

1. Aten Worship: The One True Religion of Egypt

With Atenhotep at the helm, the worship of Aten becomes the state religion, no ifs, ands, or buts. The vast pantheon of Egyptian gods—Osiris, Isis, Horus, and the like—are relegated to the status of "mythological curiosities," whispered about in dark corners but officially denounced. Akhetaten becomes a bustling metropolis, filled with temples dedicated to Aten, where priests lead daily sun rituals and everyone learns to appreciate the "one true light." The phrase "Light of Aten" replaces "God of all gods" as the ultimate expression of divine favor. Future Egyptians grow up knowing only the sun disk, with the old gods fading into the realm of folklore. The famous Egyptian Book of the Dead gets a major rewrite, now focusing on how to live a good, Aten-pleasing life rather than navigating the underworld. Tourists centuries later are baffled by guidebooks describing Akhenaten as the "Father of Monotheism" rather than the "Heretic Pharaoh."

2. The End of the Theban Priesthood: Power Shift in Egypt

The powerful priests of Amun, once the kingmakers of Egypt, find themselves out of a job—or worse. The grand temples of Karnak and Luxor are repurposed as Aten worship centers, their statues of Amun melted down and reforged into sun disks. The wealth and power once controlled by the Theban priesthood are transferred to the Aten clergy, who become the new elite of Egyptian society. The phrase "Falling from grace" is redefined by the rapid decline of the Amun priesthood, who go from being the most powerful people in Egypt to living in obscurity. Meanwhile, the Aten priests, now the wealthiest and most influential members of society, start to flex their newfound power. Future Egyptian politics is dominated by religious leaders who emphasize unity and centralized control, with the Pharaoh as the chief representative of Aten on Earth. The concept of divine kingship becomes even more pronounced, with each Pharaoh seen as a direct mouthpiece of Aten, making dissent both blasphemous and politically risky.

3. Art and Architecture: Aten Style

Egyptian art and architecture undergo a radical transformation. Gone are the old depictions of the gods in human-animal form; instead, all art is focused on the glorification of Aten, with endless scenes of rays of light extending from the sun disk, touching the Pharaoh and his family. The distinctive Amarna style, known for its naturalistic and elongated figures, becomes the dominant artistic mode, spreading throughout the empire. The phrase "The Aten look" becomes synonymous with elegance and religious devotion, as all art is mandated to reflect the glory of the sun disk. Future generations of artists are taught only how to depict Aten's rays and the Pharaoh's divine connection, leading to a more uniform and somewhat monotonous art style. Egyptian architecture also shifts, with massive sun temples dominating the landscape, their open courtyards designed to capture the maximum amount of sunlight. The Great Pyramid of Giza, if it's still remembered, is considered quaint—"Nice, but where's the sunlight?" Future archaeologists marvel at the sheer volume of sun disks and struggle to understand why Egyptians seemed so obsessed with, well, the sun.

4. International Relations: Aten and the World

The successful spread of Aten worship doesn't stop at Egypt's borders. As Egypt extends its influence over neighboring regions, Aten becomes a key part of diplomatic relations. Pharaohs send emissaries to nearby kingdoms with gifts of gold and—more importantly—sun disks, encouraging (read: pressuring) their neighbors to adopt Aten worship as well. Slowly but surely, Aten starts to gain followers outside of Egypt. The phrase "Sun worshippers" takes on a literal meaning as Aten cults spring up in Canaan, Nubia, and even as far as Mesopotamia. Kings and rulers in these regions, eager to stay on Egypt's good side, begin incorporating Aten into their own pantheons, often at the expense of their traditional gods. The spread of Aten worship creates a shared religious bond among Egypt's allies, leading to stronger political and military alliances. Future historians note the rise of "Atenism" as a precursor to later monotheistic religions, with some even suggesting that Atenism influenced the development of Zoroastrianism, Judaism, and beyond.

5. Atenism's Influence on Monotheism: A New Religious Paradigm

With Atenism firmly established in Egypt and spreading beyond its borders, the idea of monotheism gains traction much earlier in human history. Atenism lays the groundwork for future monotheistic religions, influencing the development of religious thought across the ancient world. The concept of a single, all-powerful god becomes increasingly attractive, particularly in regions where political unity is a priority. The phrase "One god, one empire" becomes a popular motto among rulers looking to centralize power and unify their domains. Future religious movements draw heavily on Atenism's emphasis on a single divine entity, leading to the rise of other monotheistic faiths that borrow liberally from Egyptian theology. Judaism, for example, might adopt Atenist practices or merge its own monotheistic beliefs with Aten worship, creating a syncretic religion that spreads throughout the Near East. The later emergence of Christianity and Islam is shaped by this early monotheistic influence, leading to a religious landscape where the idea of a single god is not only accepted but expected.

6. Social Change: The Rise of a Unified Egyptian Identity

With Aten as the sole focus of worship, the diverse and often competing religious practices across Egypt are unified under a single banner. This religious unity fosters a stronger sense of national identity, as all Egyptians, regardless of their regional origins, share the same religious beliefs and rituals. The concept of "Egyptianness" becomes closely tied to Aten worship, with loyalty to the Pharaoh and the state intertwined with devotion to Aten. The phrase "One nation under Aten" becomes the rallying cry for a unified Egypt, where regional differences are minimized in favor of a shared religious and cultural identity. The elimination of the old gods also reduces the power of local priesthoods, leading to a more centralized and efficient administration. Future Egyptian society is marked by a strong sense of cohesion and collective purpose, with less internal strife and more focus on maintaining the glory of Aten. This unity allows Egypt to remain a dominant power in the ancient world for centuries, with other civilizations looking to Egypt as a model of religious and political harmony.

7. Scientific Advancements: The Age of Enlightenment

Atenism's focus on the sun and light spurs a renewed interest in astronomy, mathematics, and other sciences. Egyptian scholars, inspired by their devotion to Aten, make significant advancements in understanding the natural world, particularly in the areas of solar observation and timekeeping. The worship of Aten, as the literal source of life and light, encourages a more systematic and empirical approach to studying the universe. The phrase "By the light of Aten" becomes the ancient equivalent of "In the name of science," as Egyptian scholars make groundbreaking discoveries in solar astronomy, leading to more accurate calendars and timekeeping methods. The emphasis on sunlight also drives innovations in architecture and engineering, with new techniques for harnessing and directing natural light in buildings. These advancements spread beyond Egypt, influencing scientific thought in other cultures and laying the groundwork for future developments in astronomy and physics. The later Greek and Roman scholars, when they encounter Egyptian knowledge, find themselves awed by the sophistication of Aten-inspired science, leading to a deep respect for Egyptian learning that influences the intellectual history of the West.

8. Cultural Exports: Atenism in Art and Literature

With Atenism firmly established as the state religion, Egyptian art, literature, and culture become heavily influenced by Aten worship. Works of literature glorify Aten, while art continues to emphasize the sun disk and its divine rays. This cultural output, promoted by the Pharaohs and the Aten priesthood, is exported across the empire and beyond, influencing the artistic and literary traditions of neighboring civilizations. The phrase "Written in the light" becomes a popular way to describe the Aten-inspired literature that spreads across the ancient world. Future generations of poets and playwrights draw on the themes of divine light and solar power, creating works that celebrate the life-giving force of the sun. This cultural export leads to the development of a shared artistic and literary tradition across the Mediterranean, with Atenism serving as a central theme. The later literary traditions of Greece and Rome are deeply influenced by these works, with the sun and light becoming recurring motifs in their own mythologies and stories. The concept of divine illumination also shapes the development of religious literature, influencing everything from hymns to sacred texts.

9. International Conflicts: The Aten Crusades

As Atenism spreads, it inevitably encounters resistance from other cultures and religions. Some neighboring states, particularly those with strong polytheistic traditions, view Atenism as a threat to their own religious practices and political autonomy. This tension leads to a series of conflicts—dubbed the "Aten Crusades"—where the Pharaohs of Egypt, in the name of Aten, launch military campaigns to spread their religion and secure their borders. The phrase "Sunset on the enemy" becomes a euphemism for the ruthless efficiency with which Egyptian armies carry out the Aten Crusades. These conflicts lead to the expansion of the Egyptian Empire, with conquered territories being forced to adopt Atenism or face destruction. The spread of Atenism through military conquest creates a deep-seated animosity among Egypt's neighbors, leading to cycles of rebellion and suppression. Future empires, inspired by the Egyptian model, also adopt religiously motivated expansionist policies, leading to a world where holy wars and crusades are common occurrences. The later development of religious tolerance is delayed, as the idea of spreading one's faith by the sword becomes entrenched in the political and religious landscape of the ancient world.

10. The Legacy of Atenism: A New World Religion

With Atenism firmly established and spread across the ancient world, it becomes one of the dominant religious traditions of the time. The legacy of Atenism shapes the development of future religions, influencing theological concepts, rituals, and religious practices for centuries to come. The worship of a single, all-powerful god, represented by the sun, becomes a foundational belief for many cultures, leading to the rise of a new world religion that draws on Atenism's principles. The phrase "In the light of Aten" becomes the ancient equivalent of "In God we trust," as Atenism's influence extends far beyond Egypt's borders. The concept of monotheism, introduced by Akhenaten and solidified by his successors, becomes a central tenet of many religions that emerge in the following centuries. Atenism's emphasis on divine light and solar worship continues to influence religious practices, with sun temples and solar festivals becoming common across the Mediterranean and Near East. The later development of Christianity and Islam is deeply shaped by Atenism, leading to a religious landscape where the sun and light are central symbols of divine power and goodness. Future historians debate the extent of Atenism's influence on the world's great monotheistic religions, with some even suggesting that Aten was the original inspiration for the concept of God in the Abrahamic faiths.

Conclusion

If Akhenaten's religious revolution had succeeded, the course of Egyptian and world history would have been dramatically altered. The worship of Aten, established as the state religion of Egypt and spread through conquest and diplomacy, would have reshaped the religious, cultural, and political landscape of the ancient world. The rise of Atenism would have influenced the development of monotheism, scientific thought, and global religion, creating a world where the light of Aten shone brightly across the ages. And somewhere in this alternate history, a future Pharaoh, basking in the glory of Aten's rays, might have chuckled and said, "Who knew that a single god could cause so much drama?"

What If the Qin Dynasty's Legalism Had Spread Throughout China?

The Background

The Qin Dynasty, though short-lived (221-206 BCE), left an indelible mark on China. It unified the warring states, standardized weights and measures, and, famously, built the first iteration of the Great Wall. But these accomplishments came at a cost: the Qin rulers, particularly the infamous Qin Shi Huang, were ardent proponents of Legalism. This philosophy emphasized strict laws, harsh punishments, and centralized, authoritarian control. The Qin's Legalist policies were so harsh that after the dynasty fell, the succeeding Han Dynasty distanced itself from Legalism, favoring Confucianism instead. But what if the Qin Dynasty's Legalism had not only survived but spread throughout China, shaping its governance and culture for centuries to come?

Let's imagine that instead of crumbling after 15 years, the Qin Dynasty, through a combination of sheer force, effective administration, and perhaps a bit of luck, manages to stabilize and entrench its rule. Legalism, with its rigid structure and iron-fisted approach to governance, becomes the dominant philosophy not just in Qin-controlled regions but throughout China. The subsequent dynasties, impressed by the Qin's ability to maintain order and suppress dissent, adopt and refine Legalism, leading to a China where authoritarianism isn't just the law of the land—it's the philosophy of life.

The 10 Possible Things That Would Happen

1. Legalism: The Gospel of Governance

With the Qin's Legalist doctrine solidified as the foundation of Chinese governance, it becomes the unchallenged political philosophy. Every ruler, from the Qin onward, is educated in the principles of Legalism: laws must be strict, punishment severe, and the state must wield absolute power. The Confucians, once the darling philosophers of Chinese culture, are relegated to the dusty corners of history—those pesky advocates of "benevolence" and "morality" now seen as hopeless idealists. The phrase "Justice is blind" takes on a whole new meaning as the courts adopt a no-nonsense approach to law enforcement. Mercy? Never heard of it. Future Chinese emperors are known not for their wisdom or virtue but for their ability to enforce the law with an iron fist. The idea of a "benevolent ruler" becomes the punchline to a joke, and instead, the ideal leader is one who keeps the people in line, whatever the cost. The scholars who once debated the nuances of Confucian ethics now spend their days trying to find loopholes in the law—unsuccessfully, of course.

2. Education: Learning to Obey

With Legalism entrenched, the Chinese education system is revamped to focus on producing loyal, law-abiding citizens. Schools teach the importance of obedience to authority, the necessity of harsh punishment, and the dangers of questioning the state. Instead of studying Confucian classics, students memorize the Legalist texts, reciting the laws and decrees of the state with the same reverence once reserved for ancient poetry. The phrase "Spare the rod, spoil the child" is upgraded to "Spare the rod, undermine the state," as education becomes less about cultivating virtue and more about enforcing conformity. Future generations of Chinese students excel at following orders and knowing exactly how many lashes come with each crime. Creativity and critical thinking are seen as suspiciously rebellious traits, best left to those who fancy a lifetime of hard labor in the state-run quarries. The later development of Chinese culture is marked by a lack of innovation and a rigid adherence to tradition, as those who dare to think outside the box quickly find themselves outside society altogether.

3. The Great Wall 2.0: A Wall to End All Walls

With the Qin Dynasty's obsession with security and control, the Great Wall of China doesn't just get built—it gets supercharged. Over the centuries, successive dynasties, driven by Legalist paranoia, continue to expand and reinforce the Wall, turning it into a monstrous, impenetrable fortress. Not just a barrier against invaders, it becomes a symbol of the state's power and the lengths it will go to keep its citizens—and ideas—within its borders. The phrase "Hitting a wall" becomes less of a metaphor and more of a daily reality for those who try to leave China without state permission. The Wall, now visible from space with the naked eye (probably), is patrolled by legions of soldiers whose main job is to ensure that no one gets any funny ideas about freedom of movement. The concept of the "Great Firewall" arrives several millennia early, as communication with the outside world is tightly controlled. Future invaders, seeing the sheer size of the Wall, decide that maybe conquering China isn't worth the effort, and instead, China remains isolated—secure, yes, but also cut off from the cultural and technological exchanges that would have shaped its development.

4. Arts and Culture: State-Approved Creativity

Legalism's grip on China doesn't just affect governance—it permeates the arts as well. The state, ever mindful of the dangers of subversive ideas, takes a hands-on approach to culture. Artists, writers, and musicians are expected to produce works that glorify the state, celebrate the law, and reinforce the values of Legalism. Those who stray from these themes are quickly silenced, either through censorship or more permanent means. The phrase "Art imitates life" is replaced with "Art imitates the state," as creativity becomes a state-controlled commodity. Future Chinese art is known for its rigid, formulaic style, with every painting, poem, and song carefully vetted to ensure it doesn't challenge the status quo. The idea of an "artist's muse" is replaced by a more practical inspiration: avoiding punishment. This leads to a cultural landscape that, while technically proficient, lacks the vibrancy and diversity seen in other societies. The great works of Chinese literature and art, when they do emerge, are often produced in secret, hidden away from the prying eyes of the state.

5. Social Structure: The Hierarchy of Control

Legalism's emphasis on strict laws and order leads to a rigid, hierarchical society where everyone knows their place—and stays there. The state's authority is absolute, with social mobility severely restricted. Citizens are categorized, registered, and monitored from birth, with each person's role in society predetermined by the state. This system ensures stability, but it also stifles individual ambition and leads to a highly stratified society. The phrase "Know your place" becomes the national motto, as everyone is expected to fulfill their role in society without question. The concept of "meritocracy" is quietly discarded, replaced by a system where one's position is determined by birth and obedience. Social harmony is achieved, but at the cost of personal freedom and ambition. The state's focus on order and control leads to a society that is stable but stagnant, with little opportunity for innovation or progress. The later development of Chinese society is marked by a deep sense of resignation, as citizens accept their lot in life without hope of change.

6. Military Prowess: The Armored Fist of Legalism

With Legalism's focus on law and order, the military becomes the ultimate enforcer of the state's will. The army, once a tool for defense and expansion, is now the primary instrument of domestic control. Soldiers are trained not just to fight foreign enemies but to maintain order within the empire, ensuring that no one dares to challenge the state's authority. The phrase "Might makes right" is taken literally as the military becomes the backbone of the Legalist state. Future Chinese emperors are known for their military prowess, with the army playing a central role in governance. The constant presence of soldiers in every town and village creates a society where dissent is nearly impossible, as any hint of rebellion is swiftly and brutally crushed. The state's reliance on military force leads to a culture of fear and obedience, with citizens conditioned to accept the state's authority without question. This militarization of society also influences China's relations with its neighbors, leading to a more aggressive and expansionist foreign policy.

7. Economic Control: The State's Hand in Everything

Legalism's insistence on central control extends to the economy as well. The state takes an active role in managing production, distribution, and trade, with all economic activity regulated by strict laws. Private enterprise is heavily restricted, and merchants, once respected for their role in facilitating trade, are now seen as potential threats to the state's control. The phrase "State-run economy" becomes the norm as the government controls every aspect of economic life. Farmers, artisans, and merchants are all subject to state oversight, with quotas, taxes, and regulations dictating their livelihoods. The state's heavy hand stifles innovation and entrepreneurship, leading to an economy that is stable but stagnant. Future economic growth is slow and carefully managed, with any deviation from the state's plan met with harsh penalties. The later development of China's economy is marked by a lack of diversity and flexibility, as the state's rigid control prevents the kind of economic dynamism seen in other regions.

8. The Suppression of Religion: No Gods, Only Law

With Legalism's emphasis on the state as the ultimate authority, religion is seen as a potential rival for the people's loyalty. The state, wary of anything that might challenge its control, takes steps to suppress religious practices and beliefs. Temples are closed, religious leaders are persecuted, and the worship of gods is replaced by the worship of the state. The phrase "In law we trust" becomes the official creed as religion is systematically eradicated from Chinese society. Future generations grow up without any concept of divine authority, instead learning to place their faith in the state and its laws. The suppression of religion leads to a society that is highly secular, with little room for spiritual or philosophical exploration. The absence of religious institutions also means that there is no organized opposition to the state's authority, making it even more difficult for dissent to take root. The later development of Chinese culture is marked by a deep sense of pragmatism and materialism, with little emphasis on spiritual or moral concerns.

9. Diplomatic Isolation: The Fortress China

Legalism's focus on internal control leads to a policy of diplomatic isolation. The state, wary of foreign influences that might undermine its authority, limits contact with other nations. Trade and cultural exchange are restricted, and foreign ideas are viewed with suspicion. The phrase "Fortress China" becomes a reality as the country withdraws from the world stage. Future Chinese leaders prioritize self-sufficiency and internal stability over engagement with the outside world. This isolation leads to a stagnation of cultural and technological development, as the state's fear of foreign influence prevents the adoption of new ideas. The later development of China is marked by a sense of insularity and conservatism, with the country falling behind other regions in terms of innovation and progress. When China does eventually re-engage with the world, it does so from a position of weakness, struggling to catch up with more dynamic and open societies.

10. The Legacy of Legalism: A Different China

With Legalism entrenched as the dominant philosophy, the legacy of the Qin Dynasty shapes the course of Chinese history in profound ways. The state's emphasis on law, order, and control creates a society that is stable but repressive, efficient but uncreative. The influence of Legalism extends far beyond China's borders, affecting the development of East Asia and shaping the region's political and cultural landscape for centuries to come. The phrase "The long shadow of Qin" becomes a common saying as the legacy of Legalism casts a pall over Chinese history. Future generations look back on the Qin Dynasty not as a short-lived experiment in tyranny but as the foundation of a thousand-year-long Legalist state. The later development of Chinese society is marked by a deep-seated fear of disorder and a rigid adherence to the law, with little room for individual expression or innovation. The influence of Legalism also extends to China's neighbors, with East Asia as a whole adopting more authoritarian forms of governance. The modern world, when it emerges, is one where freedom is seen as a dangerous luxury and where the state's power is absolute.

Conclusion

If the Qin Dynasty's Legalism had spread throughout China, the course of East Asian history would have been dramatically altered. Legalism's emphasis on strict laws, harsh punishments, and centralized control would have created a society that was stable but repressive, efficient but uncreative. The legacy of Legalism would have shaped the development of Chinese culture, governance, and society for centuries to come, leading to a world where order and control were valued above all else. And somewhere in this alternate history, a future historian, staring at a meticulously detailed but utterly lifeless painting, might have sighed and said, "In the land of Legalism, even beauty needs a permit."

What If the Roman Empire Had Successfully Conquered Germania?

The Background

Ah, Germania—the wild, untamed land of dense forests, fierce tribes, and, let's be honest, people who thought bathing was a suggestion rather than a necessity. The Romans, ever the ambitious empire builders, had their eyes on Germania from the moment Julius Caesar first scribbled about the Germanic tribes in his *Commentarii de Bello Gallico*. But despite several attempts, including the disastrous Battle of the Teutoburg Forest in 9 CE, where three Roman legions were annihilated, Rome never quite managed to bring Germania into the fold. The Germans remained a thorn in Rome's side, eventually contributing to the empire's downfall. But what if, instead of retreating back to the safety of the Rhine, the Roman legions had triumphed? What if Germania had been successfully conquered and integrated into the Roman Empire?

Let's imagine that after the Teutoburg disaster, a determined Roman general—let's call him Imperatorus Stubbornus—manages to regroup the shattered legions and pull off a stunning victory over the Germanic tribes. The Romans, with their usual efficiency, begin the systematic conquest and Romanization of Germania, pushing their borders far beyond the Rhine. The once-impenetrable forests are cleared, roads are built, and Roman baths spring up faster than you can say Veni, Vidi, Vici. Germania, now a province of the Roman Empire, is integrated into the imperial system, with all the wine, togas, and gladiator games a barbarian could ever dream of.

The 10 Possible Things That Would Happen

1. Romanization of Germania: From Barbarian to Citizen

With Germania fully conquered, the Roman Empire sets about the business of turning wild Germanic warriors into proper Roman citizens. Temples to Jupiter and Mars replace sacred groves, Latin becomes the language of the land, and the Germanic tribes, once so proud of their beards and fur cloaks, start sporting togas and debating philosophy in newly established forums. The phrase "When in Rome, do as the Romans do" is updated to "When in Germania, do as the Romans say," as the process of Romanization sweeps across the newly conquered territories. Future generations of Germans, now thoroughly Romanized, grow up reciting Virgil instead of chanting war songs around the campfire. The region becomes a hub of Roman culture, with cities like Augusta Treverorum (modern-day Trier) becoming centers of art, commerce, and politics. The once-feared Germanic tribes are transformed into loyal Roman citizens, eager to pay taxes and serve in the legions. By the time the empire faces its later crises, Germania is so thoroughly integrated that the idea of a "Germanic invasion" seems about as likely as an invasion by toga-wearing Gauls.

2. Pax Romana Extended: A Stable Northern Frontier

With Germania securely under Roman control, the empire's northern frontier is significantly more stable. The Rhine and Danube rivers, now deep within Roman territory, become less of a defensive line and more of a convenient highway for trade and movement. The legions, no longer needed to fend off constant raids, are redeployed to other parts of the empire, or perhaps even sent home to enjoy a well-deserved retirement in sunny Sicily. The phrase "All quiet on the northern front" becomes a popular saying among Roman soldiers, who find their postings in Germania to be far less hazardous than anticipated. The reduced pressure on the northern borders allows the Roman Empire to focus its resources on other threats, such as those pesky Parthians in the East. The long-term stability provided by the integration of Germania leads to a prolonged period of peace and prosperity, with trade flourishing across the empire. The Pax Romana, already impressive, is extended for several more decades, with future historians marveling at the unprecedented stability of the Roman world.

3. Cultural Fusion: The Birth of Romano-Germanic Culture

As the Roman Empire and the Germanic tribes intermingle, a new culture begins to emerge—a blend of Roman sophistication and Germanic vigor. The resulting Romano-Germanic culture is characterized by a unique combination of Roman engineering and law with Germanic traditions of hospitality, warfare, and yes, a fondness for mead. The phrase "A barbarian at heart, a Roman in manners" becomes the affectionate description of the average Romano-German. This cultural fusion leads to the development of new art forms, architecture, and even language, with Latin absorbing Germanic words and expressions. Future Roman emperors, themselves of mixed Roman-Germanic heritage, proudly embrace this dual identity, commissioning statues that depict them in Roman armor but with long, flowing Germanic hair. The Romano-Germanic culture also influences the rest of the empire, with Germanic-style feasts becoming all the rage in the imperial court. The long-term impact of this cultural blend is felt across Europe, as the region develops a unique identity that will shape its history for centuries to come.

4. Roman Law in Germania: Justice for All (or Else)

With Germania firmly under Roman control, the empire introduces its legal system to the region. Roman law, with its emphasis on order, contracts, and property rights, replaces the old Germanic tribal codes. Courts are established, and the Germans quickly learn that while Roman justice may be swift, it is also very, very thorough. The phrase "Roman law and order" becomes synonymous with the idea of a fair, if somewhat rigid, legal system. Future Germanic leaders, trained in the ways of Roman jurisprudence, become adept at navigating the complexities of contracts, land ownership, and inheritance laws. This newfound respect for the rule of law helps to further stabilize the region, reducing the frequency of violent disputes and feuds. The influence of Roman law in Germania also extends to other parts of Europe, laying the groundwork for the development of a unified legal system that will eventually become the foundation of Western legal traditions.

5. Military Integration: Germanic Legions

With Germania now a part of the Roman Empire, the legions begin to recruit heavily from the local population. The fierce Germanic warriors, once the bane of Roman generals, now serve under the eagle standard, fighting for the empire that once sought to subjugate them. The Germanic legions earn a fearsome reputation, known for their loyalty, discipline, and, of course, their terrifying battle cries. The phrase "Fighting like a Germanic legionary" becomes the highest compliment one can pay to a soldier. The integration of Germanic troops into the Roman military significantly boosts the empire's fighting capabilities, allowing it to expand and defend its borders more effectively. The Germanic legions, with their unique blend of Roman training and Germanic ferocity, become the backbone of the Roman army, feared by enemies from the deserts of Africa to the forests of Britain. This military integration also helps to further bind Germania to the empire, as the local population takes pride in their contributions to Rome's military might. The later challenges faced by the empire are met with a united and formidable force, delaying or even preventing the decline of Roman power.

6. The Spread of Christianity: A Romanized Germania Converts Early

As Germania is fully integrated into the Roman Empire, it also becomes a fertile ground for the spread of Christianity. Roman missionaries, traveling along the empire's newly built roads, bring the message of the new faith to the Germanic tribes. The process of conversion is accelerated by the region's deep ties to the empire, and soon, Christianity takes root in Germania, centuries ahead of schedule. The phrase "A Roman heart, a Christian soul" becomes a common way to describe the Romano-Germanic population. The early adoption of Christianity in Germania helps to establish the region as a stronghold of the faith, with Germanic bishops playing a key role in the early church. The spread of Christianity in Germania also influences the rest of Northern Europe, leading to a more rapid and widespread conversion of the Germanic peoples. The early Christianization of Germania strengthens the region's ties to the rest of the Roman Empire, creating a shared religious identity that helps to unify the empire in times of crisis. This early spread of Christianity also sets the stage for Germania to become a center of Christian learning and culture in the centuries to come.

7. No Barbarian Invasions: Rome's Decline Postponed

With Germania fully integrated into the Roman Empire, the threat of barbarian invasions is significantly reduced. The Germanic tribes, now Roman citizens, have no reason to invade their own empire. Instead, they become defenders of the Roman world, guarding the northern borders against any potential threats from the east or beyond. The phrase "Barbarians at the gates" never becomes part of the Roman lexicon, as the feared Germanic invasions simply never happen. The absence of these invasions leads to a much longer period of stability for the Roman Empire, delaying its eventual decline. The empire, free from the constant pressure of external threats, is able to focus on internal reforms and development, leading to a Renaissance of Roman culture and technology. Future historians debate whether the empire might have lasted indefinitely if not for the eventual rise of new threats from the east, but all agree that the successful integration of Germania bought Rome several more centuries of power and influence.

8. Economic Boom: Germania's Resources Fuel Roman Growth

With Germania under Roman control, the empire gains access to the region's vast natural resources—timber, minerals, and fertile land. The Romans, ever the industrious engineers, quickly exploit these resources, setting up mines, farms, and trade networks that bring wealth flooding into the empire. Germania becomes one of the most prosperous provinces in the Roman world, contributing to an economic boom that benefits the entire empire. The phrase "Rich as a Roman" becomes synonymous with the newfound wealth of the empire, driven in large part by the resources of Germania. The economic boom leads to a period of rapid urbanization and development, with new cities and infrastructure projects springing up across the empire. The wealth generated by Germania helps to fund the empire's military campaigns, public works, and cultural endeavors, leading to a golden age of Roman prosperity. This economic growth also strengthens the empire's political stability, as the flow of resources and wealth helps to placate potential rivals and secure the loyalty of the provinces.

9. Cultural Exchange: The Roman-Germanic Renaissance

The successful integration of Germania into the Roman Empire leads to a period of intense cultural exchange between the Roman and Germanic worlds. Germanic traditions, art, and folklore are absorbed into Roman culture, while Roman innovations in architecture, literature, and governance influence the Germanic tribes. The result is a rich, hybrid culture that combines the best of both worlds—a Roman-Germanic Renaissance. The phrase "When Rome meets the forest" becomes a popular description of the unique cultural fusion that emerges in Germania. This Roman-Germanic Renaissance leads to a flourishing of the arts, with new forms of music, literature, and visual art that draw on both Roman and Germanic traditions. The region becomes known for its vibrant intellectual life, with scholars and philosophers from across the empire flocking to Germania to study its unique cultural blend. This cultural exchange also strengthens the bonds between Germania and the rest of the empire, creating a shared identity that helps to unify the Roman world.

10. The Legacy of Rome: A Unified Europe

With Germania fully integrated into the Roman Empire, the idea of a unified Europe takes root much earlier in history. The Roman Empire, now encompassing much of the continent, becomes the foundation for a pan-European identity that transcends regional differences. This early unification has a profound impact on the future of Europe, shaping its political, cultural, and economic development for centuries to come. The phrase "The United States of Rome" is coined by a particularly forward-thinking Roman senator, who envisions a future where Europe is united under a single, Roman-inspired government. The early unification of Europe leads to the development of a shared European identity, with Latin remaining the lingua franca of the continent long after the fall of the Western Roman Empire. This early unification also lays the groundwork for future political unions, with the idea of a united Europe becoming a central theme in the continent's history. The later development of European states is marked by a sense of continuity with the Roman past, with many modern European institutions tracing their origins back to the Roman Empire.

Conclusion

If the Roman Empire had successfully conquered Germania, the course of European history would have been dramatically altered. The integration of Germania into the Roman world would have led to a more stable, prosperous, and unified empire, delaying its eventual decline and shaping the development of European culture, politics, and identity for centuries to come. And somewhere in this alternate history, a Roman-Germanic scholar, sipping on a fine vintage of Roman wine while reclining in his Germania villa, might have chuckled and said, "Who knew that taming the barbarians would turn out to be Rome's greatest triumph?"

What If the Greek City-States Had Unified Before the Persian Wars?

The Background

Ancient Greece is the land of philosophers, poets, and people who just couldn't get along. The Greek city-states, with their endless bickering, were like a dysfunctional family at Thanksgiving, except with more spears and less pie. Athens, Sparta, Corinth, and Thebes—each city-state was fiercely independent, with its own government, culture, and, of course, a deep-seated mistrust of the others. But what if, instead of squabbling over who had the best hoplites or the most impressive temples, the Greek city-states had decided to join forces? What if they had unified before the Persian Wars, presenting a united front against the might of the Achaemenid Empire?

Let's imagine that around 510 BCE, a particularly charismatic and persuasive leader—let's call him Hellenicus the Diplomatic—manages to do the impossible: he convinces the fractious Greek city-states to set aside their differences and unite under a single banner. Perhaps it's the growing threat of Persian expansion, or maybe he just throws a really great symposium, but somehow, the Greeks agree to form a unified Hellenic League. The various city-states, from Athens to Sparta, each retain some autonomy, but they pledge to cooperate on military matters, share resources, and, most importantly, stop stabbing each other long enough to deal with the Persians.

The 10 Possible Things That Would Happen

1. A United Front: Xerxes Gets a Nasty Surprise

With the Greek city-states unified, the Persian invasions of 490 BCE and 480 BCE don't go quite as planned for poor Xerxes. Instead of facing a disjointed collection of city-states, he encounters a well-coordinated, formidable Greek force. The famous battles of Marathon, Thermopylae, and Salamis still happen, but this time, the Greeks are even better prepared, with armies and navies from all over Greece fighting as one. Xerxes, instead of lounging on his golden throne and watching the action like it's some kind of reality TV show, finds himself scrambling to keep his empire intact. The phrase "Don't mess with the Greeks" becomes a popular saying in Persia, as the unified Greek forces hand Xerxes one defeat after another. The Persian Wars end sooner and more decisively, with the Greeks driving the Persians out of Europe and even launching a few counterattacks of their own. Athens, Sparta, and the other city-states, flush with victory, don't just return to their old ways—they realize the benefits of unity and start thinking about what else they can accomplish together. Future Persian kings decide that it's safer to expand eastward instead, leaving the Greeks to their olive oil and philosophy.

2. Greek Dominance: A New Superpower Emerges

With their success against Persia, the unified Greek city-states quickly become the dominant power in the Eastern Mediterranean. They establish a Hellenic League that, unlike the historical Delian League, isn't just a tool for Athenian imperialism. The League becomes a genuine alliance, with each member contributing to the common defense and benefiting from shared resources. The Greeks, with their newfound sense of unity and purpose, begin expanding their influence across the Aegean, into Asia Minor, and even further afield. The phrase "All roads lead to Athens" becomes more than just a saying as Greek influence spreads throughout the Mediterranean.

The unified Greek state starts founding colonies, not just as individual city-states, but as a collective effort. These colonies, from Sicily to the Black Sea, are loyal to the Hellenic League, creating a vast network of Greek-speaking territories that trade, cooperate, and occasionally squabble like any good family. Future historians refer to this period as the "Golden Age of Greece," where Greek culture, politics, and military power reach unprecedented heights. The Mediterranean becomes a Greek lake, with even the mighty Phoenicians and Egyptians forced to pay homage to the new superpower.

3. The Athenian-Spartan Bromance: A Love-Hate Relationship

In this timeline, Athens and Sparta don't just tolerate each other—they actually learn to work together. Sure, there's still plenty of tension (Spartans and Athenians agreeing on anything is a bit like cats and dogs forming a book club), but they manage to maintain a functional partnership. Sparta handles the land battles with their unmatched hoplites, while Athens controls the seas with its powerful navy. Together, they form an unstoppable military force. The phrase "Frenemies with benefits" becomes the perfect description of the Athenian-Spartan relationship. The two cities, while never truly best friends, learn to coexist and cooperate, each playing to its strengths. This uneasy partnership leads to a period of unprecedented stability in Greece, as the other city-states fall in line behind the two leading powers. The Peloponnesian War, that devastating conflict that historically tore Greece apart, never happens. Instead, Athens and Sparta agree to a series of compromises, maintaining the balance of power while continuing to lead the Hellenic League. Future generations of Greeks look back on this period as a time of unity and strength, marveling at how the two most powerful cities managed to keep their rivalry in check.

4. Cultural Renaissance: The Golden Age on Steroids

With the Greek city-states united and no internal conflicts to distract them, the cultural achievements of the Greeks reach new heights. The philosophers, playwrights, and artists of this era are inspired not just by their own city-states, but by the idea of a greater Hellenic identity. Athens, now the cultural capital of a unified Greece, attracts scholars and thinkers from all over the Mediterranean, leading to an explosion of creativity and intellectual achievement. The phrase "When in doubt, ask a Greek" becomes the go-to advice for anyone in need of wisdom, as the cultural and intellectual output of Greece reaches unprecedented levels. The works of Socrates, Plato, and Aristotle are not only preserved but widely disseminated across the Hellenic world. The plays of Sophocles and Euripides are performed in theaters from Athens to Byzantium, while Greek architecture and sculpture set the standard for beauty and harmony. This cultural renaissance has a profound impact on the rest of the Mediterranean, with Greek art, philosophy, and science influencing everything from Roman law to Egyptian religion. The later Renaissance in Europe, when it comes, is fueled by the rediscovery of these golden age texts, leading to a cultural revival that owes much to this earlier period of Greek unity.

5. Economic Prosperity: A Trade Empire is Born

A unified Greece, controlling key trade routes and possessing a powerful navy, becomes an economic powerhouse. The Hellenic League establishes trade agreements with powers across the Mediterranean, from the wealthy cities of Phoenicia to the burgeoning empires of the East. The Greek cities, now working together rather than competing, pool their resources to build fleets, roads, and infrastructure that benefit the entire region. The phrase "As rich as a Greek" becomes synonymous with unimaginable wealth, as the unified Greek economy thrives. The cities of Greece become bustling trade hubs, with merchants from all over the world flocking to their markets. The wealth generated by this economic boom funds public works projects, from grand temples to impressive theaters, further cementing Greece's cultural dominance. The increased trade also leads to greater cultural exchange, with Greek goods, ideas, and technologies spreading throughout the Mediterranean and beyond. The economic prosperity of the Hellenic League creates a strong middle class, leading to greater political stability and a more egalitarian society. Future historians look back on this period as the height of Greek civilization, marveling at the wealth and influence of the unified Greek state.

6. Military Might: The Hellenic Juggernaut

The unified Greek state, with its combined military resources, becomes the most formidable military power in the ancient world. The Greek hoplites, now supported by a powerful navy and advanced siege technology, are unstoppable on the battlefield. The Persians, once the greatest threat to Greece, are now on the defensive, with Greek armies pushing deep into Asia Minor and beyond. The phrase "Beware of Greeks bearing arms" becomes the ultimate warning to any would-be invaders, as the Hellenic juggernaut rolls across the ancient world. The Greeks, now confident in their military superiority, launch a series of campaigns to secure their borders and expand their influence. The Persian Empire, once the dominant power in the East, is forced to cede territory to the advancing Greeks, leading to the creation of a new Hellenic empire that stretches from the Aegean to the Euphrates. The military successes of the Greeks lead to a period of relative peace and stability in the Mediterranean, as few are willing to challenge the might of the Hellenic League. The later Roman Empire, when it emerges, finds itself facing a unified and powerful Greek state that serves as both a rival and a model for imperial ambition.

7. Political Innovation: The Birth of Federalism

With the Greek city-states unified under the Hellenic League, a new form of government begins to take shape—one that balances the autonomy of the individual city-states with the need for collective decision-making. This early form of federalism allows each city-state to retain its local traditions and governance while contributing to the common defense and foreign policy. The phrase "United we stand, divided we bicker endlessly" becomes the guiding principle of the Hellenic League, as the Greeks perfect their system of federalism. This political innovation allows the Greek city-states to maintain their unique identities while benefiting from the strength and stability of a unified government. The success of this system inspires other cultures, with the concept of federalism spreading to other parts of the Mediterranean and beyond. Future political theorists look to the Hellenic League as an early example of how diverse states can come together for mutual benefit, laying the groundwork for later federal systems in Europe and America. The later development of democratic institutions in the Western world owes much to this early Greek experiment in federalism.

8. A Pan-Hellenic Religion: The Gods Go Global

With the Greek city-states unified, their religious practices begin to merge, creating a more standardized form of worship across the Hellenic world. Temples to Zeus, Athena, Apollo, and the other Olympian gods are built in every major city, and the various local cults and mysteries are integrated into a cohesive religious system. The Greek gods, once confined to the Greek mainland, begin to gain followers across the Mediterranean. The phrase "By Zeus!" becomes the most common exclamation from Athens to Alexandria, as the Olympian gods go global. The spread of Greek religion leads to the establishment of temples and shrines throughout the Mediterranean, from the Pillars of Hercules to the banks of the Nile. The Greek gods become the deities of choice for a wide range of people, from merchants and sailors to soldiers and kings. The standardization of Greek religion also leads to the development of a more organized priesthood, with the Oracle of Delphi playing a central role in religious and political life. The later rise of Christianity is influenced by this pan-Hellenic religion, with many early Christians adopting elements of Greek worship and theology. The impact of Greek religion is felt for centuries, with the Olympian gods continuing to be worshipped well into the Roman period.

9. No Macedonian Conquest: Alexander Who?

With a unified Greece already dominating the Eastern Mediterranean, there's no need for a Macedonian upstart to come along and unite the Greeks by force. Philip II of Macedon, instead of conquering Greece, finds himself negotiating with the Hellenic League, while his son Alexander grows up with a healthy respect for Greek unity. Without the need for a conquest, Alexander's ambitions are channeled into expanding the Hellenic League's influence rather than building his own empire. The phrase "The Great Compromise" replaces "The Great Conqueror" in reference to Alexander, who becomes a key statesman in the Hellenic League rather than a world-conquering general. Instead of a brief, meteoric rise followed by the fragmentation of his empire, Alexander spends his life strengthening the bonds between the Greek city-states and expanding their influence through diplomacy and trade. The Hellenic League, under Alexander's leadership, becomes a stable and prosperous federation that dominates the Mediterranean for centuries. The later spread of Greek culture, while still significant, is more gradual and organic, with the Hellenic League's influence spreading through trade and colonization rather than military conquest. The idea of a "world empire" is replaced by a more collaborative model of international relations, with the Hellenic League serving as a model for future alliances and federations.

10. The Legacy of a Unified Greece: A Different Rome

With a powerful, unified Greece dominating the Eastern Mediterranean, the rise of Rome takes a very different course. The Romans, instead of expanding into a power vacuum left by a disunited Greece, find themselves facing a formidable rival from the beginning. The relationship between Rome and the Hellenic League is one of mutual respect and rivalry, with the two powers balancing each other and preventing either from becoming too dominant. The phrase "Rome wasn't built in a day, but it wasn't built without Greek help either" becomes a popular saying as the two great powers of the ancient world develop a complex and interdependent relationship. The early history of Rome is marked by cooperation and competition with the Hellenic League, leading to a more gradual and less aggressive expansion. The cultural exchange between Rome and Greece is even more pronounced, with Roman law, architecture, and religion heavily influenced by Greek models. The later development of the Roman Empire is shaped by this relationship, with the empire adopting many aspects of Greek governance, culture, and philosophy. The legacy of a unified Greece is felt for centuries, with the idea of a pan-Hellenic identity influencing the development of European civilization long after the fall of Rome.

Conclusion

If the Greek city-states had unified before the Persian Wars, the course of history in the ancient Mediterranean would have been dramatically altered. A unified Greece would have become a dominant power, shaping the political, cultural, and economic landscape of the region for centuries to come. The influence of this unified Greece would have extended far beyond the borders of the Hellenic world, leaving a lasting legacy that shaped the development of Western civilization. And somewhere in this alternate history, a Greek philosopher, reclining in the shade of a grand temple, might have mused, "It's amazing what a little unity can do—if only we'd thought of it sooner!"

What If the Ancient Israelites Had Established a Long-Lasting Empire?

The Background

The ancient Israelites, known for their monotheism, wandering through deserts, and a knack for building temples, were a small but resilient group nestled in the heart of the Near East. After escaping from Egypt, battling Canaanites, and eventually establishing the kingdoms of Israel and Judah, the Israelites managed to carve out a small but significant place for themselves. However, their history was marked by periods of conquest, division, and exile, with the mighty empires of Egypt, Assyria, Babylon, and Persia looming over them like an ancient version of "Who's the Boss?" But what if, instead of being a small and frequently conquered kingdom, the Israelites had managed to establish a long-lasting empire? What if King David's conquests had led to the formation of a powerful, unified state that endured for centuries, shaping the politics and culture of the ancient Near East?

Let's imagine that around 1000 BCE, after King David's successful unification of the Israelite tribes and the establishment of Jerusalem as the capital, his successors—Solomon and beyond—managed to maintain and expand this kingdom into a full-blown empire. Instead of falling into disarray and splitting into Israel and Judah, the united Israelite empire grows in power and influence, dominating the region from the Nile to the Euphrates. The

Davidic line remains strong, Jerusalem becomes a bustling imperial capital, and the Israelites are no longer the underdogs of the region but a major player in the ancient world.

The 10 Possible Things That Would Happen

1. A Regional Powerhouse: The Davidic Empire

With the Israelites unified under a powerful and enduring dynasty, the empire expands its influence across the Near East. The kingdoms of Moab, Ammon, Edom, and Aram, once troublesome neighbors, are brought under Israelite control, either through diplomacy or military conquest. Egypt, Assyria, and Babylon now have to contend with a powerful Israelite state that controls key trade routes and resources. The phrase "As mighty as David" becomes the ultimate compliment in the ancient world, as the Davidic empire becomes a formidable regional power. The Israelites, once known for their scrappy underdog status, now wield significant influence in international politics. Future historians debate whether the Assyrians, Egyptians, and Babylonians were more annoyed or terrified by the rise of this new power. The Israelites' control over trade routes brings wealth and prosperity to the empire, with Jerusalem transforming into a vibrant hub of commerce and culture. The famous phrase "Land of milk and honey" now refers to the entire Israelite empire, which is as rich as it is powerful.

2. Cultural Exchange: The Fusion of Traditions

As the Israelite empire expands, it encounters a variety of cultures, from the Phoenicians with their seafaring ways to the sophisticated Egyptians. The Israelites, while fiercely protective of their monotheistic faith, are also pragmatic enough to borrow and adapt the best elements of these cultures. The result is a fusion of Israelite, Canaanite, Egyptian, and Mesopotamian traditions that creates a unique and vibrant culture. The phrase "One God, many influences" becomes the unofficial motto of the

Israelite empire, as they blend their religious beliefs with the artistic and intellectual achievements of their neighbors. The Temple in Jerusalem becomes a marvel of architecture, adorned with Phoenician craftsmanship and Egyptian motifs, but still dedicated to Yahweh. Hebrew becomes the lingua franca of the empire, but with loanwords from Egyptian, Aramaic, and Akkadian, leading to a rich and diverse language. The empire's cultural output—literature, art, and music—reflects this blend of traditions, influencing the development of later civilizations in the Near East. Future archaeologists are baffled by the mixture of styles in Israelite artifacts, leading to endless debates about who copied whom.

3. Religious Authority: Jerusalem, the Spiritual Capital

With the Temple of Solomon at its heart, Jerusalem becomes not just the political capital of the Israelite empire but the spiritual center of the ancient world. The influence of Israelite monotheism spreads beyond the borders of the empire, attracting converts from neighboring regions. Pilgrims from across the Near East travel to Jerusalem to offer sacrifices, seek wisdom, and participate in religious festivals. The phrase "Next year in Jerusalem" becomes a popular saying centuries earlier, as people from all over the ancient world dream of visiting the city. The Israelite priests, now wielding significant religious authority, begin to codify and expand their religious texts, leading to the early development of what would become the Hebrew Bible. The spread of monotheism, driven by the success of the Israelite empire, influences the religious beliefs of neighboring peoples, with some adopting elements of Israelite worship. The later development of Judaism, Christianity, and Islam is shaped by this early expansion of Israelite religious influence, with Jerusalem maintaining its status as a holy city for millennia to come.

4. Political Alliances: The Israelite Coalition

As a major power, the Israelite empire forms alliances with other kingdoms and empires, both near and far. These alliances, forged through marriage, diplomacy, and military cooperation, help to stabilize the region and secure Israelite influence across the Near East. The empire's diplomatic efforts lead to the creation of a powerful coalition that includes Egypt, Phoenicia, and other key players. The phrase "An ally of Israel is an ally of peace" becomes the mantra of the ancient world, as the Israelite empire's alliances create a network of stability and cooperation. The coalition's combined military might deters potential invaders, while trade agreements ensure mutual prosperity. The famous marriage of Solomon to the daughter of the Pharaoh of Egypt, recorded in this timeline as a key moment in diplomatic history, becomes the stuff of legend. The alliances also lead to greater cultural and technological exchange, with the Israelite empire benefiting from the expertise of its allies. Future generations look back on this period as a golden age of peace and prosperity, driven by the strength of Israelite diplomacy.

5. Economic Boom: The Wealth of the Israelite Empire

With control over key trade routes, fertile lands, and valuable resources, the Israelite empire experiences an economic boom. The empire's wealth allows for grand building projects, including the expansion of Jerusalem, the construction of fortresses, and the development of infrastructure across the empire. Trade flourishes, with goods flowing in and out of the empire, from Egyptian gold to Phoenician purple dye. The phrase "As rich as Solomon" becomes more than just a biblical reference, as the wealth of the Israelite empire becomes legendary. The economy thrives, with bustling markets in cities like Jerusalem, Megiddo, and Hazor attracting merchants from across the ancient world. The empire's wealth funds the construction of magnificent public buildings, temples, and palaces, transforming the landscape of the Near East. This economic prosperity also leads to advancements in technology, with the Israelites developing new tools, weapons, and agricultural techniques. The later history of the region is marked by the enduring legacy of Israelite engineering and architecture, with ruins of their grand structures still standing centuries later.

6. Military Prowess: The Iron Chariots of Israel

The Israelite empire, aware of the constant threats from rival powers, develops a formidable military. The Israelite army, equipped with iron weapons and chariots, becomes one of the most feared forces in the ancient world. The empire's military campaigns expand its borders, secure its trade routes, and protect its interests from potential invaders. The phrase "The chariots of Israel and its horsemen" becomes a battle cry that strikes fear into the hearts of enemies. The Israelite military, known for its discipline and innovation, plays a key role in maintaining the empire's dominance. The use of iron technology, along with advanced tactics and fortifications, gives the Israelites a significant advantage over their rivals. The success of the Israelite military leads to the expansion of the empire's borders, with new territories being incorporated into the empire. The later development of military strategy and technology in the region is heavily influenced by Israelite innovations, with other powers adopting similar tactics and equipment.

7. Legal and Administrative Reforms: The Code of David

To govern their vast empire, the Israelites develop a sophisticated legal and administrative system. Building on the laws of Moses, the Davidic dynasty codifies a set of laws and regulations that ensure justice, order, and stability across the empire. The administration is centralized, with regional governors appointed to oversee different parts of the empire, all reporting back to the imperial court in Jerusalem. The phrase "By the law of David" becomes the standard for justice throughout the empire, as the Israelite legal code is respected and enforced in every corner of the realm.

The administrative reforms streamline governance, reduce corruption, and ensure that the empire's resources are effectively managed. The centralization of power in Jerusalem leads to a more unified and efficient state, with less regional autonomy but greater overall stability. The success of these reforms influences the development of legal and administrative systems in neighboring empires, with some adopting elements of the Israelite model. Future generations study the "Code of David" as a foundational legal text, comparable to the Code of Hammurabi.

8. The Israelite Navy: Masters of the Mediterranean

Recognizing the importance of maritime trade and defense, the Israelite empire invests in the development of a powerful navy. With the help of their Phoenician allies, the Israelites build a fleet of ships that patrol the Mediterranean, protecting trade routes and projecting power across the sea. The Israelite navy becomes a dominant force, rivaling even the great maritime powers of the time. The phrase "Rulers of the waves" is first applied to the Israelite navy, which controls key shipping lanes and protects the empire's maritime interests. The success of the navy allows the Israelites to expand their influence beyond the Levant, establishing colonies and trade outposts in strategic locations across the Mediterranean. The naval power of the Israelite empire deters piracy and ensures the safety of its merchants, further boosting the empire's economy. The development of naval technology and shipbuilding techniques by the Israelites influences later maritime powers, with the Israelite navy serving as a model for future fleets. The empire's control of the Mediterranean contributes to its long-term stability and prosperity, solidifying its position as a major player in the ancient world.

9. Cultural and Religious Influence: The Spread of Monotheism

As the Israelite empire grows, so does its cultural and religious influence. The Israelites, while respecting the traditions of their subjects, promote the worship of Yahweh as the one true God. This leads to the spread of monotheism across the Near East, with other peoples adopting elements of Israelite religion, either through conversion or syncretism. The phrase "One God, one empire" becomes the guiding principle of the Israelite state, as monotheism spreads far beyond the borders of Israel. The influence of Israelite religion shapes the development of other faiths in the region, with some adopting monotheistic practices while others incorporate aspects of Israelite theology into their own beliefs. The spread of monotheism leads to greater religious unity within the empire, reducing internal conflicts and fostering a sense of shared identity. The later development of Judaism, Christianity, and Islam is heavily influenced by this early expansion of Israelite religious ideas, with the concept of a single, all-powerful God becoming a central tenet of these faiths. The impact of Israelite monotheism is felt for millennia, shaping the religious landscape of the world.

10. The Legacy of the Israelite Empire: A Lasting Influence

The long-lasting Israelite empire leaves an indelible mark on the history of the Near East and the world. Its achievements in governance, law, culture, and religion set the stage for the development of later civilizations. The empire's legacy endures long after its decline, influencing the political, cultural, and religious landscape of the region for centuries to come. The phrase "As enduring as Jerusalem" becomes a symbol of longevity and resilience, as the legacy of the Israelite empire shapes the course of history. The achievements of the Israelites in law, religion, and governance are studied and emulated by later empires, from Rome to Byzantium. The cultural and religious influence of the Israelite empire continues to be felt in the development of Western civilization, with the Hebrew Bible serving as a foundational text for Judaism, Christianity, and Islam. The political and legal innovations of the Israelite state influence the development of modern legal systems, with the "Code of David" regarded as a precursor to later legal codes. The enduring legacy of the Israelite empire is celebrated and remembered for millennia, with Jerusalem remaining a symbol of faith, resilience, and enduring influence.

Conclusion

If the ancient Israelites had established a long-lasting empire, the course of Near Eastern and world history would have been dramatically altered. The Israelite empire would have become a dominant power, shaping the political, cultural, and religious landscape of the region for centuries. The influence of this empire would have extended far beyond its borders, leaving a lasting legacy that continues to impact the world today. And somewhere in this alternate history, an Israelite scribe, sitting in the shadow of the grand Temple in Jerusalem, might have smiled and said, "And they thought we were just a bunch of wandering shepherds—who's laughing now?"

What If the Maurya Empire Had Not Declined After Ashoka?

The Background

The Maurya Empire, founded by Chandragupta Maurya around 322 BCE, was the first to unify most of the Indian subcontinent under a single ruler. The empire reached its zenith under Ashoka the Great, who, after a particularly bloody campaign against Kalinga, had a change of heart and embraced Buddhism. He spent the rest of his reign promoting non-violence, compassion, and, of course, Buddhism, turning the Maurya Empire into a hub of Buddhist thought and culture. However, after Ashoka's death, the empire began to decline, eventually fragmenting into smaller states and losing much of its influence. But what if the Maurya Empire had not declined? What if, instead of fading into history, it continued to thrive and expand, spreading Buddhism further and deeply influencing the development of South Asia and beyond?

Let's imagine that after Ashoka's death in 232 BCE, his successors, rather than squabbling over the throne and neglecting the vast empire, are inspired by his legacy and manage to hold the empire together. They continue Ashoka's policies of governance based on dharma (moral law), maintain strong centralized control, and effectively manage the diverse regions of the subcontinent. The empire not only survives but flourishes, becoming a beacon of stability, culture, and spiritual leadership in the ancient world.

The 10 Possible Things That Would Happen

1. The Golden Age of Buddhism: Dharma Conquers the World

With the Maurya Empire continuing to thrive, Ashoka's promotion of Buddhism doesn't just maintain its momentum—it accelerates. The empire becomes the epicenter of Buddhist scholarship, missionary activity, and cultural exchange. Monasteries, stupas, and universities sprout like bamboo after a monsoon, and Buddhist monks travel far and wide, spreading the teachings of the Buddha from the Himalayas to the distant shores of Southeast Asia, and perhaps even beyond. The phrase "Spreading like Buddhism in the Maurya Empire" becomes the ancient world's version of "going viral." Buddhism, bolstered by the empire's support, spreads not just across Asia but begins to make inroads into the Mediterranean and the Middle East, thanks to the Silk Road and maritime trade routes. Future historians marvel at the sight of Greco-Buddhist statues in Athens and Buddhist temples along the Nile. The later spread of Islam and Christianity finds a more deeply entrenched and widespread Buddhist tradition, leading to fascinating syncretic religions and philosophical debates that echo through the centuries. In this timeline, "The Middle Way" becomes a global concept, influencing everything from governance to cuisine (with a lot more vegetarian options, naturally).

2. South Asia: A Unified Cultural and Political Sphere

With the Maurya Empire continuing to expand and solidify its control, South Asia develops a strong and unified cultural and political identity much earlier than in our timeline. The empire's policies of tolerance, integration, and centralized governance create a cohesive and stable region that enjoys sustained peace and prosperity. The diverse peoples of the subcontinent, from the Tamil kingdoms in the south to the tribes of the Deccan Plateau, are brought into a shared Maurya identity. The phrase "As united as the Maurya" becomes synonymous with political stability and cultural cohesion.

The early unification of South Asia leads to a more integrated economic and social system, with trade and cultural exchange flourishing across the region. The empire's efficient bureaucracy and legal system become a model for future Indian states, influencing the development of governance in the region for centuries. The shared identity fostered by the Maurya Empire also leads to the development of a more unified literary and artistic tradition, with Sanskrit becoming the lingua franca of the region. The later history of India is marked by this early unification, leading to a more stable and prosperous subcontinent that becomes a major player in global trade and politics.

3. The Maurya Navy: Masters of the Indian Ocean

Recognizing the importance of maritime trade, the Maurya Empire invests in building a powerful navy to protect its interests and expand its influence across the Indian Ocean. The empire's ships dominate the sea routes between India, Southeast Asia, and the Middle East, facilitating the exchange of goods, ideas, and culture. The phrase "As steady as a Maurya ship" becomes the ancient world's standard for reliability. The Maurya navy's dominance of the Indian Ocean leads to the establishment of Maurya colonies and trade outposts across the region, from the coast of East Africa to the islands of Southeast Asia. The wealth generated by this maritime trade funds further expansion and consolidation of the empire, while also bringing exotic goods and ideas back to the Indian subcontinent. The Maurya navy's influence extends beyond trade, with the empire playing a key role in the politics of the Indian Ocean world, from the Arabian Peninsula to Indonesia. The later development of maritime empires in the region is shaped by the legacy of Maurya naval power, with future rulers looking to the Maurya as the pioneers of oceanic exploration and dominance.

4. Cultural Renaissance: The Flourishing of Arts and Sciences

With the empire stable and prosperous, the Maurya rulers become patrons of the arts, sciences, and literature. Universities like Nalanda and Takshashila, already centers of learning, receive even more support and attract scholars from across the known world. The result is a cultural and intellectual renaissance that sees advancements in medicine, astronomy, mathematics, literature, and the arts. The phrase "Maurya Enlightenment" becomes a term used by later historians to describe this period of cultural and intellectual flourishing. The achievements of Maurya scholars in fields like mathematics (with early developments in algebra and geometry), medicine (with advancements in surgery and herbal treatments), and astronomy (with precise calendars and star maps) influence the scientific traditions of both the East and West. The literary output of the empire, from epic poetry to philosophical treatises, sets the standard for centuries to come, with future civilizations looking back to this era as a golden age of human achievement. The impact of the Maurya Renaissance is felt far beyond the subcontinent, as the empire's scholars travel to distant lands, spreading their knowledge and contributing to the intellectual development of other cultures.

5. Social Reform: A More Egalitarian Society

Continuing Ashoka's emphasis on dharma, the Maurya Empire implements a series of social reforms aimed at reducing inequality and promoting justice. The caste system, while still present, is moderated by the empire's focus on merit and dharma. Women's rights see some improvement, with more opportunities for education and participation in religious and social life. The phrase "All are equal under dharma" becomes the guiding principle of Maurya society. The empire's emphasis on social justice leads to the development of a more egalitarian society, with greater social mobility and opportunities for all citizens. The influence of Buddhism, with its teachings on compassion and non-violence, contributes to a more humane legal system, with an emphasis on rehabilitation rather than punishment. The reforms also lead to a flourishing of education, with schools and universities open to a wider range of people, including women and those from lower castes. The later history of India is marked by this legacy of social reform, with future rulers building on the foundations laid by the Maurya to create a more just and equitable society.

6. Political Stability: The Long Reign of the Maurya Dynasty

Thanks to effective governance, a strong military, and wise leadership, the Maurya Empire avoids the fragmentation and decline that plagued so many other empires. The dynasty continues to rule for several centuries, passing power smoothly from one generation to the next. The empire's stability allows for long-term planning and the completion of ambitious projects, from grand temples to extensive road networks. The phrase "Stable as the Maurya" becomes a proverb used to describe anything enduring and reliable. The long reign of the Maurya dynasty leads to a period of unprecedented political stability in South Asia, with the empire serving as a model for future Indian states. The empire's ability to maintain control over its vast territories is facilitated by a well-organized bureaucracy and an efficient system of governance that balances central authority with local autonomy. This stability allows the Maurya to undertake large-scale infrastructure projects, including the construction of roads, canals, and irrigation systems that boost agriculture and trade. The enduring nature of the Maurya Empire also provides a sense of continuity and identity for its citizens, with the empire's symbols and traditions becoming deeply ingrained in the cultural fabric of South Asia.

7. Diplomatic Relations: The Maurya Empire as a Global Player

The Maurya Empire, with its wealth, military power, and cultural achievements, becomes a major player on the global stage. The empire's rulers establish diplomatic relations with other great powers of the time, including the Hellenistic kingdoms, Persia, and even Rome. Envoys from distant lands visit the Maurya court, and the empire's influence extends far beyond its borders. The phrase "As respected as a Maurya ambassador" becomes the gold standard for diplomatic skill. The Maurya Empire's diplomatic efforts lead to the establishment of a network of alliances and treaties that help to secure the empire's borders and promote trade. The empire's influence in global affairs also leads to the spread of Maurya culture and ideas, with elements of Indian art, religion, and philosophy making their way to distant lands. The empire's diplomatic achievements are remembered and celebrated by future generations, with the Maurya serving as a model for how to balance power with diplomacy in international relations.

8. Architectural Wonders: A Legacy in Stone

With centuries of prosperity and stability, the Maurya Empire undertakes grand architectural projects that leave a lasting mark on the landscape of South Asia. The empire's rulers commission the construction of magnificent temples, palaces, and stupas that showcase the empire's wealth and artistic achievements. These architectural wonders become symbols of the empire's power and devotion to Buddhism. The phrase "Maurya magnificence" becomes synonymous with architectural splendor. The empire's grand structures, from the towering stupas of Sanchi to the elaborate palaces of Pataliputra, become the pride of South Asia and attract pilgrims, scholars, and travelers from across the world. The architectural achievements of the Maurya inspire future generations of builders and architects, with the empire's style influencing the development of temple and palace architecture across Asia. The ruins of these structures continue to stand as a testament to the empire's greatness, with later civilizations drawing inspiration from the Maurya legacy in their own architectural endeavors.

9. The Spread of Indian Influence: Cultural Exchange Beyond Borders

With the Maurya Empire continuing to thrive, its cultural influence spreads far beyond the Indian subcontinent. Indian art, literature, religion, and philosophy reach new heights and spread to neighboring regions, including Central Asia, Southeast Asia, and the Far East. The empire's cultural exports help to shape the development of these regions, creating a shared cultural heritage that transcends borders. The phrase "Maurya influence knows no bounds" becomes a common saying as the empire's cultural reach extends across Asia. The spread of Indian culture leads to the development of a shared artistic and literary tradition in the regions influenced by the Maurya, with Indian motifs and themes appearing in everything from Chinese paintings to Indonesian temples. The influence of Indian religion and philosophy also shapes the spiritual landscape of these regions, with Buddhism and Hinduism gaining a strong foothold in Southeast Asia and beyond. The later history of Asia is marked by this cultural exchange, with the Maurya Empire's legacy continuing to influence the development of art, religion, and philosophy across the continent.

10. The Legacy of the Maurya Empire: A Unified and Prosperous South Asia

With the Maurya Empire enduring for centuries, its legacy becomes deeply ingrained in the identity of South Asia. The empire's achievements in governance, culture, and religion set the foundation for future Indian states, and its influence is felt long after its eventual decline. The Maurya Empire becomes a symbol of unity, prosperity, and spiritual leadership for the region. The phrase "In the time of the Maurya" becomes shorthand for a golden age of peace, prosperity, and cultural achievement. The empire's legacy continues to shape the political, cultural, and religious landscape of South Asia for centuries, with future rulers drawing inspiration from the Maurya model of governance and administration. The enduring influence of the Maurya also contributes to the development of a shared Indian identity, with the symbols and traditions of the empire becoming central to the region's cultural heritage. The later history of South Asia is marked by a sense of continuity and pride in the Maurya legacy, with the empire's achievements serving as a benchmark for future generations.

Conclusion

If the Maurya Empire had not declined after Ashoka, the course of South Asian and global history would have been dramatically altered. The empire's continued success would have led to the spread of Buddhism, the unification of South Asia, and the development of a prosperous and stable region with a lasting cultural legacy. The Maurya Empire would have become a dominant force in the ancient world, shaping the development of Asia and leaving an enduring mark on history. And somewhere in this alternate history, a Maurya scholar, surrounded by scrolls and stupas, might have mused, "It turns out that dharma really is the best policy—who knew it would work this well?"

What If the Hittites Had Successfully Expanded into Egypt?

The Background

The Hittites, an ancient Anatolian people who made their mark by being both formidable warriors and master diplomats, were one of the great powers of the ancient Near East. Their empire, centered in modern-day Turkey, clashed with Egypt in a series of territorial disputes that culminated in the famous Battle of Kadesh around 1274 BCE. While the battle ended in a stalemate, the two powers eventually agreed to the first recorded peace treaty in history. But what if the Hittites had done more than just hold their ground? What if, through cunning strategy, military might, or sheer luck, they had successfully expanded into Egypt, turning the land of the pharaohs into a Hittite province?

Let's imagine that during the reign of Muwatalli II, the Hittite king pulls off the impossible. Perhaps it's through a brilliant military campaign that catches the Egyptians off guard, or maybe it's through clever alliances with rebellious Egyptian nobles. Either way, the Hittites manage to not only defeat the Egyptian army but also march into the heart of Egypt, capturing Memphis and ultimately taking control of the Nile Delta. The mighty Pharaoh Ramesses II finds himself in the uncomfortable position of fleeing south to Thebes, where he sets up a rump state while the Hittites consolidate their power in the north.

The 10 Possible Things That Would Happen

1. Hittite Pharaohs: A New Dynasty in Egypt

With the Hittites in control of northern Egypt, a new dynasty is born—let's call them the "Anatolian Pharaohs." These rulers, descending from the Hittite royal family, adopt Egyptian titles and traditions but with a distinct Hittite twist. Statues of pharaohs now feature the traditional Egyptian headdress with a Hittite double-plumed crown, and temples dedicated to both Egyptian and Hittite gods spring up across the land. The phrase "Two crowns, one throne" becomes the motto of the new Hittite-Egyptian rulers, who juggle the cultural expectations of both peoples. Egyptian priests, ever pragmatic, quickly incorporate Hittite deities into their pantheon, though they privately grumble about the "barbaric" customs being imported from the north. Future historians scratch their heads over the hybrid art and architecture that emerges during this period, where Hittite storm gods appear in hieroglyphic texts and Egyptian temples take on a distinctly Anatolian style. Meanwhile, the new Hittite-Egyptian dynasty faces the constant challenge of keeping both Egyptian nobles and Hittite warriors happy—a balancing act that makes the politics of the region even more complicated than it already was.

2. The Battle for the Nile: Constant Warfare and Border Disputes

Ramesses II, never one to back down, does not take the loss of Memphis lightly. He rallies his forces in Thebes and launches a series of campaigns to reclaim his lost territories. The result is a protracted conflict between the Hittites in the north and the native Egyptians in the south. The Nile becomes the new battleground, with cities and villages constantly changing hands as the two powers vie for control. The phrase "The Nile runs red" becomes the grim description of the ongoing conflict between the Hittites and the Egyptians. The constant warfare drains both sides of resources and manpower, leading to widespread suffering among the populace. The prolonged conflict also destabilizes the region, making it vulnerable to external threats from Libyan tribes in the west and the Sea Peoples in the east. The Hittite-Egyptian rivalry becomes the defining struggle of the late Bronze Age, with neither side able to secure a decisive victory. Future generations look back on this period as a time of chaos and uncertainty, with the once-mighty Nile now a symbol of division rather than unity.

3. Cultural Exchange: A Hybrid Civilization Emerges

Despite the constant warfare, the Hittites and Egyptians are not immune to each other's cultural influence. Over time, a unique hybrid civilization emerges, blending elements of Hittite and Egyptian art, religion, and governance. Hittite legal codes are introduced in Egypt, while Egyptian hieroglyphs make their way to Hattusa, the Hittite capital. The two cultures, though often at odds, begin to meld in unexpected ways. The phrase "As strange as a Hittite scribe" becomes the ancient Near Eastern equivalent of "a fish out of water," as Hittite bureaucrats struggle to learn Egyptian hieroglyphs and priests try to figure out how to integrate storm gods with sun gods. The resulting cultural fusion leads to some bizarre yet fascinating developments: temples dedicated to both the Egyptian god Ra and the Hittite god Tarhun spring up, with rituals that involve both Nile water and Anatolian beer. The hybrid art style that emerges—think sphinxes with Hittite helmets—becomes highly sought after by collectors in later centuries. The two civilizations' merging also leads to the development of a more unified legal and administrative system, albeit one that's a nightmare for anyone trying to follow the paperwork.

4. Economic Boom and Bust: The Nile Trade Route Disrupted

The Nile River, the lifeblood of Egypt, becomes a contested trade route as the Hittites seek to control the flow of goods between Upper and Lower Egypt. This leads to periods of economic boom for those under Hittite control, as they tap into Egypt's wealth, but also to periods of bust as the constant warfare disrupts trade and agriculture. The phrase "Nile gold" takes on a new meaning as the Hittites exploit Egypt's resources to fund their empire. Hittite merchants grow wealthy trading Egyptian grain, papyrus, and gold across the Mediterranean, while Egyptian farmers suffer under the burden of heavy taxation and disrupted irrigation systems. The economic disparity between the north and south deepens, leading to increased tension and periodic uprisings by disgruntled Egyptian peasants. The constant back-and-forth over control of the Nile leads to a cycle of boom and bust, with both the Hittite rulers and Egyptian elites struggling to maintain their wealth and power. Future economic historians debate whether the short-term gains of Hittite control were worth the long-term damage to Egypt's agricultural base.

5. Diplomatic Chess: The Hittites in Global Politics

With a foothold in Egypt, the Hittites become a more prominent player in the international politics of the ancient Near East. They use their control of the Nile to negotiate from a position of strength, forming alliances with other regional powers like the Mitanni and the Mycenaeans. The Hittite king, now styling himself as Pharaoh as well, becomes one of the most influential rulers of the ancient world. The phrase "Hittite diplomacy" becomes synonymous with cunning and strategic maneuvering, as the Hittite rulers expertly play off their rivals against each other. The Hittites' control of Egypt gives them leverage in negotiations with other great powers, leading to a series of alliances, betrayals, and marriages that keep the balance of power constantly shifting. The Hittite king's court becomes a hotbed of intrigue, with envoys from all over the ancient world vying for influence and favor. Future historians marvel at the complex web of Hittite diplomacy, with some suggesting that their mastery of statecraft was as important to their success as their military prowess.

6. The Exodus Reimagined: A Different Biblical Story

The Hittite control of Egypt inevitably influences the Hebrews, who, according to the Bible, were living in Egypt at the time. The story of the Exodus takes on a new dimension as the Hebrews find themselves caught between the Hittite rulers in the north and the native Egyptians in the south. The eventual flight of the Hebrews from Egypt becomes a story not just of escape from bondage but also of navigating the treacherous waters of Hittite-Egyptian rivalry. The phrase "Caught between Pharaohs" becomes a colorful way to describe a no-win situation, as the Hebrews are forced to deal with two competing powers during their time in Egypt. The biblical narrative of the Exodus is reinterpreted in this context, with Moses negotiating not just with the Egyptian Pharaoh but also with Hittite overlords. The plagues take on a more complex role, possibly seen as divine retribution against both Egyptian and Hittite oppressors. The eventual departure of the Hebrews from Egypt is depicted as a desperate flight through a war-torn land, with the Red Sea parting not just as a divine miracle but also as a tactical retreat from two hostile forces. Future religious scholars debate the implications of this dual oppression, leading to new interpretations of the Exodus story in Jewish, Christian, and even Hittite religious traditions.

7. Religious Turmoil: Clash of the Gods

The Hittite expansion into Egypt brings about a clash of religious traditions that leaves both populations bewildered. The Egyptians, deeply devoted to their gods like Ra, Osiris, and Isis, are now faced with the Hittite pantheon, which includes storm gods, sun deities, and strange rituals involving bulls and sacred stones. Religious syncretism occurs, but not without tension and occasional outright rebellion. The phrase "Worship wars" becomes an all-too-common description of the religious conflicts that plague the Hittite-Egyptian empire. Egyptian priests resist the introduction of Hittite deities into their temples, while Hittite nobles struggle to understand why anyone would mummify their dead instead of just burning them on a pyre.

The resulting religious turmoil leads to a series of reforms, decrees, and occasional purges as the Hittite rulers attempt to impose a unified religious policy. The fusion of Hittite and Egyptian religious practices results in some bizarre hybrid rituals, such as bull sacrifices followed by prayers to Osiris. Future generations are left to puzzle over ancient texts that refer to gods with both Egyptian and Hittite names, leading to endless debates among scholars and priests alike.

8. The Hittite Language in Egypt: A Linguistic Revolution

As the Hittites establish control over northern Egypt, their language begins to spread, particularly among the elite and administrative classes. The Hittite cuneiform script starts to appear alongside Egyptian hieroglyphs, and bilingual inscriptions become common. Over time, a new hybrid language emerges, blending elements of both Hittite and Egyptian, further complicating the already intricate landscape of ancient Near Eastern languages. The phrase "Lost in translation" becomes particularly relevant as scribes and officials struggle to navigate the linguistic complexities of the Hittite-Egyptian empire. The hybrid language that develops becomes the lingua franca of the ruling class, but it creates confusion and miscommunication among the general population. Future linguists have a field day trying to decipher the resulting mix of cuneiform and hieroglyphs, leading to a whole new field of study: Hittito-Egyptian philology. The linguistic blending also influences the development of other languages in the region, with traces of Hittite vocabulary making their way into Coptic and even early Greek. The later history of writing in the Near East is marked by the challenges posed by this period of linguistic experimentation, with scholars both cursing and celebrating the complexity of ancient texts.

9. Technological Exchange: Hittite Iron Meets Egyptian Craftsmanship

The Hittites, known for their advanced ironworking techniques, bring their technology to Egypt, where it is eagerly adopted and refined by Egyptian craftsmen. The combination of Hittite iron and Egyptian artistry leads to a new era of technological innovation, with advancements in weaponry, tools, and construction that benefit both Hittites and Egyptians. The phrase "Forged in iron, adorned in gold" becomes the slogan of the Hittite-Egyptian empire's new industrial age. The blending of Hittite and Egyptian techniques leads to the production of high-quality iron weapons and tools, as well as stunning works of art that incorporate both iron and gold. The military power of the empire is bolstered by these technological advancements, with the Hittite-Egyptian army becoming one of the most formidable forces in the ancient world. The influence of this technological exchange spreads beyond the empire's borders, with neighboring civilizations adopting Hittite ironworking and Egyptian craftsmanship. The later development of metallurgy in the Near East and Mediterranean is heavily influenced by this period, with the Hittite-Egyptian empire setting the standard for technological excellence.

10. The Fall of an Empire: The Hittite-Egyptian Collapse

Despite their initial success, the Hittites' expansion into Egypt eventually overstretches the empire. The constant warfare, cultural tensions, and economic strain take their toll, leading to internal strife and rebellion. The Hittite-Egyptian empire, once a formidable power, begins to crumble, with both Hittite and Egyptian factions vying for control. The collapse of the empire sends shockwaves throughout the ancient Near East, leading to a power vacuum that other civilizations rush to fill. The phrase "Too big to fail" becomes the ironic epitaph of the Hittite-Egyptian empire. The collapse of the empire leads to the emergence of new powers in the region, including the rise of the Neo-Assyrian Empire and the eventual dominance of Persia. The fall of the Hittite-Egyptian empire also accelerates the spread of new technologies, languages, and religious ideas across the Near East, as refugees and former subjects scatter to neighboring lands. The later history of the region is shaped by the legacy of the Hittite-Egyptian experiment, with future rulers both learning from and repeating the mistakes of their predecessors. The ruins of the once-great empire become a source of fascination for archaeologists and historians, who debate the causes of its downfall and the impact it had on the development of civilization in the ancient world.

Conclusion

If the Hittites had successfully expanded into Egypt, the balance of power in the ancient Near East would have been dramatically altered. The resulting Hittite-Egyptian empire would have faced constant challenges as it navigated the complexities of ruling two distinct cultures, leading to a fascinating and tumultuous period in history. The cultural, technological, and political exchanges between the Hittites and Egyptians would have left a lasting mark on the region, shaping the development of future civilizations. And somewhere in this alternate history, a weary Hittite scribe, tasked with recording yet another decree in both cuneiform and hieroglyphs, might have sighed and said, "Next time, let's just stick to Anatolia."

What If the Ancient Athenian Democracy Had Never Been Established?

The Background

In the late 6th century BCE, Athens was a hotbed of political innovation, where the seeds of democracy were sown by reformers like Solon and Cleisthenes. They laid the groundwork for a radical experiment in governance where every (male, free, land-owning, non-slave, Athenian-born) citizen had a say in how the city-state was run. This was revolutionary—a government not by the few, but by the many, or at least by a few more people than usual. Athenian democracy became the model for later democratic systems in the Western world, inspiring everything from the Roman Republic to modern-day parliaments. But what if, instead of embracing democracy, Athens had stuck to its oligarchic roots or devolved into outright tyranny? What if the birthplace of democracy had never given birth at all?

Let's imagine that around 508 BCE, just as Cleisthenes is about to introduce his groundbreaking reforms, a different faction seizes power. Perhaps it's a group of wealthy aristocrats who prefer the good old days when power was concentrated in the hands of the elite, or maybe it's a charismatic tyrant who convinces the people that democracy is too messy, too chaotic, and frankly, too much paperwork. The result? Athenian democracy is snuffed out before it even begins, leaving the city-state under the control of an oligarchy or a tyranny.

The 10 Possible Things That Would Happen

1. The Rule of the Few: Oligarchs Keep the Power

Without the establishment of democracy, Athens remains firmly in the grip of an oligarchic elite. The wealthy few continue to run the show, keeping the masses out of political decisions and maintaining their privileged status. The Assembly? More like a gathering of the city's richest families to discuss how best to keep their power intact. Ordinary Athenians, instead of debating policies in the Agora, find themselves back at work, grumbling about how the rich always get richer. The phrase "It's good to be an oligarch" becomes the ancient version of "It's good to be king," as the ruling elite enjoy their unchallenged dominance. The lack of political participation leads to widespread resentment among the common people, but without a democratic outlet, this discontent simmers beneath the surface. Future generations of Athenians grow up learning that political power is reserved for those with wealth and connections, leading to a deeply entrenched class divide. The concept of equality before the law remains a foreign idea, and the later development of Western political thought takes a very different trajectory, with oligarchy becoming the norm rather than the exception.

2. Philosophy Without Democracy: Plato's Dream, Aristotle's Nightmare

The absence of democracy in Athens has profound implications for its intellectual life. Without the vibrant debates and political experimentation of a democratic society, Athenian philosophers find themselves grappling with a more limited set of ideas. Plato, instead of critiquing democracy in his dialogues, becomes a staunch defender of the oligarchic system, arguing that the best rulers are those born to it. Aristotle, meanwhile, scratches his head trying to figure out how to categorize a city-state where political participation is limited to a select few. The phrase "Philosopher kings are the best kings" becomes Plato's rallying cry, as he writes treatises extolling the virtues of oligarchic rule. The famous "Allegory of the Cave" is reimagined as a metaphor for the common people's inability to see the light of true leadership, which of course, is embodied by the oligarchs. Aristotle, less enamored with the whole idea, ends up focusing on natural sciences instead of politics, leading to a less developed political theory in his *Politics*. The later development of political philosophy in the West is heavily influenced by this oligarchic slant, with future thinkers pondering how best to preserve the rule of the few, rather than how to empower the many.

3. No Pericles, No Golden Age: Athenian Culture Takes a Different Path

Without democracy, Athens never experiences the same cultural flourishing that marked the Age of Pericles. The great building projects—the Parthenon, the temples on the Acropolis—are either scaled back or repurposed to glorify the ruling elite rather than the city-state as a whole. The arts still develop, but they're more focused on glorifying individual patrons than celebrating the collective achievements of the polis. The phrase "Oligarch chic" becomes the style of the era, as wealthy Athenians commission grand villas and private temples instead of public monuments. The drama of Sophocles and Euripides shifts from exploring the moral dilemmas of citizens to flattering the egos of the elite. Instead of tragedies that examine the flaws and strengths of democracy, we get plays about the trials and triumphs of the rich and powerful. The famous Athenian sculpture takes on a more self-indulgent tone, with statues of the oligarchs' families filling the city's public spaces. Future historians look back at this period and see a city-state that, while culturally rich, lacked the unifying spirit and civic pride that characterized democratic Athens.

4. No Citizen Soldiers: The Military Decline

In the absence of democracy, the Athenian military doesn't evolve into the powerful citizen army that historically repelled the Persians and dominated the Aegean. The navy, too, suffers as the idea of citizens rowing the triremes seems less appealing to the oligarchs who prefer to hire mercenaries. The famous battles of Marathon and Salamis either end in defeat or are won with heavy reliance on hired soldiers, leaving Athens with a far less robust military tradition. The phrase "Mercenaries never die, they just run out of coin" becomes the oligarchs' motto as they rely more on hired hands than on citizen soldiers. The lack of civic pride and personal investment in the city's defense leads to a weaker Athenian military, which struggles to defend against external threats. The Persians, sensing an opportunity, launch more successful invasions, and Athens finds itself a pawn in the larger geopolitical struggles of the Near East. The later development of the Delian League, if it happens at all, is less of a cooperative alliance and more of a Hellenistic protection racket, with Athens constantly scrambling to maintain control. The legendary tales of Athenian military prowess never materialize, leaving Sparta to dominate the historical narrative of Greek warfare.

5. The Peloponnesian War: A Shorter, Less Tragic Affair

Without a democratic Athens to provoke it, the Peloponnesian War either doesn't happen at all or plays out very differently. Sparta, while still wary of Athens' power, doesn't feel the same ideological threat from an oligarchic neighbor. The conflict, if it occurs, is more about territory and resources than about the clash between democracy and oligarchy. As a result, the war is shorter, less devastating, and doesn't lead to the same kind of existential crisis for Athens. The phrase "War without drama" becomes the tagline for the Peloponnesian conflict, as the ideological fervor that fueled the real war is notably absent. Without the Athenian democracy to rally around, there's less at stake for both sides, leading to fewer epic battles and more drawn-out skirmishes. The war ends with a negotiated settlement rather than a crushing defeat, and Athens, while weakened, doesn't face the same catastrophic decline. The lack of a dramatic Peloponnesian War means that Thucydides doesn't write his famous history, and future generations are deprived of his insights into the dangers of hubris and the nature of power. Instead, they get a much duller account of a conflict that failed to live up to its potential.

6. No Socratic Method: Philosophy Stagnates

The lack of a democratic environment stifles the development of critical thinking in Athens. Socrates, rather than wandering the Agora engaging in provocative dialogue, finds himself sidelined or even silenced by the oligarchs, who have little patience for a philosopher who questions everything. Without the free exchange of ideas fostered by democracy, the philosophical tradition in Athens doesn't flourish in the same way, and the famous Socratic Method never takes off. The phrase "Don't ask questions, just accept" becomes the unspoken rule in oligarchic Athens, where philosophy is more about reinforcing the status quo than challenging it. Socrates, instead of becoming a martyr for free thought, ends up as a footnote in history, overshadowed by more conformist thinkers who prefer to stay on the good side of the ruling class. Plato, if he writes at all, produces far more conservative works that glorify the oligarchy rather than exploring the depths of human knowledge and morality. The later development of Western philosophy is significantly stunted, with fewer opportunities for the kind of intellectual breakthroughs that characterized classical Athens. The Enlightenment, if it comes at all, is delayed by centuries, leaving future generations with a much less robust intellectual heritage.

7. No Athenian Empire: A Lesser Influence in the Mediterranean

Without the driving force of democracy and the collective ambition it fostered, Athens never establishes the Delian League or builds an empire. The city-state remains a regional power but doesn't project its influence across the Aegean and beyond. The golden age of Athenian dominance, with its cultural and military achievements, never materializes, leaving a power vacuum that other Greek states rush to fill. The phrase "Athens, the also-ran" becomes the way historians refer to the city-state that never quite lived up to its potential. Without an empire to build or maintain, Athens remains relatively isolated, its influence limited to the immediate region. The cultural achievements of the city, while still notable, never reach the same heights as they did in our timeline. The spread of Greek culture across the Mediterranean is more fragmented, with Sparta, Corinth, and other city-states playing a larger role in shaping the Hellenistic world. The later Roman Republic, when it rises, finds less inspiration in Athens and more in the militaristic traditions of Sparta, leading to a very different development of Western civilization.

8. Sparta Dominates: A Different Hellenic World

Without a democratic Athens to challenge it, Sparta emerges as the undisputed leader of the Greek world. The militaristic and austere Spartan way of life becomes the dominant cultural force in Greece, with other city-states either aligning themselves with Sparta or facing subjugation. The Hellenic world, instead of being a patchwork of diverse political systems, becomes a Spartan hegemony where military prowess and discipline are valued above all else. The phrase "All roads lead to Sparta" becomes the new reality of the Greek world, as the Spartan model of governance and society spreads across the region. The cultural and intellectual achievements of Athens are overshadowed by the Spartan emphasis on order and stability. Future generations of Greeks grow up learning the virtues of obedience and discipline, with less emphasis on the arts, philosophy, and individualism. The later development of the Greek world is marked by a uniformity that stifles innovation and creativity, with the rich diversity of thought that characterized classical Greece never fully emerging. The legacy of the Hellenic world becomes one of military might rather than cultural brilliance, with the Roman Empire drawing more from Spartan than Athenian traditions.

9. No Western Democracy: A Different Political Evolution

The absence of Athenian democracy means that the concept of rule by the people never gains traction in the ancient world. The Roman Republic, instead of borrowing democratic elements from Athens, develops along more autocratic lines, with power concentrated in the hands of a few elite families. The idea of democracy as a viable political system remains a fringe concept, explored by only a few obscure philosophers but never put into practice. The phrase "Democracy is a dream" becomes the prevailing wisdom of the ancient world, as the concept never takes root in the political systems of the time. The Roman Empire, when it rises, is far more authoritarian, with less emphasis on public participation and more on imperial control. The later development of Western political thought is heavily influenced by this autocratic tradition, with ideas of individual rights and representative government taking much longer to emerge. The Renaissance, if it occurs, is focused more on centralizing power than on rediscovering democratic ideals. The Enlightenment philosophers have a much tougher time making their case for democracy, as the world lacks a successful historical example to point to. The modern world, when it finally develops, is marked by more centralized, less participatory forms of government, with democracy remaining a rare and fragile experiment.

10. A Darker Legacy: The Loss of Athenian Ideals

Without Athenian democracy, the values that we associate with classical Athens—freedom of speech, public debate, civic participation—never become part of the Western tradition. The idea of the "citizen" as an active participant in the governance of the state remains underdeveloped, and the concept of individual rights is much slower to emerge. The legacy of Athens is one of oligarchic rule, with little to inspire future generations to seek a different path. The phrase "Liberty is for the few" becomes the underlying principle of Western political thought, as the ideals of freedom and equality never gain widespread acceptance. The development of human rights is delayed by centuries, with most societies accepting the idea that power naturally belongs to a privileged elite. The later struggles for independence and democracy in Europe and the Americas are more difficult and bloodier, as the intellectual foundation for these movements is weaker. The modern world, when it finally embraces democratic ideals, does so more out of necessity than inspiration, with the path to freedom and equality marked by more setbacks and fewer triumphs. The Athenian ideals of civic participation and public debate remain a historical curiosity, studied by a few scholars but never fully integrated into the political systems of the time.

Conclusion

If the ancient Athenian democracy had never been established, the course of Western political thought would have been dramatically altered. The absence of democracy in Athens would have led to a more autocratic and oligarchic tradition in the ancient world, with far-reaching consequences for the development of political systems and ideas. The values that we associate with classical Athens—freedom, equality, civic participation—would have remained underdeveloped, leading to a very different trajectory for Western civilization. And somewhere in this alternate history, an Athenian citizen, gazing out over an oligarch-dominated city-state, might have muttered, "Well, at least we don't have to sit through those long, boring Assembly meetings anymore."

What If the Etruscans Had Developed a Writing System That Spread Widely?

The Background

The Etruscans, a mysterious and sophisticated civilization in ancient Italy, were already pretty advanced for their time. They had a flourishing culture, impressive art, complex religious rituals, and a knack for city-building that would later influence the Romans. However, when it came to writing, the Etruscan script didn't quite make the impact one might expect. Their writing system, which borrowed heavily from the Greek alphabet, was used mainly for religious texts, inscriptions, and the occasional shopping list. It never really spread beyond their own cities, and much of it remains undeciphered to this day. But what if the Etruscans had developed a more accessible, practical writing system that spread far and wide across Europe? What if their script became the basis for the written languages of the continent, influencing the development of European civilization in ways we can only imagine?

Let's imagine that around 700 BCE, an innovative Etruscan scribe—let's call him Linguisticus Magnificus—invents a new, streamlined version of the Etruscan script. This script is easy to learn, adaptable to different languages, and, most importantly, it's catchy. Traders, priests, and scholars across the Mediterranean and beyond start using it, and before long, the Etruscan script becomes the lingua franca of the ancient world. It spreads like wildfire, leaving its mark on the development of written language in Europe.

The 10 Possible Things That Would Happen

1. The Rise of the Etruscan Alphabet: The A-B-C's of Europe

With the Etruscan script becoming the dominant writing system, it quickly overtakes other alphabets in popularity. The Greeks, ever the trendsetters, adopt it with minor modifications, and it spreads to their colonies and beyond. The Romans, seeing a good thing when they steal it, adopt the Etruscan script for Latin, leading to the rise of a unified writing system across the Roman Empire. The phrase "It's written in Etruscan" becomes the ancient equivalent of "It's written in the stars," as the script becomes ubiquitous across Europe. Future schoolchildren in Rome grumble about having to learn their Etruscan letters, while merchants use the script to keep track of trade across the Mediterranean. The spread of the Etruscan alphabet leads to a more uniform written language across Europe, facilitating communication, trade, and the exchange of ideas. The later development of European languages is heavily influenced by this early adoption of the Etruscan script, with future linguists marveling at how one ancient alphabet could shape the course of history.

2. Etruscan Manuscripts: The Foundation of European Literature

As the Etruscan script spreads, so does the use of written language for literature, law, and record-keeping. The Etruscans, known for their religious rituals and complex ceremonies, begin to produce written manuscripts that are copied and distributed across Europe. These texts cover everything from religious hymns to epic poetry, and they become the foundation of European literary traditions. The phrase "Etruscan classics" enters the lexicon as scholars across Europe study these early texts. Future generations of writers are influenced by the themes and styles of Etruscan literature, leading to the development of a rich literary tradition that blends Etruscan,

Greek, and Roman influences. The spread of Etruscan manuscripts also helps to preserve knowledge across Europe, with ancient texts being copied and recopied by scribes in monasteries and libraries. The later Renaissance, when it comes, is fueled by the rediscovery of these Etruscan manuscripts, leading to a cultural revival that owes much to the literary achievements of the Etruscans.

3. Etruscan-Latin Hybrid: A New Lingua Franca

With the Etruscan script adopted by the Romans, the Latin language develops with a heavy Etruscan influence. Over time, a hybrid language emerges that blends elements of Latin and Etruscan, creating a new lingua franca that spreads across the Roman Empire. This hybrid language becomes the basis for the development of the Romance languages, with traces of Etruscan vocabulary and grammar persisting in modern European languages. The phrase "Speaking in tongues" takes on a new meaning as Europeans find themselves using words and phrases with Etruscan roots without even realizing it. The development of the Romance languages is marked by a strong Etruscan influence, with modern Italian, Spanish, and French retaining elements of the ancient language. Linguists in the future scratch their heads over the etymology of certain words, leading to endless debates about the extent of Etruscan influence on modern languages. The hybrid Etruscan-Latin language also serves as a unifying force in the Roman Empire, facilitating communication and governance across diverse regions.

4. Etruscan-Inspired Architecture: The Written Word in Stone

The spread of the Etruscan script leads to its use in monumental inscriptions and public buildings. The Etruscans, known for their engineering prowess, begin to incorporate their script into architectural designs, creating buildings adorned with inscriptions that tell the stories of their construction, purpose, and dedication. This practice spreads to other cultures, leading to a tradition of inscribing important texts on public monuments. The phrase "Reading the walls" becomes a literal activity as people stroll through cities filled with Etruscan-inscribed buildings. The tradition of inscribing public texts leads to the preservation of important documents and historical records, with future archaeologists finding entire histories carved into stone. The influence of Etruscan architecture spreads across Europe, with Roman, Greek, and later European buildings featuring inscriptions in the Etruscan script. This practice continues into the Middle Ages and the Renaissance, with public buildings and monuments serving as both architectural marvels and repositories of knowledge.

5. A Writing Revolution: Literacy Spreads Across Europe

The simplicity and adaptability of the Etruscan script make it accessible to a wide range of people, leading to a rapid increase in literacy across Europe. Merchants, artisans, and even common farmers begin to learn the script, using it for everything from business transactions to personal letters. This widespread literacy contributes to the spread of knowledge and ideas, laying the groundwork for future intellectual and cultural developments. The phrase "Knowledge is power" takes on new significance as literacy rates soar across Europe. The widespread use of the Etruscan script leads to the development of a more educated and informed populace, with people using their newfound literacy to engage in trade, politics, and cultural exchange. The rise in literacy also contributes to the spread of new ideas and technologies, as written instructions and diagrams become more widely available. The later development of universities and educational institutions is heavily influenced by this early writing revolution, with the Etruscan script serving as the foundation for academic study across Europe.

6. Religious Texts and Etruscan Spirituality: A New Pantheon

With the Etruscan script spreading far and wide, so too does Etruscan religion. The Etruscans, known for their elaborate rituals and pantheon of gods, begin to record their religious practices in writing. These texts are disseminated across Europe, influencing the development of religious traditions and practices in other cultures. The Etruscan pantheon, with its unique deities and rituals, becomes a part of the spiritual landscape of Europe. The phrase "In the name of Tinia" becomes a common invocation as the Etruscan god of the sky gains followers across Europe. The spread of Etruscan religious texts leads to the incorporation of Etruscan deities into the pantheons of other cultures, with gods like Tinia, Uni, and Menrva becoming household names alongside Zeus and Jupiter. The influence of Etruscan spirituality is felt in the development of Roman religion, with the Etruscan influence persisting even as Christianity begins to spread. Future religious scholars debate the extent of Etruscan influence on early Christian practices, with some arguing that certain rituals and symbols have their roots in Etruscan religion.

7. The Etruscan Codex: The Foundation of European Law

The Etruscans, known for their sophisticated legal system, begin to codify their laws in writing using their script. These legal texts are adopted and adapted by other cultures, including the Romans, who incorporate Etruscan legal principles into their own system. The result is a body of law that spreads across Europe, influencing the development of legal systems for centuries to come. The phrase "By the Etruscan code" becomes the standard for legal proceedings across Europe. The codification of Etruscan law leads to the development of a more consistent and uniform legal system, with principles of justice and fairness enshrined in written texts. The influence of Etruscan law is felt in the development of Roman law, which in turn becomes the foundation for many European legal systems. Future legal scholars study the Etruscan Codex as a foundational text, tracing the evolution of legal principles from ancient times to the modern era. The later development of constitutional law is heavily influenced by this early legal tradition, with the Etruscan emphasis on written codes and contracts shaping the way laws are understood and applied.

8. A Continent of Scribes: The Profession of Writing Flourishes

The widespread adoption of the Etruscan script leads to the rise of a new professional class: the scribes. These skilled individuals are responsible for copying texts, keeping records, and producing official documents. Scribes become highly respected and influential members of society, with their expertise in the Etruscan script giving them access to power and wealth. The phrase "The pen is mightier than the sword" becomes a reality in Etruscan-influenced Europe, where scribes wield significant power. The profession of scribe becomes one of the most sought-after careers, with young people from all walks of life aspiring to master the Etruscan script. Scribes play a key role in the administration of empires, the preservation of knowledge, and the transmission of culture, becoming indispensable to the functioning of society. The influence of scribes extends to the development of literature, science, and philosophy, as they copy and preserve important texts for future generations. The later development of printing technology is seen as a revolution in the world of the scribes, with some celebrating the increased access to knowledge, while others lament the decline of their once-exclusive profession.

9. Etruscan Script and Science: The Dawn of Written Experimentation

The spread of the Etruscan script leads to its use in scientific inquiry and experimentation. Scholars and thinkers begin to record their observations, experiments, and theories in writing, using the script to communicate their findings with others. This written record of scientific knowledge contributes to the development of early scientific methods and lays the foundation for future advancements in science and technology. The phrase "Etruscan science" becomes synonymous with early scientific inquiry, as scholars use the script to document their work. The widespread use of written records leads to the accumulation of knowledge, with scholars building on the work of their predecessors rather than starting from scratch. The Etruscan script facilitates the exchange of scientific ideas across Europe, leading to advancements in fields like medicine, astronomy, and engineering. The later development of the scientific revolution is influenced by this early tradition of written experimentation, with the Etruscan script serving as a bridge between ancient and modern science.

10. The Renaissance of the Etruscan Script: A Revival of Ancient Knowledge

The Etruscan script, having spread widely across Europe, experiences a resurgence during the Renaissance. Scholars, artists, and intellectuals rediscover ancient Etruscan texts and inscriptions, leading to a revival of interest in Etruscan culture and knowledge. The Renaissance, already fueled by the rediscovery of Greek and Roman texts, is enriched by the addition of Etruscan manuscripts, which offer new perspectives and insights. The phrase "Etruscan revival" becomes the catchphrase of the Renaissance, as scholars eagerly study the ancient texts. The rediscovery of Etruscan manuscripts leads to a renewed interest in the history, art, and science of the ancient world, with Etruscan influences permeating Renaissance culture. Artists begin to incorporate Etruscan motifs into their work, while architects draw inspiration from Etruscan designs. The revival of the Etruscan script also leads to a deeper understanding of ancient history, with scholars piecing together the connections between Etruscan, Greek, and Roman civilizations. The later development of modern European culture is heavily influenced by this Etruscan revival, with the script serving as a symbol of the enduring legacy of the ancient world.

Conclusion

If the Etruscans had developed a writing system that spread widely, the course of European history would have been dramatically altered. The Etruscan script would have influenced the development of written language, literature, law, science, and culture across the continent, leaving a lasting mark on the civilizations that followed. The spread of the Etruscan script would have facilitated communication, education, and the exchange of ideas, laying the foundation for the intellectual and cultural achievements of Europe. And somewhere in this alternate history, a Renaissance scholar, poring over an ancient Etruscan manuscript, might have smiled and said, "Who knew those mysterious Etruscans would end up writing the story of Europe?"

What If the Sumerians Had Discovered the Use of Iron Earlier?

The Background

The Sumerians, often credited as the creators of the first great civilization in Mesopotamia, were masters of many things: cuneiform writing, monumental ziggurats, irrigation systems, and, of course, the invention of the wheel. They were a busy bunch, turning the marshy lands between the Tigris and Euphrates into the cradle of civilization. However, one thing they didn't quite get to before others was the use of iron. While they were content with their bronze tools and weapons, others eventually figured out that iron, while more stubborn to work with, was far superior in strength and availability. This discovery would eventually lead to the decline of bronze-using civilizations like Sumer. But what if the Sumerians, with all their inventive spirit, had stumbled upon ironworking a few centuries earlier? What if they, instead of the Hittites, became the Iron Age trailblazers?

Let's imagine that around 2500 BCE, some enterprising Sumerian metallurgist—let's call him An-Shar the Smelter—discovers that heating certain types of ore produces a metal far stronger and more durable than bronze. An-Shar, instead of keeping this to himself (because who could keep such a secret?), shares his findings with the Sumerian elites, who, being the practical sort, quickly see the military and agricultural benefits of this new material. Soon, the Sumerians are outfitting their soldiers with iron weapons, plowing their fields with iron tools, and generally enjoying the perks of being a few steps ahead of everyone else in the metallurgy game.

The 10 Possible Things That Would Happen

1. Sumerian Supremacy: Iron-Wielding Warriors Dominate Mesopotamia

With iron weapons in hand, the Sumerians become the undisputed military power in Mesopotamia. Their armies, once comparable to their neighbors, now cut through enemy forces like a hot knife through butter. The Sumerian city-states, once prone to infighting and invasions, consolidate under a single, iron-fisted ruler who establishes a Sumerian empire stretching from the Persian Gulf to the Mediterranean. The phrase "Don't mess with Sumer" becomes the ancient equivalent of "Don't mess with Texas," as neighboring civilizations quickly learn to fear the iron-wielding Sumerians. The Akkadians, who historically conquered Sumer, find themselves on the receiving end of Sumerian expansion instead, with their once-great cities reduced to vassal states. The Sumerian Empire becomes the first true superpower of the ancient world, with its influence spreading far beyond Mesopotamia. Future generations of conquerors, from Babylon to Persia, study the military strategies of the Sumerians, leading to a tradition of iron-wielding warfare that shapes the history of the Near East.

2. The Industrial Revolution of the Bronze Age

Iron tools revolutionize agriculture, construction, and manufacturing in Sumer. Fields are plowed more efficiently, leading to increased agricultural output and population growth. Iron nails, hammers, and saws make building faster and more durable, leading to the construction of even grander ziggurats and city walls. The Sumerians begin exporting their iron goods, becoming the industrial hub of the ancient world. The phrase "It's as strong as Sumerian iron" becomes the hallmark of quality craftsmanship. The

Sumerians, now the world's leading producers of iron goods, see their economy boom as trade flourishes across the region. Merchants from as far away as Egypt and the Indus Valley come to Sumer to trade for iron tools and weapons, bringing with them new ideas, goods, and technologies. This economic prosperity leads to a golden age of Sumerian culture, with advancements in art, science, and literature rivaling anything seen in the ancient world. The later history of Mesopotamia is marked by the continued dominance of Sumerian iron, with other civilizations playing catch-up for centuries.

3. Sumerian Empire: A Dynasty of Iron Kings

The Sumerians, now armed with iron weapons and enjoying economic prosperity, establish a long-lasting dynasty of kings who rule over a unified empire. These kings, known as the "Iron Lords," oversee the expansion of Sumerian influence into neighboring regions, from Anatolia to the Levant. The empire becomes known for its centralized administration, advanced infrastructure, and iron-clad laws. The phrase "Iron rule of law" takes on a literal meaning as the Sumerian kings enforce their will with iron swords and iron fists. The Sumerian Empire, with its network of roads, canals, and fortresses, becomes the most organized and efficient state of the ancient world. The idea of a centralized empire, governed by a strong ruler and supported by advanced technology, influences the development of later empires, from Persia to Rome. Future historians look back on the Sumerian Empire as the model for all subsequent empires, with the "Iron Lords" becoming legendary figures in the annals of history.

4. The Iron Age Literacy Boom: Writing Goes Ironclad

The discovery of iron not only revolutionizes warfare and industry but also impacts writing. Sumerian scribes, tired of scratching cuneiform onto clay tablets with reed styluses, begin using iron-tipped styluses to carve more durable inscriptions into stone and metal. This leads to a proliferation of written records, legal codes, and literary works that survive the ravages of time. The phrase "Written in stone" gains new meaning as Sumerian texts, inscribed on iron tablets and stone monuments, endure for millennia. The Sumerians become known as the most literate civilization of their time, with vast libraries filled with records, laws, and epic poems. The famous *Epic of Gilgamesh*, instead of being written on fragile clay tablets, is carved into an iron pillar that becomes a wonder of the ancient world. Future archaeologists are delighted to find entire archives of Sumerian texts preserved in perfect condition, leading to a deep understanding of Sumerian history, culture, and religion. The later development of writing and record-keeping in other civilizations is influenced by this Sumerian innovation, with iron styluses becoming the tool of choice for scribes across the Near East.

5. Sumerian Iron Trade: The First Global Economy

The Sumerians, recognizing the value of their iron technology, establish extensive trade networks to export iron goods across the known world. Iron becomes the most sought-after commodity of the ancient world, with Sumerian traders setting up colonies and trade outposts from the shores of the Mediterranean to the mountains of Iran. The Sumerian economy, already prosperous, becomes the engine driving the first global economy. The phrase "As rich as a Sumerian merchant" becomes the standard for wealth and success. The trade of Sumerian iron goods leads to increased cultural exchange, with Sumerian ideas, art, and religion spreading far beyond Mesopotamia. The cities of Sumer, now thriving commercial hubs, attract traders, scholars, and adventurers from all corners of the ancient world. The prosperity generated by the iron trade funds the construction of grand temples, palaces, and public works, making Sumerian cities the envy of the ancient world. The later development of trade routes, such as the Silk Road, is influenced by these early Sumerian networks, with Sumerian iron goods remaining in high demand for centuries.

6. A New Pantheon: The Gods of Iron

The Sumerians, known for their rich pantheon of gods, begin to associate iron with divine power. Iron becomes a symbol of strength, protection, and justice, and new deities emerge in the Sumerian religion to embody these qualities. Temples dedicated to the "Iron Gods" are built across Mesopotamia, and iron weapons and tools are offered as sacred gifts. The phrase "By the hammer of the Iron God" becomes a common oath among Sumerians. The worship of the Iron Gods spreads along with the iron trade, influencing the religious practices of neighboring civilizations. The Sumerian god Nergal, traditionally associated with war and death, takes on new attributes as the "Lord of Iron," becoming one of the most feared and revered deities in the Sumerian pantheon. The association of iron with divine power influences the development of religious iconography, with iron becoming a sacred material used in the construction of temples, altars, and religious artifacts. The later development of religious symbolism in other cultures is influenced by this Sumerian innovation, with iron continuing to be associated with strength and divinity for centuries to come.

7. The Great Sumerian Wall: An Iron Defense

With their newfound ironworking skills, the Sumerians construct a massive wall around their cities, fortified with iron reinforcements. This "Great Sumerian Wall" becomes an impregnable defense against invaders, allowing the Sumerians to focus on expanding their empire without worrying about the security of their cities. The phrase "Safe as Sumer" becomes a testament to the security provided by the Great Sumerian Wall. The wall, a marvel of engineering, stands as a symbol of Sumerian power and technological prowess. Invaders, from the nomadic tribes of the steppe to the armies of rival city-states, find themselves stymied by the iron-reinforced defenses, leading to a period of unprecedented stability and peace within the Sumerian Empire. The idea of building massive defensive walls spreads to other civilizations, with the Great Sumerian Wall becoming the inspiration for later fortifications, such as the Great Wall of China. The later history of military architecture is heavily influenced by this Sumerian innovation, with iron-reinforced walls becoming a standard feature of fortified cities across the ancient world.

8. The Sumerian Renaissance: A New Age of Art and Science

The economic prosperity and stability brought about by the discovery of iron lead to a cultural renaissance in Sumer. Artists, scholars, and scientists are patronized by the wealthy elite, leading to advancements in art, architecture, mathematics, and astronomy. The Sumerians, already known for their contributions to civilization, take their achievements to new heights. The phrase "The Iron Age of Sumer" becomes synonymous with cultural and intellectual flourishing. The Sumerians develop new artistic techniques, using iron tools to create more intricate and detailed sculptures, pottery, and jewelry. Advances in mathematics and astronomy lead to the creation of more accurate calendars, improved agricultural practices, and a deeper understanding of the cosmos. The Sumerian schools, already the best in Mesopotamia, attract students from across the ancient world, leading to the spread of Sumerian knowledge and ideas. The later development of science and technology in other civilizations is heavily influenced by this Sumerian renaissance, with the achievements of the Iron Age Sumerians serving as the foundation for future advancements.

9. The Iron Throne: Sumerian Politics Reinvented

The Sumerian rulers, now wielding iron weapons and ruling over a prosperous empire, begin to associate iron with their right to rule. The "Iron Throne" becomes a symbol of the king's authority, and succession disputes are settled through displays of military prowess and strength, rather than inheritance alone. This new political culture leads to the rise of warrior-kings who lead their armies into battle and govern with an iron hand. The phrase "He who wields the iron, rules the land" becomes the guiding principle of Sumerian politics. The rise of warrior-kings leads to a more militaristic society, with the ruling elite prioritizing military strength and expansion over diplomacy and trade. The idea of the "Iron Throne" spreads to other civilizations, influencing the development of monarchical traditions in the ancient world. Future historians look back on this period as the beginning of the "Iron Age of Kings," where power is won and maintained through force rather than inheritance. The later development of feudalism in Europe is influenced by this Sumerian innovation, with the idea of land and power being tied to military service becoming a central feature of medieval society.

10. A Legacy Forged in Iron: Sumerian Influence Endures

The early discovery of iron and the resulting Sumerian dominance leave an indelible mark on the history of the ancient world. The Sumerians, once a fading civilization, become the progenitors of many of the technological, cultural, and political innovations that shape the ancient Near East. Their influence persists long after the decline of their empire, with later civilizations building on the foundations laid by the Sumerians. The phrase "Forged in Sumer" becomes synonymous with innovation and enduring legacy. The Sumerian Empire, with its advancements in ironworking, agriculture, law, and culture, becomes the model for subsequent civilizations in Mesopotamia and beyond. The later Babylonian, Assyrian, and Persian empires all trace their roots to Sumerian innovations, with iron technology continuing to play a central role in their development. The influence of Sumerian culture and technology spreads to the Mediterranean, Egypt, and even into Europe, shaping the course of history for millennia. Future historians regard the early discovery of iron by the Sumerians as one of the pivotal moments in human history, setting the stage for the rise of civilization as we know it.

Conclusion

If the Sumerians had discovered the use of iron earlier, the course of ancient history would have been dramatically altered. The Sumerians would have gained a significant technological advantage, leading to military dominance, economic prosperity, and cultural achievements that would have shaped the development of the ancient Near East. The legacy of the Sumerian Iron Age would have influenced the rise of subsequent civilizations, leaving an enduring mark on the history of humanity. And somewhere in this alternate history, a Sumerian scholar, gazing at a monument inscribed with the deeds of an iron-wielding king, might have smiled and said, "It's amazing what a little metal can do."

What If the Wars of the Diadochi Were Taken to the Next Level?

The Background

After the death of Alexander the Great in 323 BCE, the vast empire he had conquered from Greece to India suddenly found itself without a clear successor. What followed was a chaotic, decades-long series of conflicts known as the Wars of the Diadochi, where Alexander's former generals and family members (the *Diadochi*, or "successors") battled each other for control of different parts of the empire. The wars were already intense, filled with betrayals, assassinations, and epic battles, but what if they were taken to the next level? What if the Diadochi decided that instead of merely carving up the empire, they should pursue absolute dominance at any cost—escalating the conflict to levels that would make even Alexander proud (or horrified)?

Let's imagine that, instead of the somewhat reluctant acceptance of the division of Alexander's empire, one particularly ambitious Diadoch—let's call him Cassander the Calculated—decides that sharing is for the weak. Cassander rallies his forces and embarks on a campaign to not just control his portion of the empire, but to annihilate his rivals completely. His unrelenting pursuit of total power sets off a chain reaction among the other Diadochi, leading to an all-out war that makes the original conflicts look like friendly sparring. The Wars of the Diadochi escalate into a brutal, no-holds-barred struggle for absolute power, with each general aiming to reunite Alexander's empire under their own iron fist.

The 10 Possible Things That Would Happen

1. Armageddon of the Ancient World: Total War Engulfs the Empire

As Cassander declares that "There can be only one," the other Diadochi quickly realize that diplomacy and negotiation are off the table. The result is an all-consuming war that spreads across the entire empire. Forget about regional skirmishes—this is a full-blown, continent-spanning conflict that drags every city, village, and citizen into the fray. Armies the size of small nations march across the landscape, leaving nothing but destruction in their wake. The phrase "War to end all wars" is coined about 2,000 years too early. The sheer scale and intensity of the conflict devastate the known world, leading to a level of destruction that wipes out entire cities and reduces once-thriving regions to wastelands. The massive loss of life and resources leads to a dark age that lasts for generations, with future historians referring to this period as the "Great Collapse." The world's population plummets, trade routes are severed, and cultural and technological advancements come to a grinding halt. The legacy of Alexander the Great is tarnished, as people curse his name for leaving such chaos in his wake.

2. The Super Siege: Fortress Cities Become the New Normal

With every major city under threat from these supercharged armies, fortifications go from being a strategic advantage to a necessity for survival. City-states transform themselves into fortress cities, with walls that make Troy's defenses look like a picket fence. Engineers work overtime to develop new siege weapons and defensive tactics, leading to an arms race of fortification and destruction. The phrase "Safe as a city under siege" becomes a bitter joke as no city is truly safe. The escalation in siege warfare leads to increasingly brutal and prolonged battles, with some sieges lasting for years as neither side is willing to back down. The arms race results in innovations like the "super ballista," capable of hurling boulders the size of houses, and the "siege tower of doom," a rolling fortress that terrorizes defenders. The once-majestic cities of the Hellenistic world become scarred, battle-worn shells, with their populations reduced to mere survivors. Future generations grow up surrounded by the ruins of these fortress cities, leading to a culture of paranoia and constant vigilance.

3. The Betrayal Olympics: Backstabbing Becomes an Art Form

In a war where the stakes are total domination or annihilation, loyalty becomes a quaint, outdated concept. The Diadochi, already known for their treacherous tendencies, take betrayal to new heights. Alliances are made and broken on a daily basis, with generals switching sides more often than they change their tunics. Spies, double agents, and secret pacts become the norm, as trust evaporates faster than water in the desert. The phrase "Don't turn your back on a Diadoch" becomes a universal truth. The constant backstabbing and shifting alliances lead to a war where no one can predict who will be fighting whom next. Generals spend as much time watching their own backs as they do leading their armies, resulting in a climate of paranoia and mistrust. The concept of honor in warfare is replaced by cunning and deception, with the most ruthless and underhanded tactics becoming the standard. Future political treatises study this period as the epitome of realpolitik, where power is all that matters and the ends always justify the means.

4. The Birth of Mega-Mercenaries: Soldiers of Fortune Rule the Day

As the wars drag on and the regular armies are decimated, the Diadochi turn increasingly to mercenaries to bolster their ranks. But these aren't your average hired swords. These are professional warriors from all over the ancient world, forming mega-mercenary armies that fight not for loyalty, but for gold and glory. These bands of mercenaries, led by charismatic and ruthless leaders, become powers in their own right, sometimes switching sides in the middle of battle if the price is right. The phrase "In gold we trust" becomes the motto of these mega-mercenaries, who hold the true power in the Diadochi wars. The rise of mercenary armies leads to a shift in the balance of power, as these soldiers of fortune become kingmakers, deciding the fate of battles and even the war itself. The Diadochi, increasingly reliant on these mercenaries, find themselves at the mercy of their own hired guns. The most successful mercenary leaders become wealthy beyond imagination, carving out their own territories and ruling as warlords. Future historians refer to this period as the "Age of the Mercenaries," where loyalty was for sale and the highest bidder ruled the battlefield.

5. The Iron Throne of Babylon: A New Capital of Power

With the conflict dragging on and no end in sight, one of the Diadochi—let's say *Ptolemy the Persistent*—decides that if he can't win by force alone, he'll outlast his rivals by fortifying himself in the most impenetrable stronghold available: Babylon. He declares Babylon the new capital of the empire, building it up as an impregnable fortress-city, complete with walls that make the original ones look like a joke. From here, he plans to outlast all comers, turning Babylon into a symbol of unassailable power. The phrase "All roads lead to Babylon" becomes the reality as the city becomes the focal point of the Diadochi wars. The fortification of Babylon transforms it into the ultimate seat of power, where Ptolemy (or whoever claims it next) rules with an iron fist. The city becomes a mix of luxurious palaces and grim military installations, a place where politics and warfare are inseparable. The rest of the empire's cities suffer as resources and attention are diverted to maintaining Babylon's dominance. The phrase "Babylon's shadow" is used to describe the overwhelming influence the city exerts over the rest of the empire, casting a dark, long shadow over the once-diverse cultures and politics of the Hellenistic world.

6. The Rise of the Diadochi Cults: Gods Among Men

In a bid to legitimize their claims to Alexander's empire, the Diadochi start to fashion themselves not just as kings, but as living gods. Temples are erected, and state-sponsored cults promote the worship of each Diadoch as the divine heir of Alexander, mixing traditional Greek religion with the emerging personality cults. The idea is to inspire fanatical loyalty among their troops and subjects, but instead, it leads to a bizarre religious arms race, with each Diadoch trying to outdo the others in divine splendor. The phrase "Worship at the altar of power" becomes the guiding principle of the Diadochi era. These self-proclaimed god-kings demand not just obedience, but worship, leading to increasingly extravagant displays of divine favor. Cities are filled with statues and temples dedicated to these living deities, who claim to perform miracles and control the fates of men. The population, caught between rival cults, becomes deeply divided, with civil strife breaking out between followers of different Diadochi gods. The rise of these personality cults distorts traditional religious practices, leading to a fragmented and unstable spiritual landscape. Future religious movements are shaped by this period, with some adopting and others vehemently rejecting the idea of rulers as divine beings.

7. The Great Exodus: Refugees Flee the War-Torn World

As the Diadochi wars escalate into a never-ending nightmare, ordinary people begin to flee the destruction en masse. Entire populations migrate in search of safety, leading to a massive exodus from the war zones. These refugees spread out across the ancient world, bringing with them stories of the horrors of the Diadochi wars and influencing the cultures they encounter. The phrase "The wandering peoples" enters the lexicon as entire communities are uprooted by the wars. The mass migration of refugees leads to the spread of Hellenistic culture far beyond its original borders, as these displaced people bring their customs, language, and ideas to new lands. This mixing of cultures creates hybrid societies in places as far away as the western Mediterranean, Persia, and even India. The refugee crisis also leads to the development of new forms of governance and social organization, as the migrating populations seek to rebuild their lives in foreign lands. The later history of the ancient world is marked by the legacy of these wandering peoples, who leave their mark on the civilizations they encounter.

8. The Technological Arms Race: War Machines of the Diadochi

With the wars dragging on and no clear victor in sight, the Diadochi turn to technology to gain an edge. Engineers and inventors are given carte blanche to develop new and terrifying war machines, leading to a technological arms race that makes traditional battle strategies obsolete. From giant siege engines to early prototypes of warships bristling with advanced weaponry, the Diadochi armies become more like mechanized forces of destruction. The phrase "War by invention" becomes the new reality as the Diadochi armies roll out increasingly sophisticated and deadly machines. The technological arms race leads to the development of early forms of artillery, enhanced fortifications, and even rudimentary mechanical devices designed for battlefield use. The cost of war skyrockets as these machines require vast resources to build and maintain, further straining the already fragile economies of the Hellenistic world. The focus on technology over traditional tactics leads to a new class of engineers and inventors who become as powerful as the generals they serve. Future military history is shaped by this period of innovation, with many of the advances made during the Diadochi wars laying the groundwork for later developments in warfare.

9. The War of Shadows: Assassination as an Art Form

As the wars reach a stalemate on the battlefield, the Diadochi turn to more subtle methods of gaining the upper hand—assassination. The art of political murder reaches new heights as each Diadoch employs legions of assassins to eliminate rivals, sabotage enemy plans, and sow chaos behind enemy lines. The war of shadows becomes as important as the war on the battlefield, with intrigue and espionage becoming key components of the Diadochi strategy. The phrase "A knife in the dark" becomes the most feared form of attack, as assassins lurk in every shadow. The rise of assassination as a strategic tool leads to a culture of paranoia among the ruling class, with each Diadoch constantly on guard against betrayal from within. The general population, meanwhile, becomes increasingly disillusioned with their rulers, seeing them as little more than murderers in togas. The constant threat of assassination leads to the development of elaborate security measures, with rulers surrounding themselves with loyal bodyguards and constructing hidden fortresses to avoid public exposure. The later history of political intrigue is heavily influenced by this period, with assassination becoming a common tactic in power struggles across the ancient world.

10. The Collapse of the Hellenistic World: A New Dark Age

After decades of relentless warfare, the Hellenistic world collapses under the weight of its own destruction. The once-great cities of Alexander's empire lie in ruins, their populations decimated by war, famine, and disease. The Diadochi, having fought themselves into exhaustion, leave behind a shattered world with no clear ruler and no unified culture. The Hellenistic world enters a new dark age, where knowledge is lost, and the achievements of the past are forgotten. The phrase "The fall of the Diadochi" becomes synonymous with the collapse of civilization. The destruction wrought by the Diadochi wars leads to the decline of urban life, with cities shrinking or being abandoned altogether. The loss of centralized authority results in the fragmentation of the Hellenistic world into smaller, isolated communities that struggle to survive in the chaos. The advances in art, science, and philosophy made during the Hellenistic period are lost or forgotten, as the population turns its focus to basic survival. The later history of the Mediterranean is marked by the slow recovery from this dark age, with future generations having to rediscover the knowledge and culture that was lost during the wars of the Diadochi.

Conclusion

If the wars of the Diadochi were taken to the next level, the ancient world would have been plunged into a period of unprecedented chaos and destruction. The escalating conflict would have reshaped the political, cultural, and technological landscape of the Hellenistic world, leaving a legacy of war, betrayal, and devastation. The ambition and ruthlessness of the Diadochi would have led to the collapse of civilization as they knew it, creating a dark age that future generations would struggle to overcome. And somewhere in this alternate history, a weary survivor, gazing at the ruins of a once-great city, might have muttered, "Alexander conquered the world, and his successors conquered what was left of it."

What If the Romans Had Never Conquered Britain?

The Background

When Julius Caesar first set his sights on Britain in 55 BCE, he probably thought, "Why not add another rainy island to the Empire?" However, it wasn't until Emperor Claudius in 43 CE that the Romans truly committed to the idea, launching a full-scale invasion and eventually bringing Britain under Roman rule. The Roman occupation left a lasting mark on Britain—roads, baths, Hadrian's Wall, and a whole lot of Latin words for things like "wine" and "money." But what if, instead of successfully conquering Britain, the Romans had decided that the wet, foggy, and rebellious island wasn't worth the trouble? Maybe the locals were just too much of a handful, or perhaps Rome had other priorities. Either way, let's imagine a scenario where the Romans never set foot on British soil—or at least not with the intent of staying.

The 10 Possible Things That Would Happen

1. The Celts Keep Their Island: A Patchwork of Tribes and Kingdoms

Without Roman conquest, Britain remains a land of independent Celtic tribes, each with its own king, chieftain, or druid council. These tribes, from the Catuvellauni to the Iceni, continue to bicker, trade, and occasionally bash each other over the head in the name of honor or cattle. The idea of a unified Britain is as foreign as the Roman toga, and the island remains a patchwork of warring kingdoms. The phrase "A house divided" becomes more like "An island divided," as the various tribes never quite manage to get along. Future historians look back at this period and marvel at the sheer variety of tribal names and alliances, most of which change every few years because, hey, why not? The lack of Roman roads means that travel between tribes is arduous, leading to a slow development of trade and communication. The Celts continue to build their impressive hillforts, but there's no grand Roman architecture to unify or awe them. Future British monarchs look back at this period and think, "If only we'd had an empire to organize us a bit earlier."

2. No Londinium: London Remains a Swamp

The Romans famously founded Londinium on the Thames, which would eventually grow into the bustling metropolis of London. Without Roman influence, however, the site remains a swampy, misty backwater where a few hardy (or foolhardy) Celts occasionally fish or hunt, but certainly don't think of building anything permanent. The phrase "A swamp with potential" never catches on, because there's no one around to see the potential. The absence of Roman infrastructure means London as we know it simply doesn't exist. Instead, the area remains largely undeveloped, with the tribes preferring higher, drier ground for their settlements. Future British cities develop elsewhere, perhaps around existing Iron Age hillforts, but London remains an afterthought—a place people pass through but never stay. The idea of London becoming the capital of a vast empire is as far-fetched as the notion of drying out the Thames marshes.

3. No Hadrian's Wall: The Picts Keep Picturing Freedom

The Romans built Hadrian's Wall to keep the troublesome Picts out of the more "civilized" southern Britain. Without the Romans, there's no wall, and the Picts—those wild, tattooed warriors from what is now Scotland—continue to raid their southern neighbors with impunity. The border between what we now call England and Scotland remains fluid, with the Picts regularly pushing south. The phrase "Good fences make good neighbors" is completely irrelevant in a Britain without Hadrian's Wall. The constant raiding by the Picts leads to a more militarized culture in southern Britain, with Celtic tribes banding together (temporarily, of course) to fend off the northern threats. The idea of a distinct English identity doesn't develop, as the southern tribes are too busy dealing with Pictish incursions to worry about anything else. The Picts, meanwhile, enjoy their freedom and continue their proud tradition of painting themselves blue and causing trouble. Future historians refer to this period as the "Great Celtic Chaos," where the only rule was that there were no rules.

4. No Roman Roads: Britain's Infrastructure Lags Behind

One of the most enduring legacies of the Roman occupation was their extensive road network, which connected towns and cities across Britain. Without the Romans, Britain's roads remain little more than dirt tracks, suitable for ox carts but not much else. Travel is slow, trade is limited, and the idea of a national infrastructure plan is about as appealing as a bath in the Thames. The phrase "All roads lead to Rome" doesn't apply here. Instead, the Celts continue to rely on their traditional paths, which meander around hills, forests, and sacred groves rather than cutting through them. The lack of roads hampers the development of large-scale trade, and local economies remain isolated. The few traders who do venture across the island take months to complete journeys that would have taken days on Roman roads. The British Isles remain a backwater in terms of economic development, with progress moving at a snail's pace. Future British engineers look at

Roman roads in other parts of Europe and think, "Would have been nice, but we'll stick to our mud tracks, thanks."

5. The Celtic Language Dominates: No Latin Influence

The Romans left a significant linguistic legacy in Britain, with Latin influencing the development of the English language. Without Roman occupation, the Celtic languages continue to evolve without Latin interference. The language of the Britons remains firmly rooted in its Celtic origins, and Latin loanwords never enter the vernacular. The phrase "It's all Greek to me" is replaced with "It's all Celtic to me" as the island remains linguistically distinct from the rest of Europe. The absence of Latin influence means that the language spoken in Britain evolves separately from the Romance languages, leading to a very different linguistic landscape. Modern English, if it even exists, is far more Celtic in structure and vocabulary, with a guttural, sing-song quality that leaves future tourists scratching their heads. The famous "Latinization" of Europe bypasses Britain entirely, leading to a culture that is linguistically and culturally distinct from its continental neighbors. Future linguists study British languages and marvel at their resilience, while also lamenting the fact that no one outside the British Isles can pronounce anything correctly.

6. No Roman Bathhouses: The Celts Stick to Natural Spas

Roman bathhouses were a hallmark of Roman culture, bringing hygiene, relaxation, and a bit of socializing to the masses. Without the Romans, the Celts continue their own bathing traditions, which involve natural hot springs, rivers, and a general disdain for overcomplicating things. The phrase "Taking a bath" takes on a whole new meaning in Britain, where people continue to use natural bodies of water rather than building elaborate bathhouses. The absence of Roman bath culture means that the Celts never develop a taste for the communal bathing rituals that were so popular in the rest of the empire. Bathing remains a private affair, done in streams or makeshift tubs, and the idea of a public bathhouse is as foreign as, well, the Romans themselves. Future British towns built near hot springs never become spa destinations, and the concept of "taking the waters" is more about drinking than bathing. Future historians look at Roman bathhouses on the continent and think, "Nice idea, but not for us."

7. A Different Religion: The Druids Hold On

Roman occupation brought the introduction of new religions, including the worship of Roman gods and, eventually, Christianity. Without the Romans, the native Celtic religion, led by the Druids, continues to thrive. The Druids maintain their influence, presiding over religious ceremonies, legal matters, and education. The phrase "By the power of the oak" becomes the rallying cry of a Britain where the Druids still hold sway. The lack of Roman religious influence means that the Celts continue to worship their pantheon of gods, with sacred groves and stone circles remaining central to religious life. Christianity, if it arrives at all, does so much later and faces stiff resistance from the established Druidic order. The Druids, with their deep knowledge of nature and the stars, continue to be revered as the keepers of wisdom, and their influence permeates every aspect of life. Future British culture is deeply rooted in nature worship and the reverence for ancestors, with holidays and rituals centered around the cycles of the seasons. Future historians study this period and wonder how different the world might have been if the Druids had retained their power elsewhere.

8. No Roman Villas: The Celts Keep It Cozy

Roman villas, with their central courtyards, mosaic floors, and underfloor heating, never make it to Britain. Instead, the Celts continue to live in roundhouses made of wood and thatch, designed for communal living and warmth. The idea of a grand villa with all the luxuries of Roman life is as alien to them as an alien spaceship. The phrase "Home sweet home" remains humble in a Britain without Roman villas. The Celts continue to prioritize communal living and practicality over luxury, with their homes designed for warmth and protection from the elements. The lack of Roman architectural influence means that British building styles evolve along different lines, with an emphasis on wood, earth, and natural materials. Future British architecture is characterized by its organic shapes and integration with the landscape, with roundhouses eventually evolving into more complex forms, but always retaining their cozy, communal spirit. Future British homeowners look at Roman villas in other parts of Europe and think, "Nice, but who needs all that space?"

9. A Delayed British Empire: Expansion Comes Later

The Roman occupation of Britain laid the groundwork for the island's later unification and eventual empire-building. Without Roman influence, the development of a unified British identity is delayed, and the idea of a British Empire, if it comes at all, emerges much later. The various tribes and kingdoms continue to develop independently, with no single power rising to dominate the others. The phrase "The sun never sets on the British Empire" remains firmly in the future, as Britain's expansionist ambitions are stunted by its lack of early unification. The delay in forming a unified British state means that other European powers, particularly France and Spain, dominate the early exploration and colonization of the New World. Britain, when it finally gets around to expanding, finds itself playing catch-up, leading to a smaller and less influential empire. The British Isles remain something of a backwater in European politics, with their importance only gradually increasing as trade and technology advance. Future historians look at the development of the British Empire and note that it arrived late to the party, missing out on many of the early opportunities that shaped global history.

10. No Romanization: A Different Cultural Legacy

Without Roman conquest, Britain never undergoes the process of Romanization—the adoption of Roman customs, laws, language, and governance. Instead, the island's culture remains distinctly Celtic, with its own traditions, laws, and social structures. The idea of Britain as a part of the classical world is as far-fetched as the notion of Julius Caesar backing down from a fight. The phrase "When in Rome, do as the Romans do" never takes hold in Britain, because there are no Romans to emulate. The absence of Roman influence means that Britain develops its own unique cultural identity, distinct from the rest of Europe. The legal and political systems evolve from Celtic traditions, leading to a different kind of governance that emphasizes clan loyalty and tribal justice. The arts and literature reflect this cultural independence, with epic poems and sagas celebrating the deeds of Celtic heroes rather than Roman statesmen. Future British culture is marked by a deep sense of continuity with its ancient past, with traditions and rituals passed down from generation to generation. Future historians marvel at the resilience of Celtic culture, noting how it thrived and evolved in the absence of Roman intervention.

Conclusion

If the Romans had never conquered Britain, the island's cultural, political, and economic development would have taken a very different path. The Celts would have continued to shape the destiny of Britain, leading to a unique civilization distinct from the rest of Europe. The lack of Roman influence would have delayed or altered the emergence of a unified British identity and the eventual rise of a British Empire. And somewhere in this alternate history, a Druid, standing in a sacred grove, might have looked up at the stars and thought, "Perhaps we didn't need those Romans after all."

What If the Early Christian Church Had Not Split from Judaism?

The Background

In the early days of Christianity, the followers of Jesus were, for the most part, devout Jews who saw their new faith as a continuation, rather than a break, from Jewish traditions. However, as Christianity spread among Gentiles and developed its own identity, tensions arose between Jewish Christians and traditional Jews, leading to the eventual split. This separation paved the way for Christianity to become a distinct religion, ultimately growing into a dominant force in the Western world. But what if, instead of breaking away, the early Christian Church had remained firmly within the Jewish fold, never forming a separate identity? What if Christianity had continued as a Jewish sect, adhering to Jewish law and traditions while spreading the teachings of Jesus?

The 10 Possible Things That Would Happen

1. Christianity: The Jewish Sect That Conquered the World

If Christianity had remained a sect within Judaism, the religion we know today would look very different. Instead of a distinct Christian identity, we would have a form of Judaism with an emphasis on Jesus as the Messiah.

These "Messianic Jews," as they might be called, would continue to observe Jewish laws, festivals, and dietary restrictions while incorporating the teachings of Jesus. The phrase "Sunday service" becomes a bit of a misnomer, as these Messianic Jews would continue to observe the Sabbath on Saturday. Churches, as we know them, would likely be synagogues where Jesus is venerated alongside traditional Jewish figures. The New Testament might still exist, but it would be studied as part of a broader Jewish canon, with Paul's letters viewed as interpretive commentary rather than a foundational text. The idea of a global "Christianity" as a separate entity from Judaism simply doesn't take off, and instead, we have a global movement of Jesus-following Jews. Future historians scratch their heads trying to distinguish between "regular" Jews and "Jesus Jews," leading to endless debates over what exactly constitutes this expanded form of Judaism.

2. No Roman Adoption: A Jewish Religion Remains on the Fringe

Without the split, Christianity never gains the traction it did in the Gentile world, particularly in the Roman Empire. The idea of a Jewish sect becoming the official religion of Rome seems as likely as Emperor Nero taking up knitting. Instead, Rome continues to dabble in its traditional polytheism and, eventually, a variety of mystery religions. Christianity, or rather Messianic Judaism, remains largely a fringe movement, with limited influence outside Jewish communities. The phrase "When in Rome, do as the Romans do" includes a lot more sacrifices to Jupiter and a lot less monotheistic worship. The lack of Roman adoption means that the spread of Messianic Judaism is slower and more localized, with the religion maintaining a strong ethnic and cultural connection to Jewish identity. The grand basilicas and cathedrals of Europe never get built, and instead, synagogues remain the primary places of worship. The concept of a "Christian Europe" never materializes, leading to a continent where polytheism, mystery religions, and later, various forms of paganism continue to hold sway. Future European history is marked by a much more religiously diverse landscape, with no single faith ever achieving the dominance that Christianity historically enjoyed.

3. Religious Calendar Confusion: Easter and Passover Collide

With Christianity remaining within Judaism, the Christian calendar as we know it never develops. Instead, followers of Jesus continue to observe Jewish holidays, with a particular emphasis on Passover, which takes on added significance as the time of Jesus' crucifixion and resurrection. Easter, in its modern form, simply doesn't exist, and instead, Jesus' followers commemorate his resurrection during Passover. The phrase "Passover lamb" takes on a whole new meaning as the holiday becomes the central focus for Messianic Jews. The lack of a distinct Easter means that the entire Christian liturgical calendar never comes into being. Christmas, too, remains a minor observance at best, with no December 25th festivities to speak of. Future holiday traditions in Europe look vastly different, with Passover celebrated as a major religious event, complete with matzo, bitter herbs, and the retelling of both the Exodus and the Resurrection stories. The Easter Bunny? Never heard of him. Future historians puzzle over the absence of these holidays in what we would consider Christian communities, leading to confused scholarly papers with titles like "Why No Eggs? The Missing Christian Festivals of Europe."

4. Jewish-Christian Relations: Tensions That Never Boil Over

Historically, the split between Judaism and Christianity led to centuries of tension, conflict, and often outright persecution. Without the split, however, these tensions remain simmering but never reach a full boil. Jewish and Messianic communities coexist with a shared heritage, even if they occasionally eye each other with suspicion. Anti-Semitism, as we know it, doesn't develop in the same way, and the tragic history of Jewish persecution in Europe takes a very different course. The phrase "Good fences make good neighbors" is applied to the somewhat cautious but generally peaceful coexistence between Jewish and Messianic communities. The absence of a distinct Christian identity means that the harsh theological debates and accusations of deicide that fueled anti-Semitism simply don't arise. Instead, Jewish and Messianic communities continue to interact, trade, and marry within the broader context of a shared cultural and religious tradition. The Crusades? Forget it. No one's launching holy wars over a theological split that never happened. Future European history is marked by a more pluralistic society where religious diversity is the norm rather than the exception, and the dark legacy of anti-Semitism is, if not entirely absent, significantly diminished.

5. The New Testament: A Supplementary Scroll

Without the need to establish a separate religious identity, the New Testament remains a supplementary text to the Hebrew Bible rather than a standalone scripture. The Gospels, the letters of Paul, and the other writings are included in the broader Jewish canon, studied alongside the Torah, the Prophets, and the Writings. The Bible, as we know it, never comes together in the same way. The phrase "Old and New Testament" loses all meaning, as there's simply one big testament with various books that are studied by different Jewish sects. The compilation of the New Testament into a separate book never occurs, leading to a far more integrated approach to scripture. The Gospels are read in synagogues as interpretations of the messianic prophecies found in the Hebrew Bible, and Paul's letters are debated in yeshivas alongside the teachings of other Jewish sages. Future biblical scholarship is marked by a continuous tradition that blends the teachings of Jesus with the broader Jewish intellectual and spiritual heritage. The lack of a "Christian Bible" means that later religious movements, such as the Reformation, look very different, as the scriptures themselves are far less divided.

6. No Church Hierarchy: Rabbis Over Bishops

The split between Christianity and Judaism led to the development of distinct religious hierarchies, with the Christian Church establishing a complex system of bishops, priests, and later, a pope. Without the split, this hierarchy never develops. Instead, the leadership of Messianic Jewish communities remains in the hands of rabbis, who continue to teach and interpret Jewish law and tradition in light of Jesus' teachings. The phrase "As powerful as the Pope" is entirely irrelevant in this timeline. Instead, religious authority remains decentralized, with rabbis holding the most influence within their local communities. The idea of a single, centralized religious authority simply doesn't take hold, leading to a more diverse and less hierarchical religious landscape. The great church councils that defined Christian doctrine in our timeline never happen, and instead, debates over theology take place in rabbinical assemblies where differing opinions are not only tolerated but encouraged. The later history of religious schisms, from the Great Schism to the Protestant Reformation, simply doesn't occur in the same way, as there's no single institution to break away from. Future religious leaders look back at this period and marvel at the lack of dogma, noting how different the world might have been if everyone had just stayed a bit more Jewish.

7. No Christian Art: A Different Aesthetic Legacy

The distinct Christian art that emerged in the early centuries of the Church, from the catacombs of Rome to the Byzantine mosaics, never develops. Instead, religious art remains firmly rooted in Jewish traditions, with a focus on symbolic representation rather than figural depictions. The elaborate iconography of saints, angels, and the Virgin Mary never comes into being, and instead, religious art is more abstract, focusing on symbolic motifs like the menorah, the Star of David, and the Tree of Life. The phrase "A picture is worth a thousand words" has less relevance in religious art, as the emphasis remains on symbolism and scripture rather than grand visual narratives.

The absence of Christian iconography means that the great cathedrals of Europe, if they're built at all, are far less adorned with figurative art. Instead, religious spaces are filled with intricate geometric designs, calligraphy, and symbolic patterns that emphasize the divine through abstraction. The later development of Western art is marked by a stronger influence of Jewish aesthetics, with less focus on human figures and more on the interplay of light, color, and form. Future art historians study the rich tradition of abstract and symbolic art in Europe and note how different it is from the figurative art of the East, where other religious traditions still embrace human representation.

8. A Different Spread of Monotheism: Judaism Goes Global

Historically, Christianity's split from Judaism allowed it to spread rapidly among non-Jewish populations, eventually becoming a global religion. Without the split, this global spread still happens, but it takes a different form. Judaism, with its messianic branch, becomes a missionary religion, reaching out to Gentiles and converting them to a form of Judaism that includes the teachings of Jesus. The phrase "Missionary zeal" applies equally to Jews and Messianic Jews as they travel the world spreading their faith. The spread of monotheism occurs not through a distinct Christian Church, but through an expanded Jewish tradition that welcomes converts from all backgrounds. The barriers to conversion are lowered, and Judaism's emphasis on ethical monotheism becomes a global movement. The spread of this new form of Judaism leads to a world where monotheism is more unified, with fewer religious divisions and a stronger emphasis on shared ethical principles. The later development of Islam, if it occurs at all, is influenced by this unified monotheism, leading to a religious landscape where the major Abrahamic faiths are far more closely aligned. Future historians marvel at how a religion once known for its exclusivity became the world's most inclusive monotheistic faith.

9. A United Abrahamic Faith: The Birth of a New Religion

Over time, the continued integration of Messianic Judaism with broader Jewish traditions leads to the development of a new, united Abrahamic faith. This religion combines the teachings of Jesus with the foundational texts of Judaism, creating a faith that emphasizes both the law and the spirit. This united religion, let's call it "Judaism 2.0," becomes the dominant monotheistic faith across the Western world. The phrase "Three Abrahamic religions" is replaced with "One faith, many traditions," as Judaism 2.0 becomes the norm. This new religion retains the ethical monotheism of Judaism while incorporating the messianic hope of Jesus' followers. The idea of a separate Christianity simply doesn't exist, and instead, the world sees a unified religious tradition that encompasses both Jewish law and the teachings of Jesus. The development of later religious movements, such as Islam, is heavily influenced by this new faith, leading to a world where religious conflicts are far less common. Future religious leaders look back at this period as a time of great spiritual unity, noting how different history might have been if the Abrahamic religions had remained fragmented.

10. A Different Western Civilization: A More Unified Cultural Identity

The absence of a split between Judaism and Christianity leads to a very different development of Western civilization. Instead of a Europe divided by religious conflict, there is a more unified cultural identity that blends Jewish traditions with the teachings of Jesus. This unified culture influences everything from law and governance to art and literature, leading to a Western world that is more cohesive and less prone to religious wars. The phrase "Western civilization" takes on a new meaning, as the cultural identity of Europe is shaped by a unified Abrahamic faith. The legal systems of Europe are deeply influenced by Jewish law, with an emphasis on justice, charity, and community responsibility. The political systems that develop are more egalitarian, with a focus on shared leadership and ethical governance. The great religious wars that characterized European history, from the Crusades to the Thirty Years' War, simply don't happen, leading to a more peaceful and stable development of Western society. The Renaissance, when it comes, is marked by a revival of Jewish and Messianic thought, leading to a cultural flowering that emphasizes ethical monotheism and the unity of faith. Future historians look back at this period and note how the decision to remain unified led to a Western world that was far less divided and far more focused on common goals.

Conclusion

If the early Christian Church had not split from Judaism, the development of Western religion and civilization would have been dramatically different. Christianity, instead of becoming a distinct global religion, would have remained a sect within Judaism, leading to a more unified Abrahamic faith and a very different cultural and religious landscape in Europe. The impact of this decision would have shaped everything from art and literature to law and governance, creating a world where religious unity was the norm rather than the exception. And somewhere in this alternate history, a rabbi-teacher might have looked out over a congregation of Jews and Gentiles, smiled, and thought, "We really are all in this together, aren't we?"

What If the Visigoths Had Failed to Sack Rome in 410 CE?

The Background

In 410 CE, the Visigoths, led by their cunning and charismatic king Alaric, did what was previously unthinkable: they sacked the Eternal City of Rome. This event sent shockwaves throughout the Roman world, symbolizing the beginning of the end for the Western Roman Empire. The sack of Rome was more than just a military defeat; it was a psychological blow that shook the foundations of Roman civilization. But what if, through some twist of fate—whether it be a last-minute Roman defense, a diplomatic masterstroke, or Alaric simply waking up on the wrong side of the bed—the Visigoths had failed to sack Rome? How would this near-miss with history have altered the trajectory of the Western world?

The 10 Possible Things That Would Happen

1. Rome's Eternal Reputation: A City That Refuses to Fall

If the Visigoths had failed to sack Rome, the city's reputation as the unassailable heart of the empire would have been bolstered. Rome would have continued to be seen as the invincible center of civilization, a city protected by divine favor—or, at the very least, by its impressive walls and last-ditch military efforts. The phrase "All roads lead to Rome" retains its full, unblemished authority. The city's continued resilience might have bolstered Roman morale across the empire, delaying the sense of inevitable decline that had been creeping in. Future invaders would think twice before attempting to breach Rome's walls, leading to a longer-lasting, albeit still shaky, Western Roman Empire. The idea of Rome as an invincible city would have become even more deeply entrenched, leading to the perception that Rome would last forever—because, after all, who could possibly conquer a city that even the Visigoths couldn't touch?

2. Alaric's Bad Day: A Visigothic Disgrace

Alaric, having failed to sack Rome, would have found himself in a bit of a pickle. His reputation as a fearsome leader would have taken a hit, and his Visigothic followers, already a restless bunch, might have started questioning his leadership. Alaric's failed siege could have led to internal strife within the Visigothic ranks, weakening the group as a military force. The phrase "It's not you, it's me" becomes Alaric's go-to excuse as he tries to keep his disgruntled followers in line. The Visigoths, frustrated by their failure to sack Rome, might have splintered into factions, each led by a different chieftain with a different idea about how best to salvage their reputation. This division could have led to a weakened Visigothic presence in the region, allowing other barbarian groups, like the Vandals or the Huns, to fill the power vacuum and take their place as the new scourge of the Roman world. Future historians would speculate about how Alaric's failure at Rome signaled the beginning of the end for the Visigoths as a major force in Europe, possibly leading to a quieter, less dramatic decline.

3. A Delayed Decline: The Western Roman Empire Hangs On

Without the sack of Rome in 410, the Western Roman Empire might have limped along for a bit longer. The psychological and economic blow of losing the city was a significant factor in the empire's rapid decline. A reprieve from this disaster could have allowed the empire to stabilize, at least temporarily, and continue its slow decline at a more leisurely pace. The phrase "Rome wasn't built in a day, and it sure doesn't fall in one either" becomes a common refrain among Romans still clinging to the remnants of their empire. With the heart of the empire still intact, the Roman government might have had the breathing room it needed to enact a few more reforms, fend off a few more invasions, and delay the inevitable for another generation or two. This extended lifespan could have led to a slightly different map of Europe, with the Western Roman Empire holding on to a few more territories and influencing the development of early medieval states in a different way. Future historians would ponder how close Rome came to falling in 410 and speculate about how its survival—however brief—changed the course of European history.

4. Christianity's Ascendancy Slows: Paganism Hangs On

The sack of Rome in 410 was seen by many as a sign that the old gods had abandoned the city, accelerating the rise of Christianity within the empire. Without this symbolic event, paganism might have lingered a bit longer, with more Romans clinging to their traditional beliefs and rituals, convinced that their gods had given them another chance. The phrase "In the old gods we trust" remains more than just a nostalgic motto, as the failure of the sack is seen as a sign of divine favor from the traditional Roman pantheon. Christianity, while still growing, faces stiffer resistance from those who see the near-miss as proof that Jupiter, Mars, and the rest of the gang aren't ready to retire just yet. Pagan temples might receive a boost in attendance, and the old rituals continue to be practiced alongside Christian rites. The eventual Christianization of the empire happens more gradually, with a slower process of conversion that leads to a more syncretic blend of old and new religions. Future religious scholars debate how much longer the old gods could have lasted if the Visigoths hadn't almost given Rome a reason to convert en masse.

5. No Saint Augustine's "City of God": A Different Theological Legacy

The sack of Rome in 410 inspired Saint Augustine to write his monumental work, *The City of God*, which laid the theological groundwork for the idea that the fall of earthly cities was irrelevant compared to the eternal city of God. Without the sack, Augustine might have been less inspired to write this particular work, leading to a different theological emphasis in the Christian world. The phrase "The City of God" never enters the Christian lexicon in the same way, and Augustine's theological writings take a different path. Instead of focusing on the transient nature of earthly cities, Augustine might have written more about the resilience of the Roman Empire and the importance of maintaining a Christian presence within it. The absence of *The City of God* leads to a less dualistic view of the world, with Christian thinkers more focused on the here-and-now rather than the afterlife. Future theologians would look back and wonder what might have been if Augustine had never felt the need to comfort a Rome shaken to its core, leading to a more integrated view of faith and empire.

6. Roman Influence Persists: A Different Middle Ages

With Rome spared from the Visigoths, the city might have continued to exert a stronger influence over the development of Europe during the early Middle Ages. The survival of Roman institutions, laws, and culture could have led to a less abrupt transition from antiquity to the medieval period, with more continuity between the Roman past and the emerging medieval world. The phrase "Romanitas" becomes more than just a nostalgic term; it's a living tradition that shapes the development of medieval Europe. The legal codes, administrative structures, and cultural practices of the Roman Empire persist longer, influencing the emerging kingdoms of Europe. The idea of Rome as the center of the world remains strong, leading to a more centralized and unified Europe, where the legacy of Rome is preserved in a more direct way. Future historians would marvel at how the Roman Empire managed to hang on, even as the rest of the world changed around it, leading to a Middle Ages that looked a lot more like a "Roman revival" than a "Dark Age."

7. A Different Alaric: The Barbarian Who Couldn't Sack

Alaric's failure to sack Rome would have altered his legacy. Instead of being remembered as the first barbarian to breach the Eternal City's walls in centuries, he might have been seen as a leader who came close but ultimately failed. This could have led to a very different career for Alaric, possibly even changing the trajectory of the Visigothic people. The phrase "Close, but no laurel wreath" sums up Alaric's legacy, as future generations of Visigoths look back on his near-success with a mix of pride and disappointment. Alaric's failure might lead to his eventual replacement by another leader, one who is either more ruthless or more willing to negotiate with the Romans. The Visigoths, under new leadership, might have taken a different path, perhaps settling in another part of the Roman Empire or even allying more closely with Rome in exchange for land and titles. The Visigoths' eventual role in the fall of the Western Roman Empire might be diminished, leading to a different distribution of power among the barbarian kingdoms that emerged in the wake of Rome's decline. Future Visigothic leaders would tell tales of "the one that got away," with Alaric becoming a cautionary figure rather than a hero.

8. No Inspiration for Future Invaders: Rome's Aura Remains Intact

The sack of Rome in 410 sent a clear message to other barbarian groups: Rome was vulnerable. Without this event, the aura of invincibility surrounding the city might have persisted, discouraging other groups from attempting to breach its walls. This could have led to fewer invasions of the city and a more stable, if still troubled, Western Roman Empire. The phrase "If Rome can't be sacked, neither can we" becomes a rallying cry for other Roman cities, emboldened by Rome's continued resilience. The lack of a successful sack might have dissuaded other groups, like the Vandals or the Huns, from targeting Rome directly, leading them to focus their efforts elsewhere. The Western Roman Empire, though still declining, might have experienced fewer catastrophic invasions, allowing it to manage its defenses more effectively. The eventual fall of Rome, when it comes, might have been less violent and more a result of internal decline rather than external conquest. Future generations of Romans would look back with pride on their city's ability to withstand the test of time, even if that time eventually ran out.

9. A Delayed Christianization of Europe: Paganism's Last Stand

The sack of Rome in 410 was a turning point that accelerated the Christianization of Europe, as many saw it as a sign that the old gods had failed. Without this event, the spread of Christianity might have been slower, with paganism holding on longer in various parts of the empire. The phrase "Old habits die hard" applies to the persistence of paganism in a Rome that never experiences the shock of being sacked. The slower spread of Christianity means that pagan practices and beliefs remain more deeply entrenched in many parts of Europe. The Christianization of the empire happens more gradually, with a longer period of coexistence between Christian and pagan communities. This could lead to a more syncretic religious landscape, where elements of paganism are incorporated into Christian practice rather than being outright rejected. Future religious historians would note how the failure of the Visigoths to sack Rome allowed for a more gradual and less disruptive process of religious change in Europe, leading to a different blend of old and new beliefs.

10. The "What If" Industry Never Takes Off: No Sack, No Speculation

Without the dramatic event of the sack of Rome in 410, future generations of historians, writers, and armchair theorists would have one less major "what if" to speculate about. The sack of Rome has inspired countless books, articles, and debates over the centuries. If it never happened, a whole subfield of historical speculation might never have emerged. The phrase "What if the Visigoths had sacked Rome?" becomes a non-existent thought experiment in a world where the event never happened. The absence of this dramatic turning point means that historians and storytellers have to find other moments to speculate about, possibly leading to an entirely different set of popular "what if" scenarios. The sack of Rome has long been seen as a symbolic end to antiquity and the beginning of the Middle Ages—without it, the transition between these two periods might be seen as more gradual and less cataclysmic. Future historians would find themselves debating other key events, like the fall of Constantinople or the collapse of the Western Roman Empire itself, but the dramatic moment of 410 CE would remain a footnote in the long history of Rome.

Conclusion

If the Visigoths had failed to sack Rome in 410 CE, the course of Western history would have taken a very different path. The fall of the Western Roman Empire might have been delayed, and the cultural, religious, and political development of Europe would have been significantly altered. Rome's reputation as the eternal city would have been reinforced, and the psychological impact of its survival could have changed the trajectory of the Middle Ages. And somewhere in this alternate history, a Roman senator might have sipped his wine, looked out over the still-intact city, and thought, "Maybe we've got a few more centuries in us after all."

What If the Ancient Olmecs Had Developed a More Advanced Writing System?

The Background

The Olmecs, often considered the "mother culture" of Mesoamerica, laid the foundations for many aspects of later civilizations like the Maya and the Aztecs. They built massive stone heads, developed early forms of hieroglyphic writing, and were pretty much the trendsetters of ancient Mesoamerica. However, their writing system never reached the sophistication of later Mesoamerican scripts, leaving us with tantalizingly few records of their society, beliefs, and history. But what if the Olmecs, in their wisdom (and perhaps a bit of boredom with just carving stone heads), had developed a more advanced, comprehensive writing system? One that recorded their history, myths, and day-to-day dealings in exquisite detail?

The 10 Possible Things That Would Happen

1. The Olmec Chronicles: A Wealth of Written History

With a more advanced writing system, the Olmecs would have left behind detailed records of their civilization—who they were, what they believed, and how they viewed the world. This would have provided future generations, including us, with a much clearer picture of early Mesoamerican history, instead of the frustratingly vague clues we currently have. The phrase "Lost to history" no longer applies to the Olmecs. Archaeologists and historians, instead of scratching their heads over enigmatic carvings, would be poring over ancient Olmec texts that detail everything from the construction of their colossal stone heads to the day the first Olmec discovered chocolate (a day worth recording, surely). Future scholars wouldn't have to guess at the Olmec's influence—they'd have it in black and white (or rather, in whatever colors the Olmecs preferred for their glyphs). The wealth of information might even allow for a detailed understanding of Olmec governance, religion, and social structure, transforming our understanding of Mesoamerican history.

2. The Maya Take Notes: An Intellectual Legacy

The Maya, who later developed one of the most sophisticated writing systems in the ancient world, might have been directly influenced by the Olmecs' more advanced script. Instead of starting from scratch, the Maya could have built on Olmec innovations, leading to an even more complex and rich literary tradition. The phrase "Standing on the shoulders of giants" becomes literal as the Maya expand on the Olmec writing system, incorporating it into their own. The Maya might credit the Olmecs in their texts, leading to a tradition of citing sources that would make any modern academic proud. This intellectual inheritance could result in an even earlier and more detailed recording of Mayan history, astronomy, and mathematics. Maya scribes might even engage in scholarly debates over interpretations of ancient Olmec texts, leading to an academic tradition that rivals anything in the Old World. Future historians would marvel at the continuity of Mesoamerican thought, tracing complex philosophical ideas back to Olmec origins.

3. The Codices Survive: A Richer Mesoamerican Library

With a more advanced writing system, the Olmecs might have produced more codices—books made from bark paper or animal skins—that recorded their knowledge. These codices, if they survived the ravages of time and the enthusiasm of Spanish conquistadors for burning anything that looked vaguely heretical, would provide invaluable insights into Olmec life and thought. The phrase "Burning the books" would provoke even more outrage among historians as they lament the loss of Olmec codices. However, with more codices in existence, some might have survived, hidden away in remote temples or buried in tombs. The discovery of these codices in the modern era would be like finding the Rosetta Stone times ten, unlocking the secrets of the Olmecs and providing a direct link to their knowledge and beliefs. The study of Mesoamerican history would be transformed, with entire academic departments dedicated to deciphering and interpreting these ancient texts. The Olmec codices would be treated as national treasures, displayed in museums and studied by scholars from around the world.

4. A Cultural Continuum: The Olmec Influence Persists

With their ideas and knowledge more easily transmitted through writing, the Olmecs' cultural influence on later Mesoamerican civilizations would be even stronger. The Olmec script could become the basis for writing systems across the region, creating a cultural continuum that unites different Mesoamerican civilizations through a shared literary tradition. The phrase "We all speak Olmec" becomes the Mesoamerican equivalent of "We all speak Latin." The Olmec script, modified and adapted by later civilizations, becomes the lingua franca of Mesoamerica. The continuity of this script leads to a greater sense of shared identity among the diverse peoples of the region, with each civilization contributing to and drawing from a common cultural and intellectual heritage. Future historians would trace the development of Mesoamerican writing, noting the strong Olmec influence that persisted even as new civilizations rose and fell. The idea of a "Mesoamerican Renaissance" could emerge, with later civilizations consciously reviving and celebrating Olmec traditions in art, literature, and governance.

5. Religion on Record: A Detailed Account of Olmec Spirituality

The Olmecs, like many ancient civilizations, had a complex religious system involving gods, rituals, and perhaps even human sacrifices. With a more advanced writing system, they would have recorded these beliefs in detail, providing future generations with a clearer understanding of their spiritual practices. The phrase "Mystery religion" no longer applies to the Olmecs, as their detailed religious texts are uncovered and studied. These records might describe the rituals, the roles of priests, the significance of their colossal stone heads (finally, some answers!), and the myths that shaped their worldview. Future religious scholars would have a field day comparing Olmec spirituality with that of later Mesoamerican cultures, noting the continuities and divergences. The rich tapestry of Olmec religious thought could even influence modern spiritual movements, as people look to ancient wisdom for guidance in the contemporary world. The Olmecs might be seen as the original "New Age" gurus, with their texts offering insights into the cosmos, the afterlife, and the mysteries of existence.

6. Olmec Diplomacy: The Power of the Written Word

With a more advanced writing system, the Olmecs could have used written records for diplomacy, creating treaties, trade agreements, and alliances with neighboring civilizations. This might have allowed them to exert greater influence over the region, using the power of the pen to complement the power of the sword (or the obsidian blade, as the case may be). The phrase "The pen is mightier than the macuahuitl" becomes a favorite saying among Olmec diplomats. Written agreements, inscribed on stone or codices, allow the Olmecs to establish long-lasting alliances and trade networks that extend their influence far beyond their heartland. These written records could also be used to settle disputes, with neighboring civilizations respecting the authority of Olmec treaties as binding documents. The Olmec civilization might grow into a regional superpower, not just through military might but through savvy diplomacy and the strategic use of written agreements. Future historians would marvel at the Olmecs' ability to maintain a vast network of influence without the need for constant warfare, noting how their writing system played a crucial role in their success.

7. A Flourishing of Olmec Literature: The First Mesoamerican Epics

With a more advanced writing system, the Olmecs might have produced epic poetry, historical chronicles, and philosophical texts that would rival the literary traditions of the Old World. These works could provide insight into the Olmec worldview, their heroic figures, and their understanding of the universe. The phrase "The Olmec Iliad" is whispered in awe by future generations as they discover epic poems and stories that capture the imagination. These literary works, filled with tales of gods, heroes, and legendary battles, become a cornerstone of Mesoamerican culture, inspiring later civilizations to create their own epic traditions. The Olmec epics might be recited at royal courts, performed in grand ceremonies, and studied by scribes eager to preserve the wisdom of the ancients. The influence of these texts extends beyond Mesoamerica, as later civilizations adapt and reinterpret the stories to fit their own cultural contexts. The discovery of these texts in the modern era would be celebrated as one of the greatest literary finds in history, transforming our understanding of ancient Mesoamerican culture.

8. Preserving Knowledge: The Olmecs as the "Ancient Librarians" of Mesoamerica

A more advanced writing system would have allowed the Olmecs to record and preserve their knowledge of astronomy, agriculture, medicine, and other sciences. These records could have been passed down to later civilizations, creating a repository of knowledge that future societies could build upon. The phrase "Ask the Olmecs" becomes a common refrain among later Mesoamerican civilizations whenever they encounter a scientific or agricultural problem. The Olmecs' written records on topics like astronomy and agriculture become foundational texts for later civilizations, who use this knowledge to advance their own societies. The Maya, for example, might have been able to refine their already impressive calendar system even further by building on Olmec astronomical observations. The development of advanced agricultural techniques, informed by Olmec texts, could lead to greater food security and population growth across the region. Future scientists would look back at the Olmecs as the original knowledge keepers of Mesoamerica, with their texts serving as the bedrock of Mesoamerican science and technology.

9. A Stronger Legacy: Olmec Influence Shapes Future Civilizations

The Olmecs, with their more advanced writing system, could have left behind a stronger, more direct legacy. Instead of being remembered as a mysterious precursor to later civilizations, the Olmecs might be seen as the true architects of Mesoamerican culture, with their ideas and innovations directly influencing the development of later societies. The phrase "All roads lead to San Lorenzo" (or La Venta) becomes the Mesoamerican equivalent of "All roads lead to Rome." The Olmec capital cities, known for their colossal heads and impressive architecture, become pilgrimage sites for later civilizations eager to connect with their cultural roots. The Olmec legacy is felt in every aspect of Mesoamerican life, from politics and religion to art and architecture. Future Mesoamerican rulers might claim descent from Olmec kings to legitimize their power, and Olmec symbolism could be integrated into the royal iconography of later civilizations. The Olmecs would be celebrated not just as the "mother culture" of Mesoamerica, but as the intellectual and spiritual forebears of all subsequent civilizations in the region.

10. A Different Historical Narrative: The Olmecs in the Spotlight

With a more advanced writing system, the Olmecs might have recorded their history in detail, creating a narrative that would later be adopted and adapted by future Mesoamerican civilizations. This could result in a historical narrative that places the Olmecs at the center of Mesoamerican history, with later civilizations building on the foundation they laid. The phrase "In the beginning, there were the Olmecs" opens every Mesoamerican history text, placing the Olmecs at the heart of the region's historical narrative. The detailed records left by the Olmecs become the primary source for understanding the early history of Mesoamerica, influencing how later civilizations view themselves and their place in the world. The Olmecs might even be mythologized in later texts, with their kings and heroes becoming larger-than-life figures who set the stage for the glories of the Maya and Aztec civilizations. Future historians would spend their careers tracing the influence of the Olmecs on every aspect of Mesoamerican culture, noting how the advanced writing system they developed allowed them to shape the historical narrative in a way that few other ancient civilizations could.

Conclusion

If the ancient Olmecs had developed a more advanced writing system, the course of Mesoamerican history would have been significantly altered. Their detailed records and intellectual legacy would have provided invaluable insights into their civilization, influencing later cultures and creating a more unified and continuous cultural tradition in the region. The Olmecs would be remembered not just as a mysterious precursor, but as a foundational civilization whose contributions shaped the very fabric of Mesoamerican life. And somewhere in this alternate history, an Olmec scribe might have looked up from his codex, smiled, and thought, "We've really left our mark on history, haven't we?"

What If Pharaoh Ramses II Had Died Young?

The Background

Ramses II, also known as Ramses the Great, is often considered one of ancient Egypt's most powerful and celebrated pharaohs. Reigning for an impressive 66 years, he left an indelible mark on Egypt through his military campaigns, monumental building projects, and his sheer ability to outlive just about everyone who might have challenged his rule. His legacy includes the grand temples of Abu Simbel, the sprawling Ramesseum, and the famous Battle of Kadesh, where he fought the Hittites to a standstill (and then spun it into a PR victory of epic proportions). But what if Ramses II, instead of becoming the long-reigning giant of Egyptian history, had died young—before he could solidify Egypt's power and prestige? How would the ancient Near East have changed without the presence of this larger-than-life figure?

The 10 Possible Things That Would Happen

1. Egypt's Uncertain Future: A Power Vacuum in Thebes

Without Ramses II's long and stable reign, Egypt would have been left in a precarious situation. The death of a young pharaoh typically meant instability, with power struggles, regency councils, and the occasional assassination attempt becoming the order of the day. Egypt, instead of basking in the glory of Ramses's achievements, would be thrown into a period of uncertainty. The phrase "Too many cooks in the kitchen" would describe the chaos in Thebes as various factions jockey for power. Without Ramses II to hold things together, Egypt could see a series of short-lived pharaohs, each trying (and failing) to establish their own legacy. This instability could lead to weakened central authority, with regional governors (nomarchs) gaining more power and autonomy. The grand building projects that defined Ramses's reign would be reduced to half-finished monuments and grandiose plans that never saw the light of day. Future Egyptians might look back on this period as the "Lost Century," where Egypt's potential was squandered by internal divisions and weak leadership.

2. The Hittites Rise: An Uneasy Peace Broken

Ramses II's most famous military achievement was the Battle of Kadesh, where he managed to reach a stalemate with the Hittites and later negotiated one of the earliest known peace treaties. Without Ramses's military prowess and diplomatic skill, the Hittites might have seen an opportunity to expand their influence at Egypt's expense. The phrase "When the cat's away, the Hittites will play" becomes an ancient Near Eastern proverb. With Egypt in disarray, the Hittites, under a more aggressive king, might decide to break the uneasy peace and launch new campaigns into Egyptian-held territories. The balance of power in the region shifts as the Hittites push south, taking control of key trade routes and cities that once paid tribute to Egypt. The famous peace treaty of Kadesh? Never signed. Instead, historians study a series of bloody conflicts that could have dragged on for decades, with Egypt losing its grip on Canaan and the Levant. Future Hittite rulers might boast about their conquests in monumental inscriptions, while Egyptian scribes desperately try to downplay the losses.

3. No Abu Simbel: The Monuments That Never Were

Ramses II was known for his monumental building projects, most famously the temples at Abu Simbel, which were intended to awe both the gods and the Nubians to the south. Without Ramses, these colossal statues and grand temples never materialize, leaving a gaping hole in Egypt's architectural legacy. The phrase "Bigger isn't always better" takes on a whole new meaning as Egypt's monumental architecture takes a more modest turn. Without Ramses's ambitious building projects, the landscape of ancient Egypt looks very different. The towering statues that once greeted travelers along the Nile are replaced by more modest temples and tombs, reflecting the weaker central authority of a post-Ramses Egypt. The tourism industry in modern Egypt is left scratching its head, as the absence of Abu Simbel means fewer postcard-worthy sites. Future archaeologists lament the loss of these wonders, while also noting that the surviving monuments are, shall we say, a bit more "understated."

4. A Weaker Dynasty: The Ramesside Legacy Fades

Ramses II's long reign not only secured his own legacy but also bolstered the position of his descendants. His death at a young age would have left his successors with big shoes to fill—shoes they might not have been able to fill at all. The Ramesside dynasty, instead of becoming one of the most enduring in Egyptian history, could have fizzled out much sooner. The phrase "The apple fell far from the tree" becomes the Ramesside family motto as Ramses's successors struggle to live up to his nonexistent legacy. With a weaker and shorter-lived Ramses, the dynasty might face more challenges from rival claimants and regional powers. The later Ramesside pharaohs, instead of building on Ramses II's achievements, are left trying to pick up the pieces of a fractured empire. The dynasty's decline could come much sooner, with Egypt eventually falling into the hands of a different family—or even being divided into smaller, competing kingdoms. Future Egyptologists would spend their careers debating how much potential was lost due to

Ramses's untimely death, with the Ramesside dynasty remembered as one that "could have been great."

5. Cultural Impact: A Different Egyptian Religion

Ramses II's reign saw the continued promotion of traditional Egyptian religion, with massive temples dedicated to the gods and to Ramses himself as a living deity. His early death could have led to a shift in religious practices, with less emphasis on the pharaoh's divinity and more on other deities or even new religious movements. The phrase "All hail the new gods" could be heard in the temples as religious focus shifts away from the cult of the pharaoh. Without Ramses II's larger-than-life presence, the idea of the pharaoh as a living god might lose some of its luster, leading to a more decentralized religious practice. Other gods, such as Amun or Osiris, might gain more prominence, with temples dedicated to them receiving more attention and resources. This shift could also open the door to new religious movements or the revival of older, less prominent deities. Future scholars might study a more diverse and fragmented Egyptian religious landscape, noting how the absence of a strong, divinely-endorsed pharaoh changed the way Egyptians worshipped.

6. Nubian Independence: The Southern Kingdom Rises

Ramses II's campaigns in Nubia secured Egyptian control over this southern region, but without him, Nubia might have asserted its independence much earlier. A weaker Egypt would struggle to maintain its grip on Nubia, leading to the rise of a powerful and independent Nubian kingdom. The phrase "The sun rises in the south" becomes the rallying cry of an independent Nubia that capitalizes on Egypt's weakness. With Egypt's control over Nubia slipping, the region's rulers might declare independence and establish a powerful kingdom centered around Napata or Meroë. This Nubian kingdom, free from Egyptian dominance, could develop its own unique culture, art, and religion, while also expanding its influence northward into Upper Egypt.

The Nubians might even take the opportunity to reverse the historical roles, launching campaigns into Egypt and establishing their own dynasty on the throne of the pharaohs. Future historians would note the significant Nubian influence on Egyptian culture, architecture, and governance, transforming the history of the Nile Valley.

7. The Battle of Kadesh: A Different Outcome

Ramses II's leadership during the Battle of Kadesh was instrumental in turning what could have been a disastrous defeat into a strategic stalemate. Without Ramses, the battle might have gone very differently, with the Egyptians suffering a major defeat at the hands of the Hittites. The phrase "Hittite hegemony" enters the lexicon as the Hittites take advantage of their victory at Kadesh. A decisive Hittite win could lead to increased Hittite influence in the Levant, with Egypt losing control over its vassal states and trade routes in the region. The Hittites, emboldened by their victory, might push further into Egyptian territory, forcing the Egyptians into a defensive posture for the remainder of the dynasty. The Levant becomes a contested zone, with the Hittites, Assyrians, and other regional powers vying for control. Future historians would look back on the Battle of Kadesh as the turning point that shifted the balance of power in the ancient Near East, with the Hittites emerging as the dominant force—at least for a time.

8. Diplomacy Falters: The First International Peace Treaty Never Signed

Ramses II is credited with negotiating the first known peace treaty in history with the Hittites after the Battle of Kadesh. Without Ramses, this diplomatic milestone might never have occurred, leading to continued hostilities and a very different history of international relations in the ancient world. The phrase "Peace through strength" is replaced by "Peace through paper—never mind, just kidding" as the lack of a formal peace treaty leads to ongoing tensions between Egypt and the Hittites. Without this diplomatic breakthrough, both empires might remain on a war footing, with intermittent conflicts flaring up over control of key territories. This ongoing rivalry could prevent either empire from focusing on internal development, leading to a stagnation in cultural and economic growth. The concept of formalized peace treaties might take much longer to develop, with future generations of rulers preferring to settle disputes on the battlefield rather than at the negotiating table. Future diplomats might find themselves scratching their heads over the lack of precedent for peaceful resolution, leading to a more conflict-prone ancient world.

9. No Great Exodus: Biblical History Takes a Detour

Ramses II is often associated with the Pharaoh of the Exodus in popular imagination, though the historical accuracy of this association is debated. However, if Ramses had died young, the entire timeline of the Exodus (as it's traditionally conceived) could be altered, leading to a very different narrative in the Hebrew Bible. The phrase "Let my people go" might have never been uttered—or at least not in the context we're familiar with. If Ramses II is not the Pharaoh of the Exodus, or if he dies young and the Exodus story unfolds under a different ruler, the entire narrative might change. The Israelites might encounter a weaker, more disorganized Egypt, making their escape less dramatic or even unnecessary. This could lead to a different trajectory for the development of early Israelite identity, with less emphasis on the narrative of liberation from Egyptian bondage. Future biblical scholars might debate an entirely different set of questions, and the Exodus story, if it exists at all, could take on a different form in religious tradition.

10. A Weakened Egypt: Power Shifts in the Ancient Near East

Ramses II's long and stable reign helped Egypt maintain its position as a major power in the ancient Near East. His early death, however, could lead to a much weaker Egypt, with other regional powers—such as the Assyrians,

Babylonians, or even the Sea Peoples—filling the power vacuum. The phrase "The fall of Egypt" could describe a much earlier and more dramatic decline in Egyptian power. With Ramses out of the picture, Egypt's rivals might seize the opportunity to expand their influence, leading to a fragmentation of Egyptian territory. The Assyrians, known for their military might, might push into Egyptian territory, establishing a new center of power in the region. Alternatively, the Sea Peoples, who historically wreaked havoc on Mediterranean civilizations, might find a weakened Egypt easier to plunder and conquer. The result is a Near East where Egypt is no longer the dominant force, leading to a different balance of power and a very different history for the region. Future historians would study this period as the moment when Egypt's star began to fade, setting the stage for the rise of new empires and civilizations.

Conclusion

If Pharaoh Ramses II had died young, the course of ancient Egyptian history—and indeed, the history of the entire Near East—would have been dramatically different. Egypt might have faced internal instability, lost its influence over neighboring regions, and seen its cultural and architectural legacy diminished. The power dynamics of the ancient world would have shifted, with other civilizations rising to fill the void left by a weakened Egypt. And somewhere in this alternate history, an Egyptian scribe, working under a less impressive pharaoh, might have looked out over a half-built monument and sighed, "If only Ramses had lived a little longer."

What If the Ancient Chinese Had Invented the Printing Press During the Han Dynasty?

The Background

The Han Dynasty, one of China's golden ages, ruled from 206 BCE to 220 CE. This era was marked by significant advancements in science, technology, culture, and the arts. It was during the Han Dynasty that paper was invented, and the Silk Road opened, spreading Chinese goods and ideas across Asia and beyond. But what if, amid all this innovation, the ancient Chinese had stumbled upon one more world-changing invention: the printing press? Imagine a world where, centuries before Gutenberg, the Han Dynasty began churning out books, scrolls, and pamphlets at an unprecedented rate. What would this have meant for China, the world, and the course of history?

The 10 Possible Things That Would Happen

1. The Great Book Boom: An Explosion of Knowledge

With the invention of the printing press, the Han Dynasty sees an explosion of books, texts, and scrolls. What was once the domain of a few wealthy scholars becomes available to a much broader audience. Literature, philosophy, science, and even gossip spread like wildfire across the empire. The phrase "The pen is mightier than the sword" takes on a whole new meaning as the written word becomes a force to be reckoned with. The dissemination of Confucian texts, Daoist treatises, and military manuals like *The Art of War* accelerates, leading to a population that is far more literate and informed. Scholars no longer have to painstakingly copy texts by hand, and ideas can be debated, refined, and spread with unprecedented speed. The result? An intellectual golden age that makes the Renaissance look like a casual Sunday brunch. The "Great Book Boom" of the Han Dynasty becomes the stuff of legend, with future historians marveling at how quickly knowledge spread—and how much tea was spilled in the process.

2. The Confucian Comeback: A Philosophical Power Play

With the ability to mass-produce texts, Confucianism gets a significant boost. The Han Dynasty was already keen on Confucian ideals, but with the printing press, Confucian texts flood the empire, reinforcing the philosophy's dominance in Chinese culture and politics. The phrase "Confucius says" becomes a daily mantra, as the philosopher's teachings are literally everywhere—on every scroll, wall, and even public notice board. The widespread availability of Confucian texts solidifies the philosophy's role in shaping Chinese society, governance, and education. The imperial exams, based on Confucian classics, become even more rigorous, with scholars cramming from mass-produced study guides. Future Chinese dynasties remain steadfastly Confucian, and the philosophy's influence extends beyond China's borders, affecting neighboring cultures in Korea, Japan, and Vietnam. The "Confucian Comeback" of the Han Dynasty is seen as a turning point in world philosophy, with Confucius achieving a level of posthumous fame that would make any philosopher blush.

3. Bureaucracy on Steroids: The Government Gets Efficient (and a Bit Overwhelming)

The Han Dynasty's already complex bureaucracy gets a serious upgrade with the advent of the printing press. Administrative documents, legal codes, and edicts can now be produced en masse, ensuring that everyone from the emperor to the lowliest village magistrate is on the same page—literally. The phrase "Drowning in paperwork" originates in the Han Dynasty, as the empire's bureaucrats find themselves buried under a mountain of printed documents. The efficiency of government operations skyrockets, with standardized forms, reports, and decrees circulated quickly and accurately. However, this also leads to a more controlling and pervasive state apparatus, with the central government keeping an even closer eye on its subjects. Regional governors find it harder to fudge their numbers, and tax collectors become a more formidable force, armed with detailed printed records. The sheer volume of paperwork might lead to the first recorded instances of bureaucratic burnout, with future historians joking that the Han Dynasty didn't collapse—it was simply buried under its own administrative success.

4. Cultural Exchange on the Silk Road: A Printing-Powered Highway

The printing press doesn't just stay within China's borders. As books and printed materials become more common, they start to travel along the Silk Road, reaching the far corners of the ancient world. The exchange of ideas between East and West accelerates, with Chinese philosophy, science, and literature finding eager audiences in Persia, India, and beyond. The phrase "Knowledge is power" is taken quite literally as scholars from different cultures eagerly swap printed texts on everything from astronomy to agriculture. The Silk Road becomes a highway of ideas, with Chinese inventions and philosophies reaching the West centuries earlier than they would have otherwise. Greek, Persian, and Indian scholars find themselves reading Chinese texts, leading to a cross-pollination of ideas that sparks new developments in science, mathematics, and philosophy. The "Printing-

Powered Silk Road" is credited with creating an ancient intellectual melting pot, where the East meets the West in the pages of books. Future historians might even suggest that the Renaissance began a thousand years early—just in the wrong hemisphere.

5. Religious Texts Galore: Daoism and Buddhism Get a Boost

Daoist and Buddhist texts also benefit from the printing press, leading to a surge in religious literature. The teachings of Laozi and Buddha become more accessible to the masses, leading to a spiritual awakening (or perhaps a bit of confusion as people try to reconcile different philosophies). The phrase "Too much of a good thing" might apply as people find themselves juggling multiple religious texts, each offering different paths to enlightenment. The mass production of Daoist and Buddhist scriptures leads to a greater spread of these religions throughout China and beyond. Temples begin to distribute printed sutras and commentaries, making religious knowledge more accessible to ordinary people. This could lead to a flourishing of religious sects, each interpreting the texts in their own way, and potentially some doctrinal debates that make modern theological arguments look tame. The result is a more spiritually diverse China, where people can pick and choose from a buffet of beliefs. Future religious scholars would have a field day analyzing the various interpretations that emerged from this religious text boom.

6. Science Leaps Forward: The Dawn of Chinese Innovation

The printing press allows for the rapid dissemination of scientific knowledge, leading to accelerated advancements in fields like medicine, astronomy, and engineering. Han Dynasty China becomes a hotbed of innovation, with scholars building on each other's work at a pace that would make the modern tech industry jealous. The phrase "Ahead of their time" becomes synonymous with Han Dynasty inventors, who start pumping out groundbreaking technologies faster than you can say "Great Wall."

Medical texts describing advanced surgical techniques, herbal remedies, and anatomical studies circulate widely, leading to improved healthcare and longer lifespans. Astronomers produce detailed star charts, predicting eclipses and tracking comets with a precision that boggles the minds of their contemporaries. Engineers create increasingly sophisticated machines, from water clocks to early versions of seismographs, laying the groundwork for future technological revolutions. By the time the rest of the world catches up, China is light-years ahead, and future historians wonder how Europe managed to have a Renaissance at all.

7. Political Propaganda: Emperors Get a New Tool

The Han emperors quickly realize the power of the printing press for spreading their message. Imperial edicts, propaganda, and official histories are printed and distributed across the empire, helping to solidify the emperor's authority and control over his subjects. The phrase "History is written by the victors" takes on a new twist as the Han emperors use the printing press to ensure they're always the victors. The government floods the empire with printed texts extolling the virtues of the emperor, the wisdom of Confucius, and the invincibility of Han China. Dissenting voices are drowned out in a sea of official propaganda, making it difficult for any rival factions to gain traction. The centralized control of information might lead to a more stable (if somewhat Orwellian) state, where the emperor's word is law—quite literally, since it's printed on every piece of paper. Future historians might chuckle at the sheer volume of imperial self-praise that has survived, wondering how much of it was believed by the people and how much was just politely ignored.

8. Education Revolution: Schools and Scholars Multiply

With printed texts becoming widely available, education becomes more accessible to the masses. Schools spring up across the empire, and scholars have more resources at their disposal than ever before. The Han Dynasty sees a dramatic increase in literacy rates, and intellectual pursuits become a central part of Chinese society. The phrase "School's in session" becomes the motto of the Han Dynasty as education becomes a major societal focus. The rapid spread of printed textbooks and educational materials leads to the establishment of schools in even the most remote regions of the empire. The imperial examination system becomes more competitive, with scholars devouring printed study guides and past exam papers. The increased focus on education leads to a more meritocratic society, where talent and knowledge are valued over birthright. The Han Dynasty becomes known as the "Scholar's Empire," with intellectual achievement celebrated at every level of society. Future educators would look back at this period as the golden age of Chinese education, with some even suggesting that the modern university system owes a debt to Han innovations.

9. Global Influence: China's Ideas Travel Far and Wide

As Chinese printed materials make their way along trade routes, they influence not just neighboring cultures but also distant lands. Chinese philosophy, science, and art begin to shape the development of civilizations across Asia and even into Europe and Africa. The phrase "All roads lead to China" takes on new meaning as Chinese ideas become the intellectual currency of the ancient world. The spread of printed Chinese texts leads to a cultural diffusion that shapes the development of societies far beyond China's borders. Indian philosophers debate Chinese metaphysics, Persian scientists adopt Chinese astronomical techniques, and Roman engineers study Chinese designs for bridges and canals. This early globalization of knowledge could lead to a more interconnected world, where ideas flow freely across continents. Future historians might even suggest that the Renaissance began not in Florence, but in Chang'an, with Chinese innovations sparking intellectual revolutions across the globe.

10. A Different Fall of the Han Dynasty: Knowledge as Power

With the spread of knowledge comes the spread of power, and not everyone in the Han Dynasty is thrilled about this. The rapid dissemination of ideas might empower local leaders, scholars, and even commoners to challenge the central authority, leading to a more complex and possibly volatile political landscape. The phrase "Knowledge is a double-edged sword" becomes a cautionary tale as the Han Dynasty struggles to maintain control over a more informed and empowered populace. The spread of printed materials might lead to increased regional autonomy, with local leaders using their newfound knowledge to challenge the central government. Scholars, once content to serve the emperor, might begin to question his authority, leading to intellectual movements that advocate for political reform or even revolution. The Han Dynasty could face internal divisions and power struggles, accelerated by the very technology that once bolstered its power. The eventual fall of the Han might be hastened by these challenges, with future historians debating whether the printing press was a blessing or a curse for the empire.

Conclusion

If the ancient Chinese had invented the printing press during the Han Dynasty, the course of history would have been dramatically altered. The rapid dissemination of knowledge would have accelerated technological, cultural, and intellectual advancements, both within China and across the world. The Han Dynasty might have seen unprecedented achievements but also faced new challenges as power shifted and ideas spread. And somewhere in this alternate history, a Han scholar might have looked at the latest printed scroll, smiled, and thought, "This is going to change everything—whether we're ready or not."

What If the Parthian Empire Had Defeated the Romans Decisively?

The Background

The Parthian Empire, a formidable rival to Rome, was a powerhouse in the Near East from the 3rd century BCE to the 3rd century CE. Known for their exceptional cavalry and hit-and-run tactics (hello, Parthian shot!), they were a thorn in Rome's side for centuries. The Romans, despite their military prowess, found the Parthians a tough nut to crack, suffering notable defeats like the one at Carrhae in 53 BCE. But what if, instead of a series of stalemates and minor victories, the Parthians had managed to pull off a truly decisive victory, one that not only humiliated Rome but also permanently shifted the balance of power in the ancient world? Let's delve into this alternate history where Parthia becomes the dominant force in the Near East, reshaping the trajectory of Western civilization.

The 10 Possible Things That Would Happen

1. Rome Humbled: The Eternal City on Its Knees

With a decisive Parthian victory, Rome's aura of invincibility is shattered. The empire, accustomed to expanding relentlessly, suddenly finds itself on the defensive. The Roman legions, once the terror of the world, limp back to the Eternal City with their tails between their legs. The loss isn't just military—it's a psychological blow that sends shockwaves through Roman society. The phrase "All roads lead to Rome" becomes more of a cautionary tale, as the roads are now filled with retreating soldiers and worried politicians. The Senate, desperate to save face, blames the defeat on everything from bad omens to poor leadership, leading to a series of political purges and public scapegoating. The idea of Roman supremacy begins to waver, and ambitious generals and provinces start eyeing independence, sensing that the empire isn't as unshakeable as it once seemed. Future historians might refer to this period as the "Great Roman Identity Crisis," where Rome had to come to terms with not being the world's alpha dog anymore.

2. Parthia Ascendant: The New Superpower of the Near East

In the wake of their victory, the Parthians solidify their control over the Near East, expanding their influence into territories that were once hotly contested by Rome. Parthia now controls key trade routes, including the Silk Road, and their wealth and power grow exponentially. The phrase "The sun rises in the East" becomes a literal and figurative truth as Parthia emerges as the dominant superpower. The Parthians, flush with victory and spoils, start building monumental cities and palaces to rival anything in Rome. The Parthian King of Kings, now seen as the most powerful ruler in the world, demands and receives tributes from kingdoms across the Near East and beyond. The Silk Road, under Parthian control, becomes even more lucrative, with Parthian merchants and diplomats spreading their influence all the way to China. Future historians might dub this era the "Parthian Century," noting how the empire's dominance shaped the political and economic landscape of Eurasia.

3. The Roman Empire's Eastern Provinces: A Hotbed of Rebellion

With Parthia's victory, Rome's eastern provinces, always a bit of a headache, become outright rebellious. The populations of these regions, weary of Roman taxes and military conscription, see the Parthians as potential liberators. Rebellions flare up, and some provinces even attempt to switch sides, pledging allegiance to the Parthian King of Kings. The phrase "Better the devil you know" becomes the mantra of Roman governors desperately trying to keep their provinces in line. The Parthians, ever the pragmatists, support these rebellions with gold, arms, and the promise of autonomy under their rule. Rome, stretched thin by rebellions and the constant threat of Parthian invasions, begins to lose its grip on the eastern provinces. The loss of these territories deals a severe blow to Rome's economy and prestige, further weakening the empire. Future Roman emperors would lament this period as the "Eastern Catastrophe," when the empire's eastern flank all but collapsed, leaving Rome vulnerable to further incursions from the east.

4. Christianity Takes a Different Path: The Eastern Influence

The spread of Christianity, still in its infancy during this period, could have taken a different course under Parthian dominance. Instead of being shaped by Roman persecution and later adoption, Christianity might have developed under Parthian patronage, leading to a religion with a distinctly Eastern flavor. The phrase "Render unto Parthia" might replace "Render unto Caesar" in this alternate Christian tradition. With the Parthians more tolerant of diverse religious practices, early Christians find a relatively safe haven in Parthian-controlled territories. Christian theology and practices begin to incorporate more Eastern philosophical and religious ideas, leading to a version of Christianity that looks very different from the one that emerged in the Roman Empire. This Eastern Christianity might emphasize mysticism, asceticism, and otherworldliness even more strongly than its Western counterpart. The church, instead of being centered in Rome or Constantinople, might have its spiritual heart in a Parthian city like

Ctesiphon, leading to a different ecclesiastical structure and set of doctrines. Future religious scholars might debate the differences between "Western" and "Eastern" Christianity, wondering how history would have unfolded if Rome had never become the center of the Christian world.

5. Parthian-Roman Relations: A Cold War in Antiquity

The decisive Parthian victory doesn't end the rivalry between the two empires—it merely changes the nature of it. Instead of open warfare, Rome and Parthia enter into a protracted "cold war," marked by espionage, proxy wars, and diplomatic maneuvering. Both empires jockey for influence in the buffer states between them, each trying to outmaneuver the other without resorting to direct conflict. The phrase "Parthian Standoff" becomes synonymous with a tense, unspoken conflict, where neither side can afford to make the first move. Both Rome and Parthia pour resources into their intelligence networks, leading to a flourishing of ancient espionage techniques—think spies in togas and secret codes written on papyrus. Diplomatic missions become exercises in paranoia, with each side suspecting the other of double-dealing and treachery. The cold war extends to the cultural realm as well, with both empires sponsoring rival schools of philosophy, art, and literature, each trying to prove the superiority of their way of life. Future historians might describe this as the "Great Stalemate," where two superpowers were locked in a never-ending struggle for dominance without ever directly clashing on the battlefield.

6. Rome's Military Reforms: A Desperate Need for Change

The crushing defeat forces Rome to rethink its entire military strategy. Gone are the days of relying solely on heavy infantry. Instead, Rome begins to adopt more mobile and flexible units, incorporating cavalry and light infantry in ways they hadn't before. The Parthian influence becomes evident in the new Roman army, which now emphasizes speed, mobility, and adaptability. The phrase "If you can't beat them, join them" takes on a new meaning as the Romans start borrowing military tactics from their Parthian foes. Roman generals, once disdainful of the "eastern" way of war, now embrace the use of mounted archers, hit-and-run tactics, and feigned retreats. The Roman legions undergo a transformation, becoming more versatile and better suited to the vast, diverse terrains of their empire. This military reform revitalizes Rome's fighting spirit, but it also comes with its own set of challenges—chief among them, the difficulty of maintaining cohesion in a more flexible, less standardized army. Future Roman military manuals might include chapters on "Parthian Tactics," with some Roman commanders even penning treatises on the art of war inspired by their once-hated enemies.

7. Trade Routes Shift: Parthia as the Middleman

With Parthia in control of the Silk Road and other key trade routes, the flow of goods between East and West changes dramatically. Parthia becomes the middleman, reaping enormous profits from the trade of silk, spices, and other luxury goods. Rome, once a major player in the trade game, now finds itself at the mercy of Parthian merchants. The phrase "Highway robbery" is used by frustrated Roman traders who now have to pay Parthian tolls and tariffs. The Parthian monopoly on trade routes allows them to control the flow of luxury goods into the Roman Empire, driving up prices and leading to a booming black market. Roman elites, addicted to their silks and spices, grumble about the "Parthian tax" but are powerless to do anything about it. The Parthians, flush with wealth, invest in grand cities, palaces, and monuments, further solidifying their status as the richest empire in the world. Future economic historians might study this period as the "Parthian Trade Boom," noting how Parthia's control over commerce reshaped the economies of both East and West.

8. Cultural Exchange: A Fusion of East and West

With Parthia's dominance, cultural exchange between East and West accelerates. Parthian art, fashion, and customs start to influence Roman society, while Roman ideas make their way into Parthian culture. This fusion creates a unique blend of East and West that leaves a lasting impact on both empires. The phrase "When in Parthia, do as the Parthians do" becomes the motto of Roman diplomats and merchants who find themselves increasingly adopting Parthian customs. Roman fashionistas start wearing Parthian-style clothing, complete with flowing robes and elaborate headgear, while Parthian nobles develop a taste for Roman wines and architecture. The cultural fusion leads to a flowering of hybrid art forms, with Roman statues adorned in Parthian garb and Parthian palaces featuring Roman-style mosaics. This exchange also extends to the culinary world, with Roman and Parthian chefs swapping recipes and ingredients, leading to a fusion cuisine that delights (and sometimes confuses) diners on both sides of the empire. Future art historians might dub this period the "Parthian-Roman Synthesis," celebrating the cross-cultural pollination that left its mark on everything from sculpture to soup.

9. A Different Western Empire: Rome's Transformation

The Parthian victory forces Rome to rethink its identity. No longer the unchallenged master of the Mediterranean, Rome begins to look inward, focusing on consolidating its power in Europe and North Africa rather than pursuing further expansion in the East. This shift leads to a different trajectory for the Roman Empire, one that prioritizes internal stability and defense over external conquest. The phrase "Fortress Rome" becomes the guiding principle of Roman policy as the empire turns its attention to shoring up its borders and securing its heartland. The construction of massive fortifications, like Hadrian's Wall, becomes a common feature across the empire, as Rome seeks to protect itself from both external and internal threats. The Roman economy shifts to focus more on self-sufficiency, with less reliance on imports from the East. This inward focus might lead to a more cohesive and resilient empire, but it also means that Rome's days of grand conquest are over. Future historians might debate whether this shift saved Rome from a faster collapse or simply delayed the inevitable, with some arguing that Rome's best days were behind it the moment the Parthians handed them their biggest defeat.

10. The Legacy of the Parthians: A Different World Order

With Parthia's decisive victory over Rome, the history of the ancient world is rewritten. The Parthians, once seen as a rival to Rome, now become the dominant power in the Near East, shaping the development of the region for centuries to come. Their influence extends far beyond their borders, affecting the course of history in ways that are still felt today. The phrase "Pax Parthica" enters the history books as the Parthians establish a long-lasting peace in the Near East, enforced by their military might and economic power. The Parthian Empire, bolstered by its victory, becomes a beacon of culture, wealth, and stability, attracting scholars, artists, and traders from across the known world. The Roman Empire, though still formidable, is no longer the unchallenged superpower, leading to a multipolar world where power is more evenly distributed. The ripple effects of Parthia's dominance are felt throughout history, influencing everything from the rise of Islam to the development of European and Asian civilizations. Future historians might refer to this period as the "Parthian Pivot," where the course of history took a sharp turn eastward, reshaping the world in ways that no one could have predicted.

Conclusion

If the Parthian Empire had defeated the Romans decisively, the balance of power in the ancient world would have shifted dramatically. Parthia would have emerged as the dominant force in the Near East, influencing the development of Roman society, the spread of Christianity, and the course of global history. The Roman Empire, humbled and weakened, would have had to adapt to a new reality where it was no longer the unchallenged ruler of the world. And somewhere in this alternate history, a Parthian noble might have raised a glass of Roman wine, smiled, and thought, "It's good to be the King of Kings."

What If the Ancient Scythians Had Established a Lasting Empire?

The Background

The Scythians, those enigmatic and fierce nomadic warriors of the steppes, roamed the vast expanses of Eastern Europe and Central Asia from around the 7th century BCE to the 3rd century BCE. Known for their horsemanship, archery, and tendency to wear stylish gold jewelry while also being terrifying in battle, the Scythians left a mark on history without ever establishing a centralized empire. They were more of a loosely connected confederation of tribes than a unified state. But what if, instead of being content with raiding, trading, and the occasional bout of terrifying their neighbors, the Scythians had decided to settle down, build some cities (or at least well-organized yurts), and establish a lasting empire? How would this have reshaped the history of Eastern Europe, Central Asia, and beyond?

The 10 Possible Things That Would Happen

1. The Scythian Capital: A Nomadic Metropolis

The first thing the Scythians would need to do after deciding to create an empire is establish a capital. But since they're still Scythians, this wouldn't be your typical stone-and-brick affair. Instead, imagine a sprawling, semi-nomadic capital city—let's call it "Scythopolis"—built on the open steppe. This city would be a marvel of portable architecture, with entire neighborhoods able to pack up and move if the weather got too cold or the neighbors too annoying. The phrase "Home is where the herd is" becomes the city's unofficial motto as the Scythians combine their love of mobility with the trappings of empire. Scythopolis becomes a bustling hub of trade and culture, with merchants, diplomats, and warriors mingling in grand tents adorned with gold and fine textiles. The city becomes famous for its horse markets, where the finest steeds in the known world are bought and sold. Meanwhile, the administrative heart of the empire moves with the seasons, making it tricky for any would-be invaders to find (let alone conquer) the Scythian capital. Future historians might marvel at how a people known for their nomadic ways managed to create an empire without ever fully settling down.

2. The Rise of the Scythian Confederation: A New Power Bloc

With a centralized (well, sort of) capital and a shared sense of identity, the various Scythian tribes unite under a single ruler—let's call him "The Great Khan of the Steppe." This leader, chosen for his prowess in battle, wisdom, and perhaps a particularly impressive mustache, oversees a confederation of tribes that together form the Scythian Empire. The phrase "United we ride" becomes the rallying cry of the Scythian Empire as the once-fragmented tribes now ride under a single banner. The Scythians, with their unmatched mobility and fierce warrior culture, quickly expand their territory, taking control of key trade routes across the steppes and beyond. The empire stretches from the Carpathian Mountains to the Altai, with each tribe contributing to the empire's strength while retaining some autonomy. This confederation model proves surprisingly effective, with the Great Khan acting as a unifying figure who mediates disputes and organizes massive military campaigns. Future political scientists might study the Scythian Confederation as an early example of a federal system, where local autonomy and central authority are balanced in a way that keeps the empire both stable and dynamic.

3. A Scythian Cultural Renaissance: Steppe Art Goes Global

As the Scythian Empire grows, so does its influence on the arts and culture. The Scythians, already known for their exquisite goldwork and distinctive animal motifs, become trendsetters in the ancient world. Their art, characterized by dynamic depictions of animals in combat and swirling patterns, spreads across their empire and beyond, influencing the aesthetics of neighboring civilizations. The phrase "Scythian chic" enters the lexicon as people from Greece to Persia clamor for Scythian-style jewelry, weapons, and clothing. The Scythian art style, known for its vibrant energy and intricate designs, becomes the height of fashion among the elite. Workshops in Scythopolis churn out gold ornaments, intricately carved wooden items, and embroidered textiles that fetch high prices in markets from the Black Sea to the edges of China. This cultural renaissance leads to a fusion of Scythian and local styles in the regions they influence, creating a unique and lasting artistic legacy. Future art historians might dub this period the "Scythian Flourish," noting how a once-nomadic people became cultural powerhouses whose artistic influence spanned continents.

4. The Horse Lords of the Steppe: Cavalry Dominance

The Scythians, already masters of mounted warfare, take their cavalry to new heights as they expand their empire. With their empire's wealth and resources at their disposal, they breed the finest horses and develop new cavalry tactics that make them the undisputed rulers of the steppes—and a nightmare for any army foolish enough to challenge them. The phrase "The cavalry's coming—and it's Scythian" becomes a dreaded warning on the battlefield. Scythian cavalry, known for their speed, agility, and deadly accuracy with the bow, become the most feared military force of their time. They revolutionize warfare with their hit-and-run tactics, psychological warfare, and ability to outmaneuver traditional infantry-based armies.

Neighboring empires, from the Persians to the Greeks, find themselves adapting their own military strategies to deal with the Scythian threat, leading to an arms race in cavalry development. Future military historians might argue that the Scythians were the original inventors of "shock and awe," using their cavalry to demoralize and devastate their enemies long before such tactics became modern military doctrine.

5. Trade Networks Thrive: The Silk Road Before the Silk Road

As the Scythian Empire expands, it becomes a critical link in the trade routes connecting East and West. The Scythians, with their unparalleled knowledge of the steppe and its hidden paths, facilitate trade across vast distances, turning their empire into a bustling corridor of commerce. The phrase "All roads lead to Scythopolis" becomes a saying among merchants as the Scythians dominate the trade routes between Europe, Asia, and the Middle East. The Scythian Empire becomes a major player in the ancient world's economy, with caravans laden with goods from China, India, Persia, and the Mediterranean crossing their lands. The Scythians, ever pragmatic, impose taxes and tolls on these trade routes, filling their coffers and allowing them to further expand their influence. The wealth generated by trade helps fund the empire's military campaigns and cultural projects, leading to a period of prosperity that rivals that of any sedentary empire. Future economists might look back on the Scythian Empire as the "original Silk Road power," noting how they laid the groundwork for the later trade networks that would connect East and West.

6. A Different Europe: The Scythian Influence Spreads Westward

With their empire established, the Scythians don't stop at dominating the steppes—they push westward into Europe. Their influence begins to reshape the cultures of the Celtic and Germanic tribes, leading to a fusion of Scythian and European customs, art, and warfare. The phrase "When in Europe, do as the Scythians do" might become the norm as European tribes adopt Scythian fashion, cavalry tactics, and even some aspects of their social structure. The Celts, impressed by the Scythians' horsemanship and artistry, begin to incorporate Scythian motifs into their own metalwork and textiles. The Germanic tribes, inspired by Scythian military success, start forming their own cavalry units, leading to a shift in the balance of power in Northern Europe. The blending of Scythian and European cultures leads to a unique hybrid civilization, where the fierce independence of the Celts and Germans is tempered by the sophisticated nomadic traditions of the Scythians. Future historians might debate the extent of Scythian influence on early European history, with some suggesting that the rise of cavalry-dominated warfare in medieval Europe has its roots in Scythian innovations.

7. The Scythian Legal Code: Justice on the Steppes

As the Scythians transition from a loose confederation of tribes to a more structured empire, they develop a legal code to govern their diverse and sprawling territory. This code, rooted in both nomadic traditions and the needs of a vast empire, emphasizes personal honor, swift justice, and the importance of loyalty to the Great Khan. The phrase "Scythian justice" becomes synonymous with a system that is both harsh and fair (if you're on the right side of the law). The Scythian legal code, though simple by sedentary standards, is effective in maintaining order across the empire. It emphasizes the importance of resolving disputes quickly, often through mediation or trial by combat, and places a high value on loyalty to the empire and its rulers. The code becomes a model for other nomadic and semi-nomadic societies, influencing legal traditions across the steppe and beyond. Future legal scholars might study the Scythian legal code as an example of how a nomadic society can develop sophisticated systems of governance, blending traditional practices with the needs of an empire.

8. Religious Syncretism: The Scythian Pantheon Expands

As the Scythians come into contact with other cultures through conquest and trade, they begin to incorporate foreign gods and religious practices into their own spiritual framework. The result is a richly diverse pantheon that blends Scythian animism with the deities of the Greeks, Persians, and other neighboring civilizations. The phrase "In the land of many gods" describes the religious landscape of the Scythian Empire, where temples to both local spirits and foreign gods stand side by side. The Scythians, pragmatic as ever, adopt and adapt the gods of the peoples they conquer or trade with, creating a religious syncretism that reflects the diversity of their empire. This fusion of beliefs leads to a unique spiritual culture, where worshippers might offer sacrifices to both a Scythian war god and a Greek goddess of wisdom, depending on their needs. The Great Khan, seen as the divine mediator between these gods, becomes both a political and spiritual leader. Future religious scholars might view the Scythian Empire as a fascinating example of how nomadic and sedentary religious traditions can blend to create a rich and complex spiritual tapestry.

9. The Great Wall of Scythia: Defense on the Frontier

To protect their burgeoning empire from external threats, the Scythians build a massive defensive structure along their northern and western frontiers. This "Great Wall of Scythia" is not a single wall but a series of interconnected fortifications, watchtowers, and outposts manned by Scythian warriors and their allies. The phrase "The Wall keeps us safe" becomes a common refrain in Scythopolis, as the Great Wall of Scythia serves both as a deterrent to invaders and a symbol of the empire's might. The wall, though less grandiose than China's version, is highly effective in repelling raids and invasions from hostile tribes and rival empires. The construction and maintenance of the wall provide jobs and resources for the empire's people, further integrating the various tribes into a cohesive state. The wall also serves as a powerful symbol of the Scythians' transition from a nomadic confederation to a settled empire, capable of defending its borders and asserting its dominance. Future archaeologists might marvel at the ingenuity of the Scythian defenses, comparing them to other great walls in history and noting how they contributed to the longevity of the Scythian Empire.

10. The Legacy of the Scythian Empire: A Lasting Influence

The Scythian Empire, after centuries of dominance, eventually declines and falls, as all empires do. However, their impact on the history and culture of Eastern Europe and Central Asia is profound and lasting. The Scythians leave behind a legacy of art, military innovation, and cultural fusion that influences the development of later civilizations. The phrase "The Scythians were here" might be found etched into ancient ruins across the steppe, a testament to their enduring influence. The Scythian legacy lives on in the cultures of the peoples who succeed them, from the Sarmatians to the Huns to the Mongols. Their art and symbolism continue to inspire, with Scythian motifs appearing in the jewelry and weaponry of later cultures. The Scythian emphasis on mobility, adaptability, and the importance of cavalry warfare becomes a defining feature of steppe societies for centuries to come. Future historians might view the Scythian Empire as a pivotal force in the history of the Eurasian steppes, a civilization that managed to combine the best of nomadic and settled life into a powerful and lasting empire.

Conclusion

If the ancient Scythians had established a lasting empire, the history of Eastern Europe and Central Asia would have been profoundly altered. Their empire, a unique blend of nomadic traditions and centralized authority, would have reshaped the cultural, military, and economic landscape of the region. The Scythians, known for their mobility and fierce independence, would have created an empire that was both dynamic and enduring, leaving a legacy that influenced the course of history for centuries to come. And somewhere in this alternate history, a Scythian warrior, adorned in gold and seated on a fine horse, might have looked out over the vast steppe and thought, "Not bad for a bunch of nomads."

What If the Ancient Greeks Had Colonized More of North Africa?

The Background

The ancient Greeks were prolific colonizers, spreading their culture, politics, and philosophy across the Mediterranean and beyond. They established colonies in places like Sicily, southern Italy (Magna Graecia), and along the coast of modern-day Turkey. They even dipped their toes into North Africa with the founding of Cyrene in modern-day Libya. But what if, instead of just establishing a few scattered colonies, the Greeks had gone all in on North Africa? Imagine a world where the Greeks, instead of just flirting with the idea of North Africa, had established a string of thriving city-states along the entire coast, from the Libyan desert to the shores of modern-day Tunisia. How would this have reshaped the cultural, political, and economic landscape of the Mediterranean?

The 10 Possible Things That Would Happen

1. A Greek Nile Delta: Alexandria's Early Arrival

Imagine if the Greeks, seeing the fertile Nile Delta and its strategic location, had decided to set up shop centuries before Alexander the Great. Instead of Alexandria being founded by a Macedonian conqueror, it becomes a bustling

Greek city-state, perhaps named "Neopolis" (because why not have another one?). The phrase "All roads lead to Neopolis" becomes the motto of this early Greek hub in Egypt. This city-state becomes a magnet for Greek settlers, traders, and philosophers, blending Hellenic and Egyptian cultures centuries before it historically happened. The presence of this Greek city might have led to earlier and more intense interactions between Greek and Egyptian societies, with Greek scholars eagerly studying the mysteries of the Nile and Egyptian priests scratching their heads at the Greek obsession with geometry. Future historians might wonder how much of Egyptian culture was "Hellenized" and how many Greek gods picked up an Egyptian accent.

2. Carthage vs. Corinth: A Clash of Cultures

The Greeks, never ones to back down from a challenge, decide to establish colonies dangerously close to Carthage, that burgeoning power in the Western Mediterranean. What follows is a rivalry that makes the Peloponnesian War look like a friendly disagreement over a game of hopscotch. The phrase "It's not just a trade war" enters the ancient lexicon as Greek city-states like Corinth, Syracuse, and Cyrene find themselves in a cold (and sometimes hot) war with Carthage. These two powers, each proud and stubborn, engage in a series of naval battles, trade embargoes, and diplomatic shenanigans. Greek colonies in North Africa become heavily fortified, with towering walls and fleets of triremes patrolling the coasts. The Carthaginians, never ones to be outdone, step up their game, leading to an arms race that could have repercussions throughout the Mediterranean. Future historians might call this the "First Mediterranean Cold War," where Greek and Punic cultures clashed and mixed, leading to a unique hybrid culture that combined the best (and worst) of both worlds.

3. The Rise of the Greek Pharaonic Dynasties

With Greek colonies flourishing in Egypt, the local Greek elites start to get ambitious. Why stop at running a city when you can run an entire country? Before you know it, Greek dynasties begin to emerge, with local rulers claiming the title of Pharaoh—and maybe even getting into the whole "son of Ra" thing. The phrase "Pharaoh in a toga" becomes an inside joke among the Egyptian populace as Greek rulers adopt Egyptian customs, titles, and religion. These Greek Pharaohs build temples that mix Greek columns with Egyptian obelisks, creating a fusion architecture that future archaeologists drool over. The Greek influence permeates Egyptian society, leading to a unique blend of cultures where hieroglyphs and Greek inscriptions coexist on temple walls. The intellectual cross-pollination between Greek and Egyptian scholars might lead to early advancements in science, mathematics, and philosophy, with Alexandria (sorry, Neopolis) becoming the ancient world's greatest center of learning even earlier than in our timeline. Future historians might debate whether these Greek Pharaohs were truly Egyptian or just Hellenic tourists who overstayed their welcome.

4. Greek Mythology Meets African Deities: A Divine Merger

As the Greeks settle more of North Africa, their pantheon of gods comes into contact with local African deities. The result? A divine merger that sees Zeus sharing temple space with Amun, and Athena adopting a lioness head to fit in with the locals. The phrase "All gods are welcome" becomes the mantra of this new, blended religion, where Greek and African deities share the same temples and festivals. Zeus-Ammon becomes a popular god, worshipped from Greece to the heart of Africa, and shrines dedicated to this hybrid deity pop up everywhere. The Oracle of Siwa, a major religious center, might become even more influential as Greeks and Africans alike seek divine guidance. Greek and African myths begin to intertwine, leading to new epic tales where heroes navigate both the Greek underworld and African spiritual realms. Future mythologists would have a field day untangling these stories, wondering whether Hercules really did wrestle with Anubis or if that was just a later addition by some creative scribe.

5. *The Hellenistic Influence on Berber Tribes: A Cultural Renaissance*

The Berber tribes of North Africa, known for their resilience and independence, begin to adopt Greek culture, language, and political ideas. This leads to a Hellenistic-inspired cultural renaissance in the heart of the African continent, with Berber warriors quoting Homer and philosophers debating in the desert. The phrase "Philosophers in the Sahara" isn't as crazy as it sounds, as Berber tribes establish their own schools of thought, blending Greek philosophy with local traditions. The Berbers, known for their fierce independence, adapt the Greek city-state model to their own needs, creating a network of fortified towns and trade hubs across the desert. These towns become centers of learning and culture, attracting scholars, traders, and adventurers from across the Mediterranean. The Berber warriors, now equipped with Greek tactics and weapons, become a formidable force, capable of holding their own against any would-be invaders. Future historians might speak of the "Berber Renaissance," a period where Greek and African ideas combined to create a unique and enduring civilization.

6. *Trade Networks Flourish: Greek Influence Spreads Inland*

With their colonies firmly established along the coast, the Greeks begin to push inland, establishing trade routes that reach deep into Africa. These routes, dotted with Greek trading posts and settlements, bring Greek goods and culture to the farthest corners of the continent. The phrase "All roads lead to Greece" is reimagined as Greek traders establish a network of trade routes that crisscross Africa, bringing Greek pottery, wine, and olive oil to markets as far south as modern-day Nigeria. Greek influence spreads inland, with local leaders adopting Greek titles, clothing, and even political structures. The exchange of goods leads to the exchange of ideas, and soon

Greek myths, plays, and philosophies are being discussed in African courts. The reverse is also true, with African goods and ideas making their way to Greece, leading to a richer, more diverse Hellenic culture. Future economists might look back on this period as the "Greek-African Trade Boom," noting how these early trade routes set the stage for later global exchanges.

7. Greek Medicine Meets African Healing: A New School of Thought

Greek doctors, always eager to expand their knowledge, begin learning from African healers, leading to a new school of medicine that combines the best of both traditions. This new medical knowledge spreads throughout the Greek world, leading to advances in everything from surgery to herbal remedies. The phrase "Take two herbs and call me in the morning" becomes common advice as Greek doctors incorporate African medicinal herbs and practices into their treatments. The fusion of Greek and African medical knowledge leads to significant advancements in the understanding of diseases, anatomy, and treatments. Greek medical texts begin to include African remedies, and medical schools in places like Neopolis become centers for this new, blended approach to healing. Future medical historians might credit this period with laying the foundations for modern medicine, noting how the cross-cultural exchange of knowledge led to breakthroughs that wouldn't have been possible in isolation.

8. The Punic Wars Get a Greek Twist

With Greek colonies spread across North Africa, the Punic Wars between Rome and Carthage take on a new dimension. The Greeks, ever the opportunists, might play both sides against each other, or perhaps even throw their weight behind one of the contenders, turning the conflict into a three-way struggle for dominance in the Mediterranean. The phrase "A Greek in every fight" might become the catchphrase of the era as Greek city-states in North Africa find themselves entangled in the Punic Wars. Some might ally with Rome, seeing an opportunity to expand their influence, while others might side with Carthage, hoping to curb Roman power. The result is a more complex and chaotic series of wars, with shifting alliances and betrayals becoming the norm. The outcome of the Punic Wars might be very different, with Greek colonies playing kingmaker—or perhaps even emerging as the dominant power in the region themselves. Future historians might debate the true winners of the Punic Wars, wondering how much Greek meddling influenced the final outcome and how close the Mediterranean came to being dominated by a Greek-led coalition.

9. Greek Democracy Spreads to Africa: A Political Revolution

The Greeks, ever fond of their democratic experiments, bring their political ideas to North Africa. Over time, some African city-states begin to adopt democratic systems, leading to a wave of political innovation across the continent. The phrase "Democracy in the desert" doesn't sound so strange as African city-states experiment with Greek-style governance. Councils and assemblies begin to pop up in cities across North Africa, where citizens (or at least the free male ones) debate and vote on matters of state. This political innovation leads to a new era of civic engagement and public discourse, with African leaders adopting the title of "archon" or "strategos." The blend of Greek political ideas with African traditions creates unique systems of governance that emphasize both individual rights and community responsibility. Future political scientists might study this period as the "African Democratic Awakening," noting how the spread of Greek democracy influenced the political development of the continent.

10. The Roman Empire Looks Different: A More Hellenized Africa

As the Romans eventually conquer North Africa, they find a region deeply influenced by Greek culture. Instead of imposing their own ways, the Romans might adopt and adapt what's already there, leading to a more Hellenized version of Roman Africa. The phrase "When in Africa, do as the Greeks do" might become the Roman motto as they find themselves ruling over a region that is as Greek as it is African. The Romanization of North Africa takes on a distinct Greek flavor, with Roman architecture, laws, and customs blending seamlessly with the Hellenistic traditions already in place. Roman Africa becomes a melting pot of cultures, where Greek plays are performed in Roman theaters, and Roman gods share temples with their Greek counterparts. The legacy of this Hellenized Roman Africa might be seen in everything from the architecture of North African cities to the writings of local scholars who blend Roman, Greek, and African ideas into a unique philosophical tradition. Future historians might describe this as the "Greco-Roman-African Synthesis," a period of cultural fusion that left a lasting mark on the Mediterranean world.

Conclusion

If the ancient Greeks had colonized more of North Africa, the history of the Mediterranean and beyond would have taken a dramatically different course. Greek culture, politics, and philosophy would have permeated the region, leading to a unique blend of civilizations that combined the best of Greek, African, and later Roman traditions. The result would have been a richer, more diverse Mediterranean world where Greek influence was felt far beyond the Aegean, and somewhere in this alternate history, a Greek philosopher might have gazed out over the African sands, sipped his wine, and mused, "Africa? More like Afri-Greece."

What If the Ancient Celtic Tribes Had Built Cities and Centralized States Much Earlier?

The Background

The ancient Celts, known for their fierce independence, intricate art, and warrior culture, were a people of the forests and hills of Europe. They spread across a vast territory, from the British Isles to Anatolia, living in small, often isolated communities. Despite their widespread presence and rich culture, the Celts never formed large, centralized states or built cities on the scale of their Mediterranean neighbors. But what if, instead of remaining a collection of loosely connected tribes, the Celts had developed urban centers and centralized states much earlier? Imagine a world where the Celts, inspired perhaps by the Etruscans or the Greeks, began constructing walled cities, organizing armies, and establishing bureaucracies long before Rome even thought about expanding beyond the Tiber.

The 10 Possible Things That Would Happen

1. The Rise of Celtic Metropolises: From Hillforts to Cities

Instead of scattered hillforts, the Celts begin building large, fortified cities—let's call them "Celtopoli"—complete with public squares, bustling markets, and impressive temples dedicated to their gods. These urban centers become hubs of trade, culture, and political power. The phrase "Meet me at the Celtopolis" becomes the ancient equivalent of "Let's grab a coffee," as Celts flock to these new urban centers for business, politics, and a bit of socializing. The transition from hillforts to cities means that Celtic society becomes more stratified, with a distinct urban elite emerging to rival the warrior aristocracy. These cities, strategically located along trade routes, become powerhouses of commerce, attracting merchants from across Europe and even beyond. Future archaeologists might uncover the ruins of Celtopoli and marvel at how these early Celtic cities rivaled the great metropolises of the ancient world, leading to debates about whether the Celts were the true "lost civilization" of Europe.

2. Centralized Kingdoms: The Unification of the Celts

The Celts, who historically were a fractious bunch, begin to unify under powerful kings and chieftains. These rulers, based in their new cities, start to centralize power, creating early Celtic kingdoms that are far more organized and cohesive than their historical counterparts. The phrase "A king in every Celtopolis" becomes a reality as powerful monarchs emerge, each ruling over a centralized state. These kings establish courts, enforce laws, and even start minting their own currency, leading to a more integrated and unified Celtic civilization. The rivalries between these kings lead to wars of conquest and consolidation, with some kingdoms growing large enough to rival early Rome. The unification of the Celts under central authorities means that they can coordinate large-scale military campaigns and fortification projects, making them a formidable force in Europe. Future historians might refer to this period as the "Celtic Kingdoms Era," a time when the Celts transformed from a loose confederation of tribes into a network of powerful states.

3. Celtic Architecture: A New Style Emerges

With the rise of cities and centralized states, Celtic architecture undergoes a transformation. The Celts, inspired by their own artistic traditions and borrowing ideas from neighboring cultures, develop a unique style of monumental architecture, characterized by intricate stonework, towering structures, and ornate carvings. The phrase "Celtic stonecraft" becomes synonymous with architectural brilliance as Celtic builders create structures that stand the test of time. Temples, palaces, and public buildings are adorned with the swirling, interlacing patterns that define Celtic art, while massive stone walls encircle their cities, making them virtually impregnable. The Celts also develop advanced engineering techniques, building bridges, aqueducts, and roads that connect their urban centers. The result is a landscape dotted with impressive stone cities, each reflecting the power and wealth of its rulers. Future architects might study Celtic ruins alongside those of Rome and Greece, noting how the Celts brought their own unique flair to the art of building.

4. A Celtic Army to Rival Rome: Professional Soldiers and Organized Warfare

The Celts, no longer just a collection of warriors who showed up when called, develop a professional army. This force, trained and equipped by the centralized state, is capable of organized warfare on a scale previously unseen among the Celts. The phrase "The Celts are coming" sends shivers down the spines of their enemies as this new, professional Celtic army takes to the field. Armed with iron weapons and clad in armor, these soldiers march in disciplined formations, using tactics and strategies developed by their kings' military advisors. The Celts also invest in cavalry and chariot units, creating a mobile and versatile force that can strike fear into even the most seasoned Roman legions. The development of siege engines and fortifications means that the Celts are now a match for any army in Europe, capable of both defending their cities and launching devastating offensives.

Future military historians might credit the Celts with pioneering some of the techniques later used by the Romans, leading to speculation about how much of Rome's military prowess was borrowed from their earlier Celtic foes.

5. The Celtic-Roman Wars: A New Rivalry

With their new urban centers and organized states, the Celts become a much more formidable opponent for Rome. The historical raids and skirmishes are replaced by full-scale wars between the two powers, each vying for dominance in Europe. The phrase "Celtic defiance" enters Roman literature as the two civilizations clash in a series of brutal wars. These conflicts, fought across Gaul, Britain, and the Alps, become legendary for their intensity and scale. The Celts, now equipped with fortified cities and a professional army, manage to hold their own against Rome, even scoring some major victories that shake the Roman Senate to its core. The rivalry between the two powers leads to an arms race, with each side adopting and adapting the other's tactics and technologies. Future historians might debate whether Rome's eventual dominance was ever inevitable or if the Celts came within a hair's breadth of turning the tables on their Mediterranean rivals.

6. A Celtic Intellectual Renaissance: Druidic Schools and Philosophical Thought

With the rise of cities and centralized states, the Celts begin to invest more in education and intellectual pursuits. Druidic schools, already centers of learning, expand their curricula to include philosophy, mathematics, and astronomy, creating a Celtic intellectual renaissance. The phrase "Druids and scholars" becomes more than just a description of wise men in white robes—it becomes a hallmark of Celtic society. The Druidic schools, now supported by the state, attract students from across Europe, eager to learn the secrets of the natural world, the stars, and the human mind. Celtic scholars begin to write down their teachings, creating a rich body of literature that blends traditional Druidic knowledge with new ideas borrowed from Greek and Roman thinkers. This intellectual blossoming leads to innovations in medicine, engineering, and philosophy, with the Celts making significant contributions to the broader European intellectual tradition. Future scholars might study the "Celtic Enlightenment," marveling at how a people once considered barbarians became a beacon of knowledge and wisdom.

7. Celtic Trade Networks: A Commercial Powerhouse

The establishment of cities and centralized states leads to the development of extensive trade networks. The Celts, already skilled craftsmen, begin to export their goods—fine metalwork, textiles, and pottery—across Europe and beyond. The phrase "Celtic gold" becomes a byword for quality and craftsmanship as Celtic goods flood the markets of the ancient world. The Celts establish trade routes that stretch from the British Isles to the Mediterranean, bringing in wealth that fuels further urban development and military expansion. Celtic merchants, savvy and well-connected, become some of the richest people in Europe, rivaling their Greek and Roman counterparts. The influx of foreign goods and ideas leads to even greater cultural exchange, with the Celts adopting new technologies and artistic styles while spreading their own culture far and wide. Future economists might look back on this period as the "Celtic Commercial Boom," a time when the Celts became a major economic power in the ancient world.

8. A Celtic Naval Power: Dominance of the Atlantic

With their newfound wealth and organization, the Celts don't just stick to land—they take to the seas. Celtic shipbuilders, inspired by the need to protect and expand their trade routes, develop a formidable navy that dominates the Atlantic and even challenges Roman control of the Mediterranean. The phrase "Celtic sails on the horizon" becomes a common sight for coastal towns from Iberia to Britannia. The Celtic navy, equipped with fast, maneuverable ships and crewed by experienced sailors, patrols the Atlantic coast and conducts raids deep into Roman territory. These naval expeditions disrupt Roman supply lines and establish Celtic dominance over key maritime trade routes. The Celts also begin to explore distant lands, establishing colonies in the far reaches of the Atlantic and even venturing into the Mediterranean, where they set up trading posts and challenge Roman naval supremacy. Future maritime historians might refer to this period as the "Celtic Age of Sail," noting how the Celts became the dominant naval power of their time, rivaling even the legendary fleets of Carthage and Rome.

9. Celtic Religion: A New Pantheon Emerges

The Celts, always a deeply spiritual people, begin to formalize and centralize their religious practices with the rise of their cities and states. New temples are built, and a more organized priesthood emerges, leading to the creation of a standardized Celtic pantheon that blends old tribal gods with new deities that reflect the changing nature of Celtic society. The phrase "In the name of the gods" takes on new significance as the Celts establish a unified religious system. Grand temples dedicated to gods like Lugus, Brigid, and Taranis dominate the skyline of Celtopoli, becoming centers of worship, pilgrimage, and political power. The Druids, now a formalized priestly class, hold sway over religious and political matters, advising kings and leading rituals that unite the people in a shared faith. This new pantheon becomes a symbol of Celtic identity, reinforcing the unity of the Celtic kingdoms and providing a spiritual foundation for their society. Future religious scholars might study the "Celtic Reformation," a period when the Celts created a cohesive religious system that reflected their newfound power and unity.

10. The Fall of Rome: A Different History

With the Celts more organized, urbanized, and militarized, Rome's expansion into Gaul and Britain faces fierce resistance. Instead of falling easily to Roman legions, these regions become battlegrounds where the Celts hold their ground, leading to a much slower and more costly Roman conquest—or even a different outcome altogether. The phrase "The Celtic Wars" becomes the focus of Roman history, a series of protracted and brutal conflicts that drain the resources of the Roman Empire. The Celts, now masters of both land and sea, launch counterattacks that threaten Rome's hold on its western provinces. The Roman Empire, overstretched and bogged down in a costly war with the Celts, begins to show cracks much earlier than in our timeline. The eventual fall of Rome might be hastened by this relentless Celtic resistance, leading to a world where the Celts, not the Romans, become the dominant force in Western Europe. Future historians might debate the "Celtic Factor" in the fall of Rome, arguing that the rise of a powerful and organized Celtic civilization played a key role in bringing down one of history's greatest empires.

Conclusion

If the ancient Celtic tribes had built cities and centralized states much earlier, the history of Europe—and indeed, the world—would have taken a radically different course. A more urbanized and organized Celtic civilization would have posed a formidable challenge to Roman expansion, potentially altering the balance of power in the ancient world. The Celts, once seen as the wild barbarians of the north, might have become the rulers of a vast, powerful empire that shaped the future of Europe. And somewhere in this alternate history, a Celtic bard might have sung tales of a world where the Celts, not the Romans, built the greatest cities, won the greatest wars, and left the greatest legacy.

What If the Byzantine Empire Had Reconquered the Entire Western Roman Empire?

The Background

The Byzantine Empire, the Eastern Roman Empire that stubbornly clung to its Roman heritage while the West crumbled into feudal chaos, was a force to be reckoned with. Under Emperor Justinian I in the 6th century, the Byzantines embarked on an ambitious campaign to reconquer the lost territories of the Western Roman Empire. They made some impressive gains, reclaiming parts of North Africa, Italy, and even parts of Spain, but the dream of fully restoring the Roman Empire was never realized. But what if Justinian's generals had gone all the way, reconquering the entire Western Roman Empire? Imagine a world where the Byzantine Empire, flush with victory, reestablishes Roman control over the West, knitting together a fractured Europe under the golden banner of the double-headed eagle.

The 10 Possible Things That Would Happen

1. A United Roman Empire: The Revival of the Eternal City

With the Western territories fully reclaimed, the Byzantine Empire could restore the glory of Rome, reestablishing it as the political and cultural heart of the empire. Rome becomes a bustling metropolis again, filled with senators, philosophers, and—of course—corrupt politicians. The phrase "All roads lead to Rome" gets a literal revival as the city, once again, becomes the center of the known world. With Byzantine funding and expertise, Rome's crumbling infrastructure is rebuilt, aqueducts flow with water, and the Colosseum echoes with the roar of chariot races and political debates (which, let's be honest, are equally bloody). The city's rebirth as a hub of power might overshadow Constantinople, leading to a rivalry between the two great cities that keeps the empire on its toes. Future historians would marvel at how the ancient capital rose from the ashes, only to descend once again into the same old political squabbles, proving that some things never change.

2. The Byzantine Feudal System: A Twist on Medieval Europe

The Byzantines, having reasserted control over the West, begin to impose their own brand of centralized bureaucracy on Europe, but they can't avoid adopting some elements of the feudal system that had taken root in their absence. This leads to a bizarre hybrid where Byzantine emperors rule over a patchwork of feudal lords who are required to wear togas during official ceremonies. The phrase "Byzantine complexity" takes on new meaning as Europe's feudal lords struggle to navigate a system that combines the worst of both worlds—Byzantine red tape and feudal obligations. Local barons and dukes find themselves drowning in imperial decrees written in Greek, while trying to maintain their medieval power structures. The Byzantine influence could lead to a more centralized and stable Europe, but also one where every minor dispute requires an imperial council, three scrolls of ancient law, and an official seal that takes a year to get from Constantinople. Future medieval historians might joke that the Byzantines didn't so much conquer Europe as they buried it under a mountain of parchment.

3. A Byzantine-Latin Cultural Fusion: The Renaissance Comes Early

The reunification of East and West under Byzantine rule leads to a blending of Greek and Latin cultures, sparking an early renaissance. The fusion of Byzantine intellectual traditions with Western art and literature creates a cultural explosion that redefines Europe's identity. The phrase "When in Rome, do as the Greeks do" becomes the cultural mantra as Byzantine philosophy, art, and theology mix with Western creativity. Scholars in newly restored libraries translate ancient Greek texts into Latin, sparking a revival of classical learning that spreads across the empire. Gothic cathedrals get a Byzantine makeover, complete with domes, mosaics, and more gold leaf than anyone knows what to do with. This early renaissance leads to advancements in science, philosophy, and the arts, setting the stage for an even more brilliant cultural flowering centuries later. Future art historians might argue over whether the Mona Lisa would have looked better with a Byzantine halo, while philosophers debate whether Aristotle would have approved of medieval knights quoting Plato.

4. Religious Unity—or Not: The Great Schism Gets Delayed

With the West under Byzantine control, the tension between the Eastern Orthodox Church and the Roman Catholic Church could either be smoothed over or exacerbated. Either way, the Great Schism, which historically split Christianity into East and West in 1054, would be delayed or altered. The phrase "One empire, one church" becomes a Byzantine slogan, though how successful this unification effort would be is anyone's guess. The Byzantines, keen to assert their religious authority, might impose their Orthodox practices on the Western Church, leading to conflicts over everything from the use of leavened bread in the Eucharist to the proper way to bow before icons. On the other hand, a compromise might be reached, with the Pope becoming a sort of Byzantine-appointed bishop who's just a little too independent for Constantinople's liking. The delayed or different Schism might mean that Christianity remains more unified—or that the eventual split is even messier. Future theologians would have a field day debating what might have been, with some lamenting the lost chance for a united Christendom while others breathe a sigh of relief that it only took a thousand years for the inevitable breakup to happen.

5. The Holy Roman What? A Different Germanic Legacy

With the Byzantine Empire in full control of the West, the historical rise of the Holy Roman Empire under Charlemagne in the 9th century could be drastically altered or even prevented. The Germanic tribes, now under Byzantine rule, might develop very differently. The phrase "Charlemagne, who?" might become a historical curiosity as the Byzantine administration keeps the Germanic tribes in check, preventing the rise of a rival empire in Western Europe. Instead of the patchwork of kingdoms that historically developed, the Germanic territories might be integrated into the Byzantine system, with local rulers appointed by the emperor in Constantinople. This leads to a more unified and stable central Europe, but also one where the distinct Germanic identity is subsumed under the broader Roman (Byzantine) culture. Future historians might lament the loss of the Holy Roman Empire's colorful political drama, but they'd probably appreciate the fewer wars fought over who gets to wear the imperial crown.

6. The Byzantification of Britain: From Angles to Emperors

With the Western Roman Empire fully restored, the Byzantine influence might reach even the distant shores of Britain. Instead of being left to fend for themselves against waves of Anglo-Saxon invaders, the Britons receive Byzantine support, leading to a unique blend of Roman and local traditions. The phrase "Byzantine Britons" might become a shorthand for the island's hybrid culture. Byzantine influence in Britain could mean that the country's famous hillforts get an upgrade into full-blown walled cities, complete with

Orthodox churches and bathhouses. The local kings and chieftains find themselves answering to Byzantine governors, and the Celtic cross might gain a few more Byzantine flourishes. Arthurian legends could take on a distinctly Eastern flavor, with knights embarking on quests for holy relics under the banner of the double-headed eagle. Future British historians might ponder the effects of this alternate history, where London boasts a grand cathedral dedicated to Saint Sophia and where Arthur's knights wear lamellar armor instead of chainmail.

7. Economic Revival: A Byzantine Golden Age in the West

The reconquest of the West brings a flood of wealth back into the empire, leading to an economic revival. The Western territories, once plagued by barbarian invasions and economic decline, experience a resurgence under Byzantine rule. The phrase "All that glitters is Byzantine gold" could be heard across Europe as the empire's coffers fill with the riches of the West. The Byzantines, always keen on trade, reestablish old Roman trade routes, leading to a boom in commerce across the Mediterranean. Cities like Ravenna, Rome, and Carthage become thriving economic centers, exporting goods to the East and importing luxury items from Constantinople. The economic revival also leads to advancements in technology and infrastructure, with aqueducts, roads, and public buildings being restored or rebuilt. Future economic historians might refer to this period as the "Byzantine Boom," a time when the restored Roman Empire once again became the economic powerhouse of the ancient world.

8. Byzantine Law and Order: The Codex Justinianus Expands

The Byzantine legal system, already sophisticated and detailed thanks to Justinian's Code, gets implemented across the newly reconquered Western territories. This brings a level of legal uniformity to Europe that it hadn't seen since the days of the early Roman Empire. The phrase "Justice is blind, and Byzantine" might be used to describe the sprawling legal system that now governs Europe. The Codex Justinianus becomes the law of the land from Britannia to Hispania, leading to a more orderly and structured society. This legal uniformity helps stabilize the empire and reduce conflicts between different regions, as everyone now plays by the same Byzantine rulebook. The influence of Byzantine law might also mean that European legal traditions develop differently, with a stronger emphasis on Roman legal principles rather than the more localized systems that historically evolved. Future legal scholars might debate the long-term effects of this "Byzantine Unification," noting how it set the stage for the modern legal systems of Europe.

9. A New Byzantine Military: The Cataphracts of Gaul

With the Western territories fully reconquered, the Byzantine military needs to adapt to the new realities of ruling such a vast empire. This leads to the development of a more versatile and diverse army, combining the best of Roman, Byzantine, and Western military traditions. The phrase "Cataphracts in Gaul" becomes a reality as the heavily armored Byzantine cavalry, known for their effectiveness in the East, are deployed in the Western provinces. These cataphracts, along with a mix of Roman legions, Germanic infantry, and local militias, form a formidable military force that secures the empire's borders. The Byzantines might also adopt and improve upon Western military innovations, such as the use of stirrups, leading to an even more powerful and mobile army. This new military force could deter invasions from beyond the empire's borders, delaying or preventing the rise of the medieval kingdoms that historically replaced the Roman Empire. Future military historians might look back on this period as the "Byzantine Renaissance in Warfare," where the empire's military might was unmatched across Europe and the Mediterranean.

10. The Preservation of Roman Legacy: A Different Middle Ages

With the Byzantine Empire's successful reconquest, the Western Roman Empire's fall is effectively reversed. This leads to a preservation of Roman culture, technology, and governance that fundamentally alters the course of European history. The phrase "Dark Ages? What Dark Ages?" might be heard as the traditional narrative of medieval Europe is upended. With Roman institutions preserved and reinforced by Byzantine rule, Europe avoids the severe fragmentation and decline that historically characterized the early Middle Ages. Instead of a patchwork of feudal states, Europe remains a more centralized and cohesive entity, with Roman law, culture, and infrastructure continuing to influence daily life. The preservation of Roman learning and technology means that Europe remains more connected to its classical past, potentially leading to an earlier and more seamless transition into the Renaissance. Future historians might refer to this as the "Continued Classical Age," a period where the echoes of Rome never faded, and Europe remained a beacon of Roman civilization.

Conclusion

If the Byzantine Empire had successfully reconquered the entire Western Roman Empire, the history of Europe and the Mediterranean would have been dramatically altered. The restoration of Roman control over the West would have led to a more unified and stable Europe, preserving Roman culture and institutions well into the Middle Ages. The Byzantine influence would have reshaped everything from law and religion to military and economic systems, creating a world where the legacy of Rome endured in ways that our own history only briefly glimpsed. And somewhere in this alternate timeline, a Byzantine emperor might have looked out over his vast, restored empire and mused, "Who said you can't put Rome back together again?"

What If the Ancient Mayans Had Established a Vast Empire?

The Background

The ancient Mayans, renowned for their advanced knowledge of astronomy, mathematics, and their complex calendar, were a collection of city-states scattered across the jungles of Mesoamerica. They built towering pyramids, developed a sophisticated writing system, and engaged in intricate trade networks. But despite their many achievements, the Mayans never united into a single, vast empire like the Aztecs or the Incas. Instead, they remained divided, with city-states like Tikal, Calakmul, and Palenque often at war with each other. But what if, instead of a loose network of rival cities, the Mayans had forged a powerful and unified empire? Imagine a world where the Mayan civilization not only survived but thrived, dominating Mesoamerica and potentially even influencing regions beyond.

The 10 Possible Things That Would Happen

1. The Founding of Mayapolis: The Heart of the Empire

The first step in establishing a Mayan empire would be the creation of a central capital—let's call it "Mayapolis." This grand city, strategically located at the heart of the Yucatán Peninsula, becomes the seat of the emperor, a hub of trade, culture, and political power. The phrase "All roads lead to Mayapolis" replaces "All roads lead to Rome" as the empire's influence spreads across Mesoamerica. Mayapolis becomes a sprawling metropolis, with grand temples, palaces, and an observatory so advanced that it makes Stonehenge look like a glorified garden gnome. The city's population swells as people flock to the capital for opportunities, whether in trade, scholarship, or simply to avoid being sacrificed to the gods. Future archaeologists might uncover the ruins of Mayapolis and wonder if the city's engineers had a side gig consulting for Atlantis.

2. The Rise of the Mayan Emperor: A New Kind of Ruler

A unified Mayan empire requires a strong central figure, and so the title of "K'uhul Ajaw" (Divine Lord) is born. This emperor, seen as both a political and spiritual leader, wields unprecedented power, uniting the previously warring city-states under a single banner. The phrase "The Divine Lord commands" becomes the most effective way to end any argument, as the emperor's word is law. The K'uhul Ajaw oversees everything from trade agreements to religious ceremonies, ensuring that the empire runs like a well-oiled sacrificial altar. With the emperor's authority recognized across the land, rival city-states finally put aside their differences, or at least pretend to while plotting in the shadows. The establishment of a central ruler also means that succession becomes a big deal, with royal intrigue, palace coups, and the occasional bout of poisoning making Mayan politics more exciting than a Mesoamerican soap opera. Future historians might look back on the Mayan emperors and debate whether they were more like benevolent philosopher-kings or just really good at managing a thousand-year-long popularity contest.

3. Cultural Golden Age: The Mayan Renaissance

With the empire united and stable, a cultural renaissance blossoms. The arts, sciences, and architecture flourish like never before, with Mayan cities competing not through war but through monumental construction projects and intellectual achievements. The phrase "Build it bigger!" becomes the unofficial motto of the empire as Mayan architects push the boundaries of what's possible. Temples and pyramids rise to dizzying heights, decorated with intricate carvings that make other civilizations' art look like doodles. Mayan mathematicians, having already invented the concept of zero, start toying with more advanced mathematical theories, while astronomers predict celestial events with uncanny accuracy. The empire's scribes produce a flood of codices, recording everything from poetry to medical knowledge, ensuring that Mayan culture and achievements are immortalized for future generations. Future archaeologists might compare the Mayan Renaissance to the Italian one, except with fewer plagues and more human hearts offered to the gods.

4. Trade Networks Expand: From the Gulf to the Andes

The unification of the Mayans leads to the expansion of trade networks that stretch across Mesoamerica and beyond. Mayan merchants establish trading posts as far north as the Gulf of Mexico and as far south as the Andes, exchanging goods, ideas, and—let's be honest—a few sharp words over the price of obsidian. The phrase "Mayan merchants are here!" becomes both a welcome and slightly nervous greeting across the continent as the empire's influence spreads. The Mayans trade cacao, jade, and textiles for gold, silver, and exotic feathers, creating a vibrant economy that fuels further expansion. Trade routes are protected by the empire's military, ensuring that merchants can travel safely and that no one cheats the emperor's tax collectors. The flow of goods also means the flow of ideas, leading to a cross-cultural exchange that enriches the entire region. Future economic historians might refer to this as the "Mayan Commercial Revolution," noting how the empire's trade networks laid the groundwork for later civilizations to connect the Americas long before Columbus ever sailed the ocean blue.

5. Military Might: The Jaguar Warriors of the Empire

To maintain control over such a vast territory, the Mayan emperor builds a formidable military. The elite Jaguar Warriors, known for their ferocity and discipline, become the backbone of the empire's army, ensuring that no city-state gets any funny ideas about independence. The phrase "Send in the Jaguars" becomes the empire's version of "Release the hounds," as these warriors are deployed to crush rebellions and expand the empire's borders. Clad in jaguar skins and armed with obsidian blades, they strike fear into the hearts of anyone foolish enough to challenge the K'uhul Ajaw's authority. The empire's military might also deters external threats, keeping rival civilizations like the Zapotecs and Toltecs at bay. With a strong army to back up its diplomatic efforts, the Mayan Empire enjoys a period of relative peace and stability, though the occasional border skirmish keeps the Jaguars on their toes. Future military historians might compare the Jaguar Warriors to the Spartans, except with more colorful outfits and better taste in jewelry.

6. Religious Unification: One Pantheon to Rule Them All

With the empire unified, the Mayan religion undergoes a transformation. The pantheon of gods, once varying from city to city, is standardized across the empire, with a central temple in Mayapolis serving as the religious heart of the empire. The phrase "All gods are welcome, as long as they fit the official narrative" becomes the empire's religious policy. The priesthood, now centralized and powerful, enforces a uniform set of rituals and ceremonies, ensuring that everyone worships the same gods in the same way. The Great Pyramid of Mayapolis becomes the center of the religious universe, where the most important rituals are conducted, and where the emperor himself communes with the divine. The unification of the religion strengthens the empire's cohesion, creating a shared spiritual identity that binds the people together. Future religious scholars might debate the merits of this religious standardization, wondering whether it stifled local traditions or simply made it easier to keep the gods on the same page.

7. Diplomatic Relations: The Mayan Embassy in Rome

With their empire firmly established, the Mayans begin to engage in diplomacy with distant lands. Ambassadors from Mayapolis are sent to the courts of far-flung civilizations, including—why not?—Rome. The sight of a Mayan embassy arriving in the Eternal City is enough to make even the most jaded Roman senator sit up and take notice. The phrase "When in Rome, bring cacao" becomes a diplomatic truism as the Mayans exchange gifts and knowledge with the Romans. The two civilizations, despite their vast differences, find common ground in their shared love of architecture, mathematics, and good old-fashioned imperialism. The Mayans, intrigued by Roman engineering, bring back ideas for new construction techniques, while the Romans develop a taste for Mayan chocolate (because who wouldn't?). This cultural exchange leads to a fascinating blend of styles, with Roman villas in Gaul featuring Mayan-inspired murals, and Mayan pyramids incorporating arches and aqueducts. Future historians might write about the "Mayan-Roman Connection," marveling at how two great empires on opposite sides of the world managed to influence each other without ever going to war—or at least not a war anyone survived to write about.

8. The Preservation of Knowledge: Mayan Libraries and Codices

The unification of the Mayan Empire leads to the establishment of great libraries in cities across the empire. These libraries house vast collections of codices, recording everything from astronomy to agriculture, ensuring that the empire's knowledge is preserved for future generations. The phrase "Knowledge is power, especially if it's written down" becomes the guiding principle of Mayan intellectual life. The scribes of Mayapolis, trained in the art of writing, produce thousands of codices that document the empire's history, scientific achievements, and religious beliefs. These libraries become centers of learning, attracting scholars from across the empire who study, debate, and expand on the knowledge contained within. The preservation of this knowledge ensures that the Mayan civilization remains intellectually vibrant, with each generation building on the discoveries of the last. Future archaeologists might stumble upon these libraries and, after years of painstaking work, finally be able to decipher the Mayan script, leading to a renaissance of Mayan studies and a new appreciation for this once-mighty empire.

9. A Mayan Calendar That Doesn't End in 2012

With a unified empire and a thriving intellectual culture, the Mayans refine their already sophisticated calendar system. This new, improved calendar extends far into the future, avoiding the whole 2012 debacle and saving us all from a lot of unnecessary panic. The phrase "The world ends when the calendar says so" becomes less of a concern as the Mayans create a calendar that accounts for cosmic cycles far beyond the year 2012. This extended calendar becomes a point of pride for the empire, symbolizing their mastery of time and the heavens. The new calendar is so accurate that Mayan astronomers can predict solar eclipses, planetary alignments, and the occasional celebrity scandal centuries in advance. Future conspiracy theorists might still latch onto the calendar for their doomsday predictions, but at least they'll have to work a lot harder to find an apocalyptic date. Historians, meanwhile, might wonder why the rest of the world didn't just adopt the Mayan calendar, considering how good the Mayans were at this whole timekeeping business.

10. The Fall of the Mayan Empire: A Different Ending

Even with all their advancements, the Mayan Empire is not immune to the forces of history. Over time, internal strife, environmental changes, and the arrival of new external threats begin to challenge the empire's stability. But instead of a sudden collapse, the Mayan Empire experiences a gradual decline, leaving behind a legacy that continues to influence the region long after its political power has waned. The phrase "All empires fall, but some take their time" might describe the slow, dignified decline of the Mayan Empire. As the empire's power wanes, it fractures into smaller, but still culturally vibrant, city-states that maintain their traditions and knowledge. The legacy of the Mayan Empire endures in the art, architecture, and religious practices of the region, which continue to influence the successor states that emerge in its wake. The Mayan language remains in use, and their calendar, mathematics, and astronomy are preserved by scholars who revere the achievements of their ancestors. Future historians might look back on the Mayan Empire as one of the great civilizations of the ancient world, noting how it managed to leave a lasting impact even as its political power faded, and how, in some ways, the Mayan spirit never truly disappeared.

Conclusion

If the ancient Mayans had established a vast empire, the history of Mesoamerica—and possibly even the world—would have been dramatically different. A united Mayan civilization would have achieved remarkable cultural, scientific, and military advancements, creating a powerful and enduring empire that could have influenced neighboring regions and even distant civilizations. The Mayan Empire, with its grand cities, centralized rule, and vibrant culture, might have become one of the greatest civilizations of the ancient world, leaving behind a legacy that would resonate through the ages. And somewhere in this alternate timeline, a Mayan scribe might have looked up from his codex, smiled at the thought of the empire's enduring glory, and noted, "It's good to be immortalized in stone—and on paper."

What If the Roman Empire Had Fully Integrated Christianity with Traditional Roman Religion?

The Background

The Roman Empire, ever pragmatic and always on the lookout for ways to keep its vast and diverse population under control, was known for its ability to absorb and adapt various religious practices from the lands it conquered. When Christianity began to spread throughout the empire, it was initially met with persecution. But after Constantine's conversion and the Edict of Milan in 313 CE, Christianity gained official tolerance and later became the state religion under Theodosius I. But what if, instead of adopting Christianity as the sole religion of the empire, the Romans had decided to fully integrate it with their traditional polytheistic practices? Imagine a world where Jesus and Jupiter share temple space, and where Christian saints are just as likely to be invoked alongside Mars, Minerva, or Bacchus.

The 10 Possible Things That Would Happen

1. The Rise of the Pantheon Plus: A Divine Merger

In this alternate timeline, the Roman Pantheon doesn't just include the gods of Olympus but also features Jesus, Mary, and an array of Christian saints, who are now officially recognized as divine figures in the empire's religious mosaic. Temples to Jupiter also house statues of the Virgin Mary, while altars to Mars have space for Saint George—because who better to fight dragons and enemies alike? The phrase "Pray to whoever works" becomes a common Roman saying as citizens hedge their bets by offering sacrifices to both old and new gods. Festivals become even more extravagant, with a new holiday calendar that includes both Saturnalia and Easter, as well as celebrations honoring "Jovian Jesus" and "Mars the Martyr." Religious processions become a chaotic blend of Roman and Christian symbols, with priests of Jupiter and Christian bishops debating theology in the streets. Future theologians might debate the finer points of "Jovian theology," wondering whether it was really a good idea to mix monotheism with polytheism or if it was just a brilliant way to cover all spiritual bases.

2. Saints and Gods: The Romanization of Christian Figures

The Roman habit of associating local deities with their own gods takes on a new twist as Christian saints are officially "Romanized." Saint Peter becomes the patron of fishermen alongside Neptune, Saint Sebastian is associated with Mars (for obvious reasons), and Saint Anthony is linked with Bacchus—because who else could protect you from overindulging at a feast? The phrase "When in Rome, invoke a saint" becomes the new norm as Christian figures are assimilated into Roman religious practices. Churches dedicated to saints often share space with temples dedicated to their associated Roman gods, leading to some interesting architectural mashups. This syncretism might lead to a more inclusive and flexible religious system, where worshippers feel free to mix and match their prayers depending on their needs. Future art historians might marvel at frescoes depicting Saint Peter fishing with Neptune or Saint Anthony trying to keep

Bacchus from turning water into too much wine.

3. Christian Sacrifices: A New Twist on Old Traditions

In this blended religious system, Christian rituals incorporate elements of traditional Roman sacrifice. While animal sacrifices might decline, offerings of bread and wine to both the Christian God and the Roman gods become a common practice, with some priests even claiming that the gods appreciate a good loaf of bread as much as the Eucharist. The phrase "Give unto Caesar, give unto Christ, and give unto Jupiter" becomes a catchy slogan, as Roman citizens juggle their offerings. Public ceremonies might include prayers to Jesus followed by the ritual slaughter of a bull for Jupiter—because why not cover all bases? The integration of Christian practices with Roman sacrifices could lead to some awkward moments, such as when a bishop and a priest argue over who gets the first sip of wine at a communal feast. Future anthropologists might scratch their heads over this curious blend of practices, trying to determine whether it was a sign of religious tolerance or just the Romans' inability to give up a good party.

4. Christian Emperors and Divine Status: The Ultimate Power Play

With Christianity and Roman religion fully integrated, Christian emperors are now seen not just as political leaders but also as divine figures, in line with the tradition of the Roman emperors being deified. Emperor Constantine, already hailed as the first Christian emperor, is worshipped as "Constantinus Divus," with statues erected in his honor that show him holding both a cross and a lightning bolt. The phrase "Hail Caesar, Son of God" becomes the imperial salute, blending Christian reverence with Roman imperial tradition. Emperors after Constantine are routinely deified upon their deaths, with Christian bishops and Roman priests presiding over the ceremonies. The imperial cult becomes a strange fusion of Christianity and Roman state religion, where emperors are both vicars of Christ and embodiments of divine power. This could lead to a situation where loyalty to the emperor becomes both a religious and political obligation, creating a more unified—but also more rigid—society. Future historians might ponder whether this practice strengthened the empire or simply made it more susceptible to the whims of increasingly divine (and increasingly eccentric) rulers.

5. Monasticism Meets Mithraism: A New Kind of Asceticism

The monastic tradition, which begins to flourish in this alternate world, is heavily influenced by Roman mystery religions like Mithraism. Monks not only retreat to remote locations to pray but also engage in secret rituals and initiations that draw on both Christian and Roman traditions. The result is a monastic order that's part hermit, part soldier, and part mystic. The phrase "Monks of Mithras" becomes synonymous with these new religious warriors who combine Christian asceticism with Roman martial discipline. These monastic orders might take vows of poverty and chastity, but they also train in combat and engage in elaborate initiation rites that involve both fasting and feats of strength. The integration of Mithraic elements into monasticism could lead to the rise of a new kind of spiritual warrior, one who sees the battle against sin as both a physical and spiritual struggle. Future scholars might compare these monk-warriors to the later knights of the Crusades, noting how this early blend of asceticism and militarism paved the way for the concept of "holy war."

6. Theological Debates Get Even More Complicated: Enter the Philosophers

With the integration of Christianity into Roman religion, theological debates become even more complex as Christian theologians and Roman philosophers clash over questions of divinity, morality, and the nature of the universe. Plato, Aristotle, and Cicero are now quoted alongside the Gospels in sermons, leading to some very confused congregations. The phrase "As Plato said to Paul" becomes a popular way to start an argument, as everyone from priests to philosophers tries to reconcile these disparate traditions. Christian doctrine begins to incorporate elements of Greek philosophy, leading to a version of Christianity that's deeply intellectual but also bewilderingly complex. The concept of the Trinity might get a Platonic makeover, while the idea of the Logos becomes even more central to theological discussions. The integration of Roman philosophy into Christian thought could lead to an early flowering of scholasticism, where reason and faith are seen as complementary rather than contradictory. Future theologians might spend centuries untangling the resulting doctrines, debating whether Christianity's Platonic elements made it more accessible to intellectuals—or just more confusing to everyone else.

7. A Different Kind of Martyrdom: Gladiators for God

In this alternate timeline, the concept of martyrdom takes on a new meaning as Christian heroes are celebrated not just for their piety but also for their prowess in the arena. Christian gladiators, who fight for their faith and their lives, become the ultimate symbols of the new syncretic religion. The phrase "Fight the good fight" becomes literal as Christians take to the arena to prove their devotion. These gladiator-martyrs, who see their combat as a form of spiritual warfare, are venerated as saints after their deaths—if they don't survive long enough to become trainers for the next generation of holy fighters. The spectacle of Christian gladiators might become a popular form of entertainment, drawing crowds who cheer for their favorite saints-in-training. The integration of Christianity with Roman martial traditions could lead to a more militant version of the faith, one that sees physical combat as a legitimate way to demonstrate spiritual strength. Future historians might look back on this period as the "Age of the Gladiator Saints," a time when Christianity's message of peace and love got a bit lost in the clash of swords and the roar of the crowd.

8. A Syncretic Scripture: The Gospel According to Jupiter

The integration of Christianity with Roman religion might lead to the creation of new religious texts that blend elements of the Bible with Roman myths. The result is a syncretic scripture that features stories of Jesus performing miracles with the help of Roman gods, apostles who consult the Sibylline Oracles, and letters from Paul that include footnotes from Cicero. The phrase "As it is written, so shall it be interpreted" takes on a whole new meaning as scholars try to make sense of these hybrid texts. The new syncretic scripture might include tales of Jesus calming storms with a nod from Neptune, or Saint Paul receiving divine guidance from both the Holy Spirit and Mercury. These stories could become the foundation of the new religion, leading to a version of Christianity that's as much about myth as it is about history. Future biblical scholars might debate the authenticity of these texts, with some arguing that they represent a corruption of the original message, while others see them as a creative adaptation to the Roman world. In any case, the resulting religion would be a fascinating—and possibly bewildering—mix of Christian and Roman traditions, with a scripture that's as diverse as the empire it serves.

9. The End of Paganism? Not So Fast

While Christianity might become fully integrated into Roman religion, that doesn't mean traditional paganism just fades away. Instead, pagan practices continue to thrive, albeit in a more Christianized form. Temples to the old gods remain standing, but they're now adorned with crosses, and priests of Jupiter might find themselves sharing duties with Christian bishops. The phrase "Old habits die hard" becomes the watchword of the time, as the Roman people continue to practice their traditional rites alongside their new Christian ones. Festivals like Saturnalia might still be celebrated, but with a Christian twist, leading to some very confused worshippers who aren't sure whether they're honoring Saturn or Jesus (or both). The persistence of pagan practices could lead to a more diverse and tolerant religious environment, where different beliefs coexist relatively peacefully—at least until someone tries to outlaw animal sacrifices again. Future historians might refer to this period as the "Pagan-Christian Continuum," a time when the lines between the old and new religions were blurred in ways that left everyone a little bit confused but generally content.

10. A Different Spread of Christianity: East and West United

With Christianity fully integrated into the Roman religious system, its spread across the empire and beyond takes on a different character. Instead of being seen as a distinct and often oppositional force, Christianity is embraced as part of the Roman identity, which might lead to its spread being more rapid and less contentious. The phrase "Roman Christianity" becomes a redundant term as the faith spreads seamlessly across the empire. Missionaries might find their work easier, as they can present Christianity as simply another aspect of Roman culture, rather than a radical new faith. This integration could lead to a more unified religious landscape across the empire, with fewer internal conflicts over doctrine and practice. The spread of Christianity into the Eastern Roman Empire (Byzantium) and beyond could be smoother, leading to a stronger and more cohesive Christian world by the time of the empire's later years. Future religious scholars might debate whether this smoother integration made Christianity more resilient—or if it diluted the faith's original message in the name of imperial unity.

Conclusion

If the Roman Empire had fully integrated Christianity with traditional Roman religion, the result would have been a fascinating—and possibly chaotic—blend of beliefs, practices, and traditions. This syncretic religious system would have altered the development of both Christianity and Roman culture, creating a world where the divine and the mundane, the old and the new, were inextricably intertwined. The Roman Empire might have enjoyed a more stable religious landscape, but at the cost of some serious theological confusion and a few gladiator saints. And somewhere in this alternate timeline, a Roman citizen might have looked up at a statue of Jesus holding Jupiter's lightning bolt, shrugged, and said, "Well, when in Rome..."

What If the Huns Had Settled and Established a Kingdom in Europe?

The Background

The Huns, the fearsome nomadic warriors who rode out of the steppes of Central Asia, struck terror into the hearts of late Roman Europe in the 4th and 5th centuries. Under the leadership of Attila, they became one of the most formidable forces in Europe, wreaking havoc on Roman territories and contributing to the eventual fall of the Western Roman Empire. However, after Attila's death in 453 CE, the Huns quickly disintegrated as a unified force and faded from the historical stage. But what if, instead of scattering to the winds, the Huns had decided to settle down and establish a kingdom in Europe? Imagine a world where Attila's successors built a lasting state, blending their warrior culture with the sedentary life of Europe.

The 10 Possible Things That Would Happen

1. The Founding of Hunland: The Birth of a New Kingdom

Instead of riding off into historical oblivion, the Huns, under a strong successor to Attila, decide to settle in the fertile plains of Pannonia (modern-day Hungary) and establish a kingdom—let's call it "Hunland." This new state becomes a formidable power in Central Europe, blending Hunnic nomadism with the settled agricultural lifestyle of the region. The phrase "All roads lead to Hunland" might have been whispered in fear rather than awe, as this new kingdom becomes the epicenter of power in Central Europe. The Huns, no longer just marauding horsemen, begin to build fortified towns and establish a capital—perhaps in the location of modern-day Budapest—where they construct a grand palace in a style that blends Roman, Gothic, and their own nomadic influences. The Hunnic aristocracy, while still preferring their horses and mobile lifestyle, start to enjoy the comforts of settled life, with feasts, hunts, and perhaps even a primitive form of Hunnic bureaucracy. Future archaeologists might dig up the ruins of Hunland's capital and scratch their heads at the mix of steppe culture and European urban planning, wondering if Attila's descendants had finally traded in their stirrups for city walls.

2. A Hunnic-Aristocratic Fusion: Nobility by the Sword

As the Huns settle, they begin to intermarry with the local Gothic, Roman, and other tribes, creating a new hybrid aristocracy. The new noble class blends the Hunnic emphasis on martial prowess with the administrative and cultural traditions of the Romans and Goths. The phrase "Nobility by the sword" becomes literal, as the Hunnic ruling class values both lineage and the ability to swing a blade with precision. This new aristocracy takes pride in both its Hunnic heritage and its ability to govern, leading to a unique social structure where warrior skills are as important as land ownership. The fusion of Hunnic and Roman-Gothic traditions might also lead to an interesting mix of clothing, with noblewomen combining Gothic brooches with Hunnic furs, while the men sport a mix of chainmail and steppe-style leather armor. Future medieval historians might chuckle at the odd sartorial choices in Hunland, noting how the kingdom's aristocrats managed to look both fierce and fabulously overdressed at the same time.

3. The Preservation of the Roman Legacy: A Curious Twist

Unlike other barbarian tribes that dismantled Roman institutions, the Huns, ever the pragmatists, decide to keep some aspects of Roman governance. They recognize the value of Roman infrastructure, such as roads, aqueducts, and legal systems, and incorporate these into their new kingdom. The phrase "When in Hunland, do as the Romans do" becomes a guiding principle for the kingdom's administration. The Huns, while fiercely independent, realize that Roman tax collection methods and legal codes could be quite useful—especially when it comes to keeping the local population in line and the coffers full. Roman engineers and administrators are retained or quickly retrained under Hunnic rule, ensuring that the transition from a nomadic to a settled society is as smooth as possible. This preservation of Roman traditions might lead to a more stable and prosperous kingdom, with a bureaucracy that is a strange but effective mix of Hunnic directness and Roman red tape. Future legal scholars might debate whether Hunland's legal code represents the last gasp of Roman law or the first step towards something entirely new.

4. The Hunnic Influence on European Warfare: Heavy Cavalry and the Bow

The Huns, famous for their horse archers, bring their military tactics into the settled life of Europe. As they establish their kingdom, these tactics evolve, leading to a new style of warfare that combines the speed and mobility of their cavalry with the heavy armor of their European neighbors. The phrase "Strike like a Hun" becomes the motto of Hunland's military, as their armies become a fearsome blend of light horse archers and heavily armored cataphracts. The Huns' expertise in mounted warfare spreads across Europe, influencing the development of cavalry tactics in neighboring regions. European kingdoms might adopt these new techniques, leading to an arms race in which everyone is trying to out-Hun the Huns. The heavy cavalry of the Middle Ages, known for their devastating charges, could develop earlier and more intensely due to the Hunnic influence. Future military historians might look back at this period and wonder how many knights took a crash course in horse archery before donning their suits of armor and charging into battle.

5. Diplomatic Relations: The Huns as Power Brokers

With their newfound power and influence, the Huns become key players in European diplomacy. Hunland's rulers are sought after as allies by both Eastern and Western Roman remnants, as well as by emerging Germanic kingdoms. The Huns, ever the opportunists, play both sides, securing their kingdom's place in European politics. The phrase "Hunnic handshake" comes to signify a deal struck with a powerful but potentially treacherous ally. Hunland's rulers become adept at balancing the demands of their neighbors, making strategic marriages and alliances to keep their kingdom secure. This diplomacy might involve sending ambassadors to Constantinople and Ravenna, while hosting envoys from the Franks, Visigoths, and Lombards at the Hunnic court. The Huns' ability to negotiate with both the East and West might lead to a more stable Central Europe, but also one where the Hunnic kingdom becomes the ultimate kingmaker—determining the fates of its neighbors with a flick of the emperor's whip. Future diplomats might study Hunnic diplomacy as a masterclass in maintaining power through strategic flexibility and a well-timed threat.

6. Religion in Hunland: A Syncretic Spiritual Landscape

As the Huns settle and interact with their Christian and pagan neighbors, their own spiritual practices begin to blend with those of the local population. A unique syncretic religion develops in Hunland, combining elements of traditional Hunnic shamanism with Christianity and local pagan beliefs. The phrase "Pray to the sky and the cross" becomes a common saying in Hunland, as the kingdom's spiritual life becomes a complex tapestry of beliefs. The Hunnic elite might continue to venerate their traditional sky gods and ancestors, while also adopting certain Christian rituals to appease their new subjects and allies. Churches and shamanic shrines coexist, and festivals might feature both Christian saints and Hunnic spirits. This blending of religions could lead to a more tolerant society, where religious diversity is the norm rather than the exception. Future religious scholars might write volumes on the "Hunland Heresy," debating whether it was a true spiritual synthesis or just a convenient way to keep everyone happy—and under control.

7. The Huns' Impact on Feudalism: A Different Power Structure

The settlement of the Huns and their establishment of a kingdom might delay or alter the development of feudalism in Europe. The Huns' emphasis on loyalty to the chieftain and their mobile warrior culture could result in a more centralized and less feudal society. The phrase "Loyalty to the Khan" becomes a pledge taken by all Hunnic warriors, emphasizing their direct allegiance to the king rather than to local lords. This could lead to a more centralized power structure in Hunland, where the king's authority is absolute, and land is granted in exchange for military service rather than hereditary rights. Neighboring regions might adopt elements of this system, leading to a different form of feudalism in Europe—one where loyalty to a central ruler is paramount, and the autonomy of local lords is less pronounced. Future political historians might speculate on how the "Hunnic Model" of governance influenced the later development of European monarchies, possibly leading to stronger, more centralized states much earlier in history.

8. Cultural Exchange: The Spread of Hunnic Art and Crafts

As the Huns settle and interact with their neighbors, their unique artistic traditions begin to influence European art and crafts. Hunnic motifs, such as intricate animal designs and steppe-inspired patterns, start to appear in the metalwork, textiles, and jewelry of Europe. The phrase "Hunnic chic" might be used to describe the latest trends in European fashion and decoration. The distinctive styles of Hunnic art, with its emphasis on dynamic movement and bold, abstract forms, could inspire new artistic movements across Europe. Gothic and Roman artisans might incorporate these motifs into their own work, leading to a fusion of styles that becomes the hallmark of the period. This cultural exchange might also extend to music, dance, and storytelling, as Hunnic traditions blend with local customs to create a rich and diverse cultural landscape. Future art historians might look back on this period as a time of great innovation, where the "Barbarian Influence" revitalized European art and laid the groundwork for later medieval aesthetics.

9. Education and Literacy: The Huns Get Scholarly

As the Huns settle, they begin to recognize the value of education and literacy, particularly as a means of administering their growing kingdom. Schools are established in Hunland, where Hunnic children learn not only the traditional skills of horsemanship and warfare but also reading, writing, and mathematics. The phrase "The pen and the sword" might be inscribed above the entrance to Hunland's first school, symbolizing the kingdom's commitment to both intellectual and martial prowess. The adoption of literacy leads to the creation of written records, legal codes, and literature in the Hunnic language, preserving the kingdom's history and culture for future generations. The Huns' emphasis on education might inspire neighboring kingdoms to follow suit, leading to a broader spread of literacy across Europe. Future historians might find well-preserved manuscripts from Hunland's scribes, marveling at the blend of Hunnic oral traditions and written scholarship, and wondering how the Huns managed to go from illiterate nomads to scholars in just a few generations.

10. The Legacy of Hunland: A Different Medieval Europe

With the Huns firmly established in Europe, the political landscape of the continent is fundamentally altered. Hunland becomes a major power in Central Europe, influencing the development of neighboring kingdoms and possibly preventing the rise of certain medieval states, such as the Holy Roman Empire or the Frankish Kingdom. The phrase "Hunland at the heart of Europe" might be used by future historians to describe the kingdom's central role in shaping the continent's history. The presence of a strong Hunnic state might deter the rise of other powerful kingdoms, leading to a more fragmented and diverse political landscape in Western Europe. The Huns' influence on military tactics, governance, and culture could spread far and wide, leaving a lasting mark on the medieval world. The Holy Roman Empire might never form, or it could develop in a very different way, with a stronger emphasis on centralized authority rather than the loose confederation that historically existed. Future historians might debate whether Hunland's dominance was a stabilizing force or a disruptive one, but there's no doubt that the kingdom's legacy would be felt for centuries to come.

Conclusion

If the Huns had settled and established a kingdom in Europe, the history of the continent would have been profoundly different. A lasting Hunnic kingdom would have influenced everything from the development of feudalism and warfare to art, religion, and education. The political landscape of Europe might have been more centralized and less feudal, with the Huns playing a key role as power brokers and cultural influencers. And somewhere in this alternate timeline, a Hunnic scribe might have looked up from his parchment, smiled at the thought of the kingdom's enduring legacy, and noted, "It's good to be both feared and learned."

What If the Ancient Polynesians Had Discovered the Americas Before Columbus?

The Background

The Polynesians were extraordinary navigators, mastering the vast expanses of the Pacific Ocean long before most Europeans even dared to venture beyond the sight of land. They settled islands scattered across thousands of miles, from Hawaii to New Zealand, using only the stars, ocean currents, and a keen sense of adventure. But what if, instead of stopping at Easter Island, they kept going and made landfall on the west coast of the Americas—centuries before Columbus ever set sail? Imagine a world where Polynesians, with their canoes and rich cultural heritage, established contact with Native American civilizations, leading to a fusion of ideas, technologies, and possibly even languages.

The 10 Possible Things That Would Happen

1. The Founding of Polynesia-America: The Pacific Meets the Americas

Instead of Columbus planting a flag for Spain, imagine a Polynesian chief planting a carved tiki statue on the shores of what is now California. Polynesians establish settlements along the coast, forming the first Polynesian-American communities. These settlements, though small at first, become hubs of trade and cultural exchange between the Pacific Islanders and Native American tribes. The phrase "Aloha, amigos" might become the greeting of choice as Polynesians and Native Americans blend their languages and cultures. Polynesian outrigger canoes become a common sight along the Pacific coastline, with Native American traders eager to exchange goods like maize, beans, and obsidian for Polynesian tools, fishhooks, and tapa cloth. These early settlements might grow into bustling port towns, where totem poles and moai statues stand side by side. Future archaeologists might dig up artifacts that seem oddly out of place—like a feathered headdress adorned with Polynesian seashells—and wonder what kind of party they missed.

2. A Culinary Fusion: Taro Meets Maize

The meeting of these two cultures would lead to a unique culinary exchange. The Polynesians, masters of cultivating taro, breadfruit, and coconut, would introduce these staples to the Americas. In return, they'd take back maize, beans, and chili peppers to their Pacific islands. The phrase "Tacos with a side of poi" might be the menu special in these coastal settlements, as the fusion of Polynesian and Native American cuisines creates dishes that are both delicious and a bit confusing to modern palates. Imagine a world where tamales are wrapped in banana leaves and topped with a spicy coconut sauce, or where poke bowls feature corn and chili-lime seasoning. This culinary exchange could lead to new farming practices in both regions, with Polynesians introducing terraced farming techniques to the Americas and Native Americans teaching their Polynesian counterparts the secrets of the

Three Sisters (maize, beans, and squash). Future food historians might credit this early contact with revolutionizing the diets of both cultures, though they might also wonder how anyone managed to get anything done with all that delicious food around.

3. Polynesian Navigation Meets Native American Engineering

The Polynesians were unparalleled navigators, while Native American civilizations, such as the Incas and Aztecs, were master builders and engineers. The exchange of knowledge between these two cultures could have led to remarkable advancements in both fields. The phrase "Let's take the scenic route—by canoe and road" might describe the new transportation networks that spring up as a result of this exchange. Polynesian navigators, with their star charts and ocean-going canoes, might teach the Native Americans how to explore the Pacific, while the Native Americans introduce the Polynesians to the concept of paved roads and bridges. This exchange could lead to the development of a unique transportation system that combines the best of both worlds—think highways that lead directly to well-established port cities where Polynesian canoes are ready to set sail. Future historians might marvel at the intricate network of trade routes that crisscross the Americas and the Pacific, wondering how much sooner globalization would have kicked off if these two cultures had teamed up.

4. A Religious Blend: Gods of the Pacific Meet the Spirits of the Land

The Polynesians had a rich pantheon of gods, many of whom were associated with the sea, the land, and the sky. Native American tribes also had complex spiritual systems tied to the natural world. The meeting of these two spiritual traditions could lead to a fascinating syncretism, where Polynesian gods and Native American spirits coexist and even merge. The phrase "May the gods and spirits guide you" could become a common blessing as these two religious traditions blend together. Imagine a world where Maui, the Polynesian demigod known for fishing up islands, is worshipped alongside

Coyote, the Native American trickster spirit. Rituals might involve both Polynesian chants and Native American dances, performed in front of altars adorned with both tikis and totem poles. This syncretic religion could lead to a more harmonious relationship between the two cultures, with shared beliefs fostering cooperation and mutual respect. Future religious scholars might study the "Polynesian-American Spiritual Tradition," noting how it combined the best elements of both faiths while keeping everyone guessing as to which god or spirit was actually in charge.

5. A United Pacific-Atlantic Trade Network

The Polynesians, with their incredible seafaring abilities, could establish trade routes not only across the Pacific but also connecting with existing Native American trade networks that span the continent. These routes might even reach the Atlantic, creating a vast trade network that links the Pacific Islands, the Americas, and possibly even Europe and Africa. The phrase "All oceans lead to trade" might become the mantra of the new world economy, as goods flow freely between the Pacific, the Americas, and beyond. Polynesian navigators, using their knowledge of ocean currents and winds, could map out new trade routes that make the Silk Road look like a country lane. Native American traders, with their vast networks stretching from the Great Lakes to the Gulf of Mexico, could tap into this oceanic trade, bringing goods from the Pacific to the Atlantic coast. This could lead to an early form of globalization, with goods, ideas, and even diseases spreading more rapidly across the globe. Future economic historians might refer to this as the "Pre-Columbian Trade Revolution," noting how it set the stage for the world's first truly global economy—long before Columbus ever got lost on his way to India.

6. The Spread of Agriculture: New Crops for New Lands

The introduction of Polynesian crops like taro, breadfruit, and sweet potatoes to the Americas could lead to new agricultural practices and a more diverse diet for Native American civilizations. Similarly, Native American crops could spread across the Pacific, leading to changes in Polynesian agriculture. The phrase "Grow local, eat global" might describe the new agricultural landscape that emerges from this exchange. In the Americas, farmers might start cultivating taro in terraced fields, while breadfruit becomes a staple crop in coastal regions. Meanwhile, Polynesian islands could see fields of maize and beans sprouting up alongside their traditional crops, leading to new farming techniques and a more varied diet. This exchange of crops could lead to increased food security and population growth in both regions, with more diverse agricultural systems capable of supporting larger and more complex societies. Future agricultural historians might marvel at how this early exchange of crops reshaped the diets of entire civilizations, wondering why it took so long for the rest of the world to catch on to the benefits of a diverse and interconnected food system.

7. The Polynesian Influence on Native American Art and Architecture

The Polynesians were known for their intricate wood carvings, tattoo art, and monumental stone structures like the moai of Easter Island. Contact with Native American civilizations, known for their own impressive artistic traditions and architecture, could lead to a unique fusion of styles. The phrase "Moai meets Mesa Verde" might describe the new artistic and architectural styles that emerge from this fusion. Imagine cliff dwellings in the American Southwest adorned with Polynesian-inspired carvings, or massive stone heads reminiscent of the moai standing watch over Mesoamerican cities. The Polynesian love of intricate patterns and bold, symbolic designs could influence Native American pottery, textiles, and even body art, leading to a new, hybrid style that becomes the hallmark of this cross-cultural exchange. Future art historians might refer to this period as the "Polynesian Renaissance," noting how the meeting of these two artistic traditions led to an explosion of creativity that left a lasting mark on the visual culture of the Americas.

8. Language Exchange: A New Lingua Franca

The contact between Polynesians and Native Americans would likely lead to the exchange of languages, resulting in a new lingua franca that incorporates elements of both linguistic traditions. This new language could facilitate trade, diplomacy, and cultural exchange across the Pacific and the Americas. The phrase "Talk story" might take on a whole new meaning as this new language spreads across the continents. Traders, diplomats, and storytellers might all use this hybrid language to communicate, blending Polynesian words with Native American grammar and syntax. The resulting lingua franca could be rich in metaphor, imagery, and oral tradition, making it as much a tool for diplomacy as for storytelling. This new language might also influence the development of written scripts, leading to a fusion of Polynesian and Native American writing systems that could be used to record everything from trade agreements to epic poems. Future linguists might study this "Polynesian-American Creole," marveling at its complexity and wondering how many syllables it took to order a simple bowl of taro and beans.

9. The Polynesian Exploration of the Americas: The Next Frontier

With their navigational skills, the Polynesians might not stop at the Pacific coast but continue to explore inland, establishing contact with civilizations such as the Aztecs, Incas, and Mississippians. Their exploration could lead to new alliances, trade routes, and possibly even the spread of Polynesian cultural practices across the Americas. The phrase "From the islands to the mountains" might describe the Polynesians' journey as they make their way inland, exploring new territories and forging new relationships with

Native American civilizations. The Polynesians might be welcomed as exotic visitors, bringing gifts from the Pacific and sharing their knowledge of the sea in exchange for learning about the vast empires of the Aztecs and Incas. This exploration could lead to the creation of new trade networks that connect the Pacific coast to the heart of the Americas, with goods and ideas flowing freely between these distant cultures. Future historians might refer to this period as the "Polynesian-American Age of Discovery," noting how it reshaped the cultural and economic landscape of the Americas long before Europeans even knew what they were missing.

10. A Different Encounter with Europe: The Polynesian Perspective

When Europeans eventually arrive in the Americas, they find not only Native American civilizations but also well-established Polynesian communities along the Pacific coast. These Polynesians, already accustomed to long-distance travel and cultural exchange, might play a crucial role in mediating between Native Americans and the newcomers. The phrase "Aloha, conquistadors" might greet the first European explorers as they land on the shores of a very different New World. The Polynesians, with their knowledge of seafaring and their experience in cross-cultural interaction, could serve as intermediaries, guiding the Europeans through this unfamiliar territory and helping to broker alliances (or perhaps steering them clear of trouble). This could lead to a more complex and nuanced encounter between the Old World and the New, with the Polynesians playing a key role in shaping the course of history. Future historians might debate how much of Europe's eventual dominance in the Americas was due to Polynesian assistance—or how much trouble the Polynesians caused by teaching the Europeans about long-distance navigation.

Conclusion

If the ancient Polynesians had discovered the Americas before Columbus, the course of history in both regions would have been profoundly altered. The early contact between these two rich and diverse cultures could have led to a fusion of traditions, technologies, and ideas that reshaped the Americas long before European influence arrived. The resulting Polynesian-American civilizations would have been vibrant, interconnected, and possibly even more resilient in the face of later challenges. And somewhere in this alternate timeline, a Polynesian chief might have looked out over his thriving coastal city, smiled at the sight of canoes and totem poles lining the shore, and thought, "We really should have brought more taro."